in company 3.0

PRE-INTERMEDIATE STUDENT'S BOOK

B1

MACMILLAN

in company 3.0 at a glance

Third edition Student's Book:

15 Business communication units focusing on current business issues and everyday skills for the workplace

Learning objectives to track your progress

Fluency and communication activities on every page

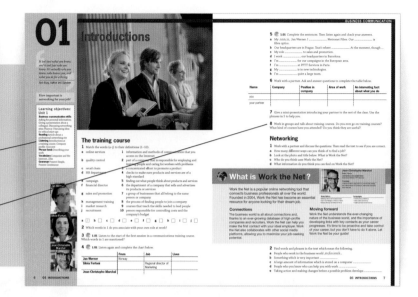

5 People skills units focusing on functional Business English language and interpersonal skills

Useful language boxes support the roleplays

Roleplay activities consolidate the skills learnt

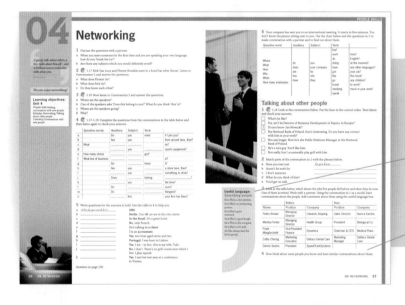

5 Workplace scenarios offering challenging case studies that simulate business situations and allow interaction with the language in a dynamic way

Engaging videos illustrate true-to-life scenarios

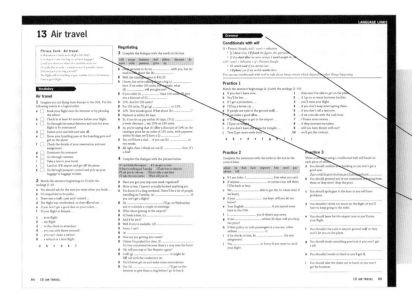

Extra material

- Irregular verb list
- Additional material for communicative activities
- Self-evaluation forms for Workplace scenario activities
- Listening scripts

New Online Workbook and Student's Resource Centre

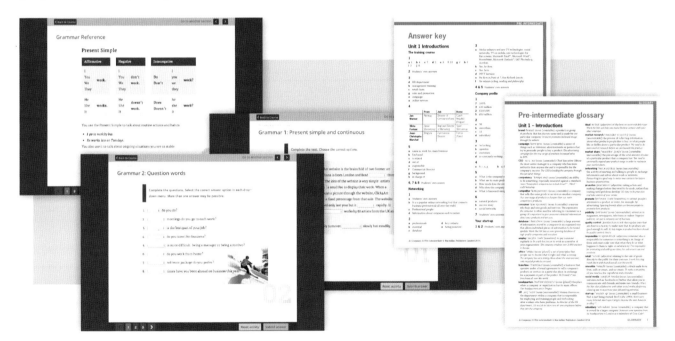

Online Workbook

Everything you need to build and expand on the Student's Book material outside the classroom, and all accessible online:

- Interactive activities to practise:
  - Vocabulary
  - Grammar
  - Reading
  - Writing
  - Listening
- Automatic markbook
- Grammar reference

Student's Resource Centre

An extensive collection of resources, all available to download:

- Student's Book audio
- 'In company in action' – Student's Book scenario videos
- 'In company interviews' – additional video material
- Glossary
- Answer key
- Phrase banks

Contents

01 Introductions

> It isn't just what you know, and it isn't just who you know. It's actually who you know, who knows you, and what you do for a living.

Bob Burg, Author and Speaker

How important is networking for your job?

Learning objectives: Unit 1

Business communication skills
Asking for personal information; Giving a presentation about a colleague; Discussing networking sites; Fluency: Discussing ideas for ethical start-ups
Reading Article about a professional networking site
Listening Introductions at a training course; Company profile: Innocent
Phrase bank Describing your work
Vocabulary Companies and the Internet, Jobs
Grammar Present Simple, Present Continuous

Jan Werner

Silvia Fortuni

Jean-Christophe Marchal

The training course

1 Match the words (a–j) to their definitions (1–10).

a	online services	1	information and methods of communication that you access on the Internet
b	quality control	2	part of a company that is responsible for employing and training people and caring for workers with problems
c	retail chain	3	a concentrated effort to promote a product
d	HR department	4	checks to make sure products and services are of a high standard
e	campaign	5	finding out what people think about products and services
f	financial director	6	the department of a company that sells and advertises its products or services
g	sales and promotion	7	a group of businesses that all belong to the same person or company
h	management training	8	the process of finding people to join a company
i	market research	9	courses that teach the skills needed to lead people
j	recruitment	10	person responsible for controlling costs and the company's budget

a ☐1 b ☐ c ☐ d ☐ e ☐ f ☐ g ☐ h ☐ i ☐ j ☐

2 Which words in 1 do you associate with your own role at work?

3 🔘 1.01 Listen to the start of the first session in a communications training course. Which words in 1 are mentioned?

4 🔘 1.01 Listen again and complete the chart below.

	From	Job	Lives
Jan Werner	Norway		
Silvia Fortuni		Regional director of Marketing	
Jean-Christophe Marchal			

5 🔘 1.01 Complete the sentences. Then listen again and check your answers.

a My _name is_ Jan Werner. I _____ Metronet Fibre. Our _____ is fibre optics.

b Our headquarters are in Prague. That's where _____. At the moment, though …

c My role _____ to sales and promotion.

d I work _____ our headquarters in Barcelona.

e I'm _____ for our campaigns in the European area.

f I'm _____ at PPTT Services in Paris.

g My _____ is in new technologies.

h I'm _____ quite a large team.

6 Work with a partner. Ask and answer questions to complete the table below.

Name	Company	Position in company	Area of work	An interesting fact about what you do
you				
your partner				

7 Give a mini-presentation introducing your partner to the rest of the class. Use the phrases in 5 to help you.

8 Work in groups and talk about training courses. Do you ever go on training courses? What kind of courses have you attended? Do you think they are useful?

Networking

1 Work with a partner and discuss the questions. Then read the text to see if you are correct.

a How many different ways can you think of to find a job?

b Look at the photo and title below. What is Work the Net?

c Who do you think uses Work the Net?

d What information do you think you can find on Work the Net?

What is Work the Net?

Jean-Christophe Marchal
Paris, France
MARKETING AND ADVERTISING
Commercial Director, *PPTT Services*

Overview
Commercial Director responsible for promoting and pitching new online products and services for major public companies in the Paris area.

Work history	Languages
Marketing Director at Thomson Europe	• French (native proficiency)
Export Area Manager at Thomson France	• Italian (native proficiency)
Business Manager at Berlusconi Group	• English (professional proficiency)

Work the Net is a popular online networking tool that connects business professionals all over the world. Founded in 2004, Work the Net has become an essential resource for anyone looking for their dream job.

Connections

The business world is all about connections and, thanks to an ever-growing database of high-profile companies and recruiters, Work the Net can help you make the first contact with your ideal employer. Work the Net also collaborates with other social media platforms, allowing you to maximize your job-seeking potential.

Moving forward

Work the Net understands the ever-changing nature of the business world, and the importance of developing links with key contacts as your career progresses. It's time to be proactive and take control of your career, but you don't have to do it alone. Let Work the Net be your guide!

2 Find words and phrases in the text which mean the following.

a People who work in the business world _professionals_

b Something which is very important _____

c A large amount of information which is stored on a computer _____

d People who you know who can help you with work _____

e Taking action and making changes before a possible problem develops _____

3 Jean-Christophe Marchal has a profile on Work the Net. Look at his page and answer the questions.

a What are Jean-Christophe's competencies and skills?

b Does he have a degree?

c Is he married?

d Who is his current employer?

e Where does he live?

f What things does he enjoy doing in his spare time?

Jean-Christophe Marchal

Paris, France

MARKETING AND ADVERTISING

Commercial Director, *PPTT Services*

Overview

Commercial Director responsible for promoting and pitching new online products and services for major public companies in the Paris area.

Work history

Marketing Director at Thomson Europe

Export Area Manager at Thomson France

Business Manager at Berlusconi Group

Education

Università Luigi Bocconi – Milan, Italy

Académie Carat Espace – Paris, France

École Centrale Paris (ECP) – Paris, France

Competencies and skills

- Media Industry and new TV technologies
- Social networks
- TV on mobile
- New technologies for flat screens
- Excel
- Word
- PowerPoint
- Outlook
- SAP
- Photoshop
- Acrobat

Languages

- French (native proficiency)
- Italian (native proficiency)
- English (professional proficiency)
- German (limited professional proficiency)
- Mandarin (elementary)

Interests

cycling, reading, philosophy

Personal details

Phone: 00 33 167464748

Address: 7, Rue Richard-Lenoir, Paris

Birthday: 24 May 1965

Marital status: Married

4 Now ask a partner the same questions.

What are your competencies and skills?

5 Work in groups and discuss networking sites.

a Do you have a profile on a social or professional networking site?

b Do you think these sites are useful for people in business? How might they be useful?

c What problems do you think there might be with using these sites?

Company profile

1 💿 **1.02** Listen to an extract from a radio programme. The speaker is talking about a company. Number the figures in the order you hear them.

- [ ] 100%
- [ ] £30 million
- [ ] £250,000
- [ ] £60 million
- [8] 10%
- [ ] 10,000
- [1] £500
- [ ] 58%

2 💿 **1.02** Listen again and complete the details in the company profile.

Name of company:
Innocent

💿 **innocent**

Founders:
Richard Reed and friends

Established in:
(a) 19_____

Main product:
(b) _____ (fruit-based drinks)

Main market:
Europe, in (c) _____ countries

Operations:
As a (d) _____ of Coca-Cola®

Brand image:
Promoted through website and (e) _____

Location:
Headquarters in (f) _____

Company ethics:
Gives (g) _____ of profits to charity

3 💿 **1.02** Complete the sentences. Then listen again to check your answers.

a This month we _____ at the role of ethics in business.

b Innocent now _____ from its headquarters in London as a subsidiary of Coca-Cola®.

c Innocent _____ to innovate.

d The company _____ on new lines.

e Innocent _____ to over ten thousand retailers in thirteen European countries, …

f … and its market _____.

g It _____ only 100% natural products …

4 Match the sentences (a–g) in 3 to the descriptions.

a Present Simple to describe a stable situation: __*b*__ _____ _____ _____

b Present Continuous to describe a current situation or activity: _____ _____

c Present Continuous to describe a situation of change: _____

5 Write questions for these answers using the prompts.

a Innocent Drinks. (What / name?)
What is the company's name?

b Fruit-based smoothies and fruit juices. (What / main products?)

c Ten per cent of its profits. (How much / give / charity?)

d Over 10,000 retailers in 13 countries. (Who / sell to?)

e The combination of ethics and clever marketing. (What / recipe / success?)

6 Combine a word from box A with a word from box B to complete each sentence.

A

detailed   natural   negative   product   social   success

B

information   networks   products   publicity   range   story

a Consumers like _natural products_ with no additives or chemicals in them.
b Facebook is a _____ which will be difficult for others to imitate.
c Companies now rely on _____ to promote and market their products.
d _____ can put a company out of business.
e It's important to give consumers _____ about your products and services.
f You need to continually expand your _____ in order to maintain your market share.

7 Do you agree with the sentences in 6? Why / Why not?

Your start-up

1 You are going to develop an idea for your own ethical start-up (new company).
a Think of ideas for your own start-up. It can be either serious or humorous.
b Complete the 'Your start-up' column in the table below.
c Work with a partner and ask questions to complete the 'Your partner's start-up' column.

	Your start-up	Your partner's start-up
Name of company		
Product or service		
'Ethical' selling point		
Location		
Markets		
Competition		

2 Use the framework below to write a description of your new partner's company.

(name of company) _____ is a (type of company)
_____.
The main activity of the company is _____.
Its 'ethical' selling point is _____.
The company is based in _____.
Its main markets are _____ and its main competitor is
_____.

01 Introductions

Phrase bank: Describing your work

I work for (IBM / a pharmaceutical company).
I work in (a bank / an office / London).
My job involves …
My role is to …
I'm head of (marketing) / in the (marketing) department.

I am responsible for (accounts).
I have (five) years of experience in (sales).
I'm based in …
Our headquarters are in …

Vocabulary

Companies and the Internet

1 Complete the sentences using the words in the box.

> employs   franchises   headquarters   Internet
> investment   network   promote   responsible   retail
> sales   website

a Sporting brands often use famous people to _____ their products.

b McDonald's® has _____ all over the world.

c My department is _____ for marketing and sales in Eastern Europe.

d Our company _____ provides information about our services and products, but we don't sell anything online.

e We need more _____ to finance our expansion in China.

f The _____ of Nestlé are in Geneva.

g In my opinion, the BBC has one of the best websites on the _____.

h For the company to survive, our _____ need to grow by 20% this year.

i I have a much better _____ of contacts since I started using LinkedIn®.

j The company _____ over 2,000 workers in Europe, located in four different factories.

k Online stores like Amazon have completely transformed the _____ sector.

Jobs

2 Unscramble the letters to form words related to jobs. Then complete the sentences using the words.

> acontcaunt   cnaharim   dsptreinoci   etxecuvie
> mnagrea   pdenistre   psoioint   rdritee   tlite

a She's the chief _____ officer.

b As _____ of the board, he has the final decision on all issues.

c He doesn't work; he's _____.

d The CEO is the top _____ in the company.

e Her job _____ is 'vice president'.

f I'm the _____ of a small team; I lead six people.

g The financial director is a qualified _____.

h The _____ of our company is based in the company headquarters in Paris.

i My job _____ outlines my role and responsibilities.

Grammar

Present Simple

Affirmative		Negative		Interrogative		
I		I			I	
You		You	**don't**	**Do**	you	
We	**work.**	We	**work.**	**Don't**	we	**work?**
They		They			they	
He		He			he	
She	**works.**	She	**doesn't**	**Does**	she	**work?**
It		It	**work.**	**Doesn't**	it	

You use the Present Simple to talk about routine actions and habits.
- *I **go** to work by bus.*
- *He **works** late on Tuesdays.*

You also use it to talk about ongoing situations you see as stable.
- *We **live** in London.*
- *They **employ** over 250 people.*

Present Continuous

Affirmative		Negative		Interrogative		
I'm (am)		I'm not		Am / Aren't	I	
You're (are) We're (are) They're (are)	working.	You aren't We aren't They aren't	working.	Are / Aren't	you we they	working?
He's (is) She's (is) It's (is)		He isn't She isn't It isn't		Is / Isn't	he she it	

You use the Present Continuous to talk about activities happening at the moment of speaking.
- *Don't interrupt me, please. I'm trying to concentrate.*
- *He's wearing a grey suit, a white shirt and a blue tie.*
- *What are you doing?' 'I'm preparing this month's sales figures.'*

You can also use it for activities or situations you see as temporary.
- *We're using this office until the new one is ready.*
- *I'm working from home today, so don't phone me at the office.*

You use the Present Continuous for situations which are changing.
- *The economic situation is getting better.*
- *Our company share price is steadily improving.*

You often use the Present Continuous with time expressions – for example, *at the moment, this week/ month/year*, etc.
- *We are having a lot of problems with our suppliers at the moment.*
- *I'm doing a course this month, but it's not very interesting.*

Practice 1

Complete the sentences using the verbs in the box in the correct form – Present Simple or Present Continuous. Use each verb twice.

do   get   live   sell   think   work

a   Normally, I am in the office in the afternoon, but this month I _____ a course. [T]
b   In the winter, the reps _____ more than in the summer. [ ]
c   Our most important market is the Far East. We _____ business with several companies there. [ ]
d   Our new product line _____ very well this year. [ ]
e   Our boss _____ very long hours. [ ]
f   He _____ of changing his job because he's not very happy. [ ]
g   'What's your address?' 'I _____ in a hotel until we find a nice flat.' [ ]
h   In June, the weather _____ hot there, so take some cool clothes. [ ]
i   He _____ his job is really interesting. [ ]
j   It _____ hotter. We need to get some air conditioning for this office. [ ]
k   At present, we _____ on new products and services for the future. [ ]
l   During the week, he _____ in his city flat and at the weekend he goes to the country. [ ]

Now mark each sentence with a letter to show which rule applies.
H – routine actions and habits
O – ongoing situations you see as stable
M – activities happening at the moment of speaking
T – activities or situations you see as temporary
C – situations which are changing

Practice 2

Write questions about the information which is missing.
a   The company makes money by ...
    How does the company make money?
b   Our business is expanding because ...
    Why _____
c   They are setting up a business in ...
    Where _____
d   We are looking for $ ...
    How much _____
e   He has previous experience in the ... business.
    What kind _____
f   Their unique selling point is ...
    What _____
g   My company employs ... people.
    How many _____
h   The manager of the company is ...
    Who _____
i   They are talking to ... about further investment.
    Who _____

02

How many hours do you work each week?

Work–life balance

1 Complete this extract from an article about work–life balance with the numbers in the box.

| 2̶ | 1,625 | 3 | 48 | 76,700 |

A new study shows that full-time male workers in Britain work (a) __2__ hours per week longer than the European average. The long hours culture is still a problem for many workers in this country, despite the recent growth of part-time jobs.

Despite a fall in the number of people working *very* long hours, (b) _____ million employees still work more than (c) _____ hours – around 1 in 8. Excessive working time is linked with the development of health problems like heart disease, diabetes, stress and depression. It can also lead to poor performance and absenteeism, and takes time away from things like training and education, which are necessary for economic success.

The average UK worker spends (d) _____ hours a year at work, yet only produces (e) $_____ in GDP value.

Source: http://touchstoneblog.org.uk/2013/01/british-men-are-working-the-longest-hours-in-europe/

2 Look at page 130 to check your answers in 1. Then discuss the questions with a partner.

a What is the situation like in your country?

b Do you think this situation will change in the future?

3 Read the profile of a leading executive and answer the questions.

a What time does Sally McDermott start work in the morning?

b What time does she normally get to the office?

c How long does she take off for lunch?

d Why does she prefer to call people rather than send an email?

e How often does she have to work at the weekend?

A day in the life of Sally McDermott

Sally McDermott is the international operations manager of a major telecoms company, with operations in most of Europe and Latin America. Her career has included periods of work in Portugal, Paris and London. She speaks Spanish, French and Russian, as well as English.

'People <u>often</u> ask me how I manage to combine a successful career with family life. The secret is that I don't need much sleep! Five hours is enough, so by 5.30 am I am usually up, reading reports and checking emails on my smartphone. Then I have breakfast at 8 am, together with my husband, Derek, and my 15-year-old daughter, Katie.

I go to work in a taxi which picks me up at 8.30 am every day. On the way to work I look through the daily papers. It normally takes us about 20 minutes to get to the office. When I arrive my secretary joins me and we go through any correspondence and plan the day. I make decisions about appointments and organize meetings.

I drink a lot of coffee and mineral water. I usually have just a sandwich for lunch, or sometimes something in a nearby restaurant, but I am never out for more than an hour. Then, in the afternoon, it's back to the office and more meetings, although once a month I take an afternoon off, if it's possible. When I'm not in a meeting I am constantly on the phone. I use the phone whenever possible because it's nearly always quicker than using email. Even if I'm in the office, I prefer to use my smartphone. I hardly ever send text messages except to my daughter – it's just too time-consuming.

I like to pick Katie up from school when I can, but most days I work until at least 8 pm. Weekends are reserved for my family. I don't often have to work, but sometimes something comes up which I just can't avoid. All in all, it's hard work, but I enjoy my job.'

4 How typical do you think Sally McDermott's life is? Does she have a good work–life balance? Why / Why not?

5 <u>Underline</u> all the phrases in the profile on page 13 which say how often something happens. The first one has been done for you.

6 Read the rules below and <u>underline</u> the correct option.

a In most cases, adverbs of frequency (*sometimes*, *often*, *never*, etc) go **before** / **after** the main verb.

b Adverbs of frequency go **before** / **after** the verb *to be*.

c Time phrases (*twice a year*, *every day*) can go at the **beginning** / **end** / **beginning or end** of a sentence or clause.

7 Add a word or phrase from the box to each sentence so that it is true for you. You may need to change the verb form.

| always | every day | every week | hardly ever | never | not often | often | once a month |
| sometimes | twice a year | usually | | | | | |

a I go to work by car.   *I don't often go to work by car.*
b I get home late.   _____
c I work at the weekend.   _____
d I have a holiday.   _____
e I feel bored with my job.   _____
f My boss leaves work before me.   _____
g My computer crashes.   _____
h I find time to relax and enjoy myself.   _____
i I have arguments with people at work.   _____
j I read the financial papers.   _____

8 Complete the 'Action' and 'You' columns in the chart below. Then ask questions to complete the 'Your partner' column.

	Action	You	Your partner
	eat out	*once a week*	
How often do you ...?			
Do you ... much?			
Do you ever ...?			

9 Present your partner's routine to the rest of the class.

What's in a new job?

1 1.03 Two friends meet and talk about someone's new job. Listen to their conversation and answer the questions.

a What is the relationship between Eddie (the man) and Fiona (the person with the new job)?

b How does Eddie feel about the new job?

2 1.03 Write questions for the answers using the prompts. Listen again to check your answers.

a (involve / long hours?) *Does it involve long hours?*

Officially 40 hours, but she often works late. We don't see her at home much.

b (What / do?)

_____

... she's regional marketing manager for Latin America now.

c (What / involve?)

_____

Quite a lot!

d (mean / lot / travelling?)

_____

It seems to. At least a couple of trips a month.

e (have / work / weekends?)

_____

Not every weekend, but we can never make plans.

f (How / holiday?)

_____

Three weeks a year.

g (she / enjoy?)

_____

It's hard work, but I think she enjoys the challenge.

3 Work with a partner. Ask questions like the ones you wrote in 2 to complete your chart.

Speaker A: Look at the chart on page 132.

Speaker B: Look at the chart on page 140.

4 Ask your partner similar questions about their job or the job of someone they know.

Taking things easy

1 Do you take regular exercise? Do you think it's important? Work with a partner and complete the questionnaire below.

a	Taking exercise is the best solution for stress.	true ☐	false ☐
b	Sport is the key to a healthy and long life.	true ☐	false ☐
c	People who get up early suffer from stress.	true ☐	false ☐
d	People who have a sleep during the day live longer.	true ☐	false ☐
e	People in their 50s need to save their energy.	true ☐	false ☐
f	Brisk walks are the healthiest form of exercise.	true ☐	false ☐

2 Now read the article to see if your answers are the same as the author's.

They say that a healthy body is a healthy mind, but according to a German expert it is lazy people who lead longer and healthier lives. Professor Peter Axt recommends avoiding strenuous activity like aerobics or working out in a gym. 'People who prefer to laze in a hammock instead of running a marathon or who take a midday nap instead of playing squash have a better chance of living into old age,' says this scientist. They are also less likely to suffer from professional stress.

He co-wrote *On the Joy of Laziness* with his daughter, who is also a doctor. In the book he advises people to 'waste half your time. Just enjoy lazing around.' Those who get up early in the morning usually feel stressed for the rest of the day, so his advice is to take it easy.

However, Professor Axt stresses that laziness is only one of the keys to a longer life. In fact, the subtitle of his book is *How best to use your energies*. He argues that if you are too fat, you need more energy to maintain body functions, and is in favour of moderate exercise like 'meditative' jogging or brisk walks to 'relax body and spirit at the same time.'

On the other hand, any exertion is not recommended, especially for middle-aged people who should be particularly careful about doing too much sport. Professor Axt believes we have only a limited amount of energy, and people who use up their supply more quickly live shorter lives. 'Research shows that people who run long distances into their 50s are using up energy they need for other purposes.'

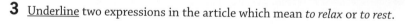

3 <u>Underline</u> two expressions in the article which mean *to relax* or *to rest*.

4 Choose the best title for the article.
a All work and no play makes Jack a dull boy
b Health risks for the over 50s
c Siesta or marathon?
d _____ (your own idea)

5 Discuss the following questions with other people in the class.
a Do you agree with any of Professor Axt's suggestions? Which ones?
b What do you do to relax?
c Do you find it easy to relax?
d Do you do more or less exercise than you would like to? Do you do more or less exercise than you think is good for you? Why?

02 Work–life balance

Phrase bank: Talking about routines

We work (37) hours a week.

They work an average of (five) hours of overtime.

The average user saves (45) minutes a day by being able to check emails on the move.

I always go to work (by car).

I usually just have (a sandwich) for lunch.

I hardly ever send (text messages).

She sometimes has to work at the weekends.

It involves long hours.

It means a lot of travelling.

We get (three) weeks' holiday a year.

Vocabulary

Work and routines

1 Complete the sentences with the pairs of words in the box.

check + emails	full-time + work	get + off	productive + day
ratio + to	takes + hour	work + overtime	

a We only _____ half an hour _____ for lunch.

b More than four million _____ employees _____ more than 48 hours a week.

c I _____ an average of 6 hours _____ a week.

d It _____ me an _____ to get to work.

e I _____ my _____ at least ten times a day.

f The _____ of men to women is two _____ one in my job.

g Nobody can be _____ sixteen hours a _____.

2 Match the sentence beginnings (a–h) with the endings (1–8).

a Professor Axt thinks that lazing ...

b Doing as little as possible is better ...

c Being lazy is the key ...

d Take a midday break instead ...

e He's in favour ...

f Try to take ...

g We only have a limited ...

h If you get up early, you are likely to ...

1 ... around is good for you.

2 ... of playing squash or going for a run.

3 ... amount of energy.

4 ... it easy this weekend.

5 ... than going to the gym.

6 ... to a long and healthy life.

7 ... of moderate exercise like walking.

8 ... feel stressed for the rest of the day.

a   b   c   d   e   f   g   h

Do as an auxiliary

3 Complete the conversation using *do, does, don't* or *doesn't*.

A (a) _____ you do a lot of exercise?

B Yes, I suppose I (b) _____. Why do you ask?

A Well, it's better if you (c) _____, according to a German scientist.

B What (d) _____ he say about it?

A He (e) _____ say that exercise is bad for you exactly, but that if you do too much, you use up all your energy.

B That (f) _____ make sense. Sport is good for you and makes you feel better.

A Yes, but according to him people who run a lot and play squash (g) _____ usually live to an old age.

B Well, I (h) _____ believe it. He probably just (i) _____ like sport.

Phrasal verbs

4 Combine a verb from box A with a preposition from box B to complete each sentence below. You may need to change the verb form.

A

give	go	pick	switch	use	work

B

off	out	through	up	up	up

a Please can you _____ your mobile phones before the presentation begins?

b After a long day at the office. I like to _____ at the gym before I go home.

c I want to _____ smoking because I know it's bad for my health.

d The taxi _____ me _____ every morning at half past nine.

e I don't want to _____ all my energy doing strenuous exercise.

f She _____ her correspondence with her secretary every morning.

Expressing frequency

To say how often something happens you can use adverbs of frequency.

always	hardly ever	never	not often	often	sometimes	usually

The adverb comes **before** the main verb but **after** the verb *to be*.

I You He She We They	(don't/doesn't) **usually** (don't/doesn't) **often** **sometimes** **never**	drive(s) to work. go(es) out for lunch.

I You He She We They	am are is	(not) **usually** (not) **often** **sometimes** **never**	late. tired.

You can also use time phrases.

every day	every week	once a day	once a week	twice a month	three times a year

These phrases come **at the beginning** or **end** of the sentence/clause.

I You He She We They	have (has) a break go (goes) on holiday	**every day.** **once a day.** **twice a week.** **three times a month.** **four times a year.**

Every day **Once a day** **Twice a week** **Three times a month** **Four times a year**	I you he she we they	have (has) a break. go (goes) on holiday.

Practice 1

Reorganize the words to make correct sentences.

a abroad times I a year travel four

_____

b a on department meeting we always have Monday morning

_____

c often he to Germany doesn't go

_____

d manager the department usually leaves on Friday early

_____

e I use the car never can't because drive I

_____

f has the office canteen she always lunch in

_____

g often they for work aren't late

_____

h always Microsoft® is the news in

_____

i my every I change mobile year

_____

j ever do you have parties office ?

_____

k often to how gym you the do go ?

_____

l you your do use much laptop ?

_____

Practice 2

Rewrite the questions using question words *what, who, when, how long,* etc.

a Do you go to work by car? On foot?
   How do you go to work?

b Do you use the phone a lot? Ever?

_____

c Do you get to work at 8.30 am? 9 am?

_____

d Does he do the housework because he likes it? Because he has to?

_____

e Does he play squash every day? Every week?

_____

f Does she go to work with her husband? A friend?

_____

g Do you spend the morning making plans? Having meetings?

_____

h Do you work 35 hours a week? 40 hours a week?

_____

i Does it take you 20 minutes to read the newspaper? Half an hour?

_____

j Do you work so hard because it's fun? Because you need the money?

_____

Telephone talk

1 🔊 **1.04–1.08** Listen to the extracts and write the phone numbers.

a _0837_____ d _____

b _____ e _____

c _____

2 🔊 **1.04–1.08** Listen again and number the phrases in the order that you hear them.

a ☐ I'd like to speak to Derek LaMotte, please.

b ☐ You have one message from 903586759 at 18.30 on April 1.

c ☐ Ring now on 090 238 6980. I'll repeat that for you. If you know the answer, phone us now on 090 238 6980.

d ☐ Can you give me the number of Budget Car Rental, please?

e ☐ No, I'm afraid you've got the wrong number.

f ☐ I'm sorry. Could you say that again more slowly?

3 <u>Underline</u> the phrases in the sentences in 2 that you think are useful to know.

4 Write down five different telephone numbers and dictate them to your partner as fast as possible. Who gets the most correct?

Polite questions

1 🔊 **1.09** A customer phones an airline for some information. The dialogue includes the questions (a–c) below, but in a more polite form. Listen to the conversation and write down the actual questions you hear.

a What's the flight number?

Do you _____?

b What time does it get in?

Could you _____?

c Is there any delay?

Do you _____?

> *Telephone communication may be slower than its new-media counterparts, but it still has benefits in an increasingly impersonal world. The telephone call, which connects a caller with a human voice, is still an important business component.*

Mary Nestor-Harper, Demand Media

Is the telephone an important communication tool for you?

Learning objectives: Unit 3

Business communication skills Using telephone phrases; Roleplay: Telephoning for information; Discussing telephone frustrations; Roleplay: Making an order by telephone

Reading Article about effective telephone communication

Listening Telephone numbers; Requests for information and orders; Telephone customer service

Phrase bank Telephoning

Vocabulary Numbers, Telephone phrases

Grammar Polite questions

📺 **In company interviews** Units 1–3

2 Use the model in 1 and the prompts on page 130 to have a conversation with your partner. Use polite questions.

3 Look at the chart below. Then rephrase the questions to make them polite using *Do you know ...?* or *Could you tell me ...?*

Do you know ...	how long it takes?
	where the airport is?
Could you tell me ...	if she got my message?
	if you'll finish the order on time?

a What time does the flight leave?
   Could you tell me what time the flight leaves?
   (NOT ~~Could you tell me what time does the flight leave?~~)

b Which terminal does it leave from?

_____

c How far is the factory from the airport?

_____

d How long is the meeting with Mr Fuentes?

_____

e Which car hire company is it?

_____

f Which models do they have available?

_____

g Do I need an international driving licence?

_____

h Where are we staying?

_____

i Is it a nice place?

_____

j How far is the hotel from the nearest town?

_____

k Have they booked a meeting room?

_____

4 Work with a partner.
Speaker B: Look at page 136.
Speaker A: Read the information below and follow the instructions.

a Ring your office to get the necessary information.
b Use the questions in 3 to get the information you need.
c Make a note of all the information.

You are travelling on business in the UK. When you finish there, you are going straight to another country for a special sales conference. You expected to receive an email with information about this trip from your office, but there seems to be a problem with the company server and you can't access your email account.

Telephone frustrations

1 Complete the list of possible telephone frustrations using the verbs in the box.

| call | get (x 3) | listen | play | put | repeat | return | take | transfer |

a They _____ irritating music when you're put on hold.

b You _____ cut off in the middle of your call.

c People you call _____ a long time to answer.

d They _____ you on hold and forget about you.

e They _____ you to another person and you have to _____ your enquiry.

f They don't _____ properly to what you are saying.

g You continually _____ an engaged tone when you _____ someone.

h People don't _____ your calls.

i You _____ through to a voicemail system.

2 With a partner, decide which of the problems in 1 are the five most frustrating. Then look on page 136 to compare your answers with the results of a survey. Are there any other things that frustrate you when using the telephone?

3 Work with a partner and answer the questions.

a With the growth of the Internet, email and text messaging, how important is the telephone in business these days?

b What skills do staff who answer the phone need to have?

c Does bad telephone customer service have an impact on the success of a business?

4 Now read the article. According to the author, what are the answers to the questions in 3?

5 The author suggests, 'More business is lost through bad service than by poor product performance.' Do you agree? Discuss with a partner.

Effective Phone Communication

In this age of the Internet, email and electronic communication, the telephone is still one of the most important business tools. Customers expect to be dealt with professionally and competently, so effective phone communication skills are vital. Good customer service can give a company a competitive edge, while ineffective telephone behaviour can cost millions in lost sales opportunities.

Apart from a positive attitude, whatever business you are in, staff dealing with phone enquiries need training in a number of essential skills. These include transferring a call, placing a call on hold, dealing with angry callers, responding to enquiries about correspondence, using a caller's name and taking messages correctly. Callers should not hear informal expressions like 'Oh, she's just gone out' or 'Sorry, he's not with us anymore'. Customers want a prompt response from a real person (not a machine) who is friendly, helpful and can make a decision.

More business is lost through poor service than by poor product performance, and the quality of a company's response to a call is one of the chief factors in creating a perception of good or bad service.

6 🔘 **1.10–1.15** Listen to six extracts from telephone calls. Identify which skill listed in paragraph 2 of *Effective Phone Communication* is being used.

a *placing calls on hold*

b _____

c _____

d _____

e _____

f _____

7 🔘 **1.10–1.15** Listen again and complete the missing phrases.

a **A** Can I have _____ 305, please?

    B I'm afraid the line _____. Will you hold?

b **A** Could I _____? You need 50 units by Friday, and Mr Johansson can contact you on 943 694726.

    B Yes, that's correct.

    A Right, Mr Smith. I'll _____ as soon as he's free.

c **A** ... and it really isn't good enough.

    B Yes, Mr Wright. I understand what you're saying and _____ the error. As soon as Mr Downs is back, I'll ask him to get in contact with you. _____ about this.

    A Right, thank you. I realize it's not your fault.

d **A** Could I have the sales department, please?

    B One moment, please. Just _____ now.

e **A** Shonagh Clark speaking.

    B Hello, I'm _____ your letter of 12th June.

f **A** This is Jorgen Bode here. Could I speak to Jean Simmons, please?

    B Oh, I'm sorry, Mr Bode, but Ms Simmons _____ right now. Can I ask her to call you back? Or I can contact her _____ if it's urgent.

8 Match the words and phrases to make telephone expressions. Add three of your own expressions to the list.

Could you ...	put	a message?
	repeat	that, please?
	read	me through to (Accounts)?
	give	me your name?
	take	that back to me?

Could I ...	leave	to Mr Wilson?
	speak	over that again?
	have	extension 103, please?
	check	a message?
	go	that?

I'm phoning ...	to	your advertisement.
	about	make an appointment.
	to	some information.
	for	confirm our meeting.
	to	see if you could attend a meeting on the 20th.

_____

_____

_____

Sales contacts

1 🔘 **1.16** The sales team at JD Graphic uses the form below to record the details of all phone calls with potential clients. Listen to the conversation and complete the form.

GRAPHIC   PHONE CONTACT FORM

DATE:	Wednesday 14 May
CALL INITIATED BY:	Client
CALL HANDLER:	Barry White
CLIENT:	AMC Elevator
ADDRESS:	(a) _54 Eisenhower Lane North, Lombard_
CONTACT:	Mr Schmidt
POSITION:	Head of (b) _____
TEL:	(c) _____
EMAIL:	schmidt@amcelevator.com
NATURE OF BUSINESS:	Elevator manufacturer
PURPOSE OF CALL:	Wants estimate for printing a (d) _____ of (e) _____ pages. Copies: (f) _____ Estimates also for (g) _____ and (h) _____ copies. Size: (i) _____ in black and white. Cover in colour. Will supply material on memory stick.
COMMENTS:	They are updating all their manuals, so could give us more work if the price is right.
ACTION REQUIRED:	Visit client with (j) _____
BY WHOM:	B. White
DATE AND TIME:	(k) _____ May at 10 am.

In company interviews
Units 1–3

2 Work with a partner and practise telephoning for information and taking notes.

Speaker A: Look at page 142.

Speaker B: Look at page 146.

03 Telephone talk

Vocabulary

Numbers

1 Write the full form of the numbers and figures.

a 321   *three hundred and twenty-one*

b 69% _____

c 3,428 _____

d £3M _____

e $9.39 _____

f 24,678,902 _____

Telephone phrases

2 Put the conversation below in the correct order.

☐ Hello, BDC electronics.

☐ Yes, please. Could you ask him to phone John Clarkson from Duraplex? He has the phone number.

☐ Just one moment … I'm sorry, there's no answer.

☐ Yes, of course. Could I just check your name? John Clark from Duraplex.

☐ Thank you. Goodbye.

☐ Oh, dear. I'm phoning for some information. It's quite urgent. Do you know where I can contact him?

☐ Oh, good morning. Could I speak to Peter White, please?

☐ No, sorry, I'm afraid I don't. Can I take a message?

☐ No, it's Clarkson. He knows what it's about.

☐ Oh, sorry, Mr Clarkson. I'll tell him as soon as he's available.

3 Complete the conversation using the words and phrases in the box.

bad line   call me   Can I take a message?
Could I speak to   dialled the wrong number   engaged
hold   put me through   This is   You're through

A Sales Department. Can I help you?

B Oh! I must have (a) _____. Can you (b) _____ to Customer Services, please?

A I'm sorry, it's a (c) _____. Did you say Customer Services?

B Yes, that's right.

A Just one moment. I'm sorry, but the line is (d) _____. Do you want to (e) _____?

B All right.

A (f) _____ now.

B Hello. (g) _____ the department manager, please?

C I'm afraid he's not in the office this morning. (h) _____?

B Yes, please. (i) _____ George Smith. Could you ask him to (j) _____?

C Yes, of course. Goodbye.

B Bye.

4 Match the sentence beginnings (a–f) with the endings (1–6).

a Tell her it's Mr Jenkins. I'm returning …

b Typical! I got cut …

c I hate it when they put you …

d I keep getting an engaged …

e Could you say …

f Can you read that …

1 … on hold, and then forget about you.

2 … back to me, just to check?

3 … tone. Maybe his phone is off the hook.

4 … her call this morning.

5 … that again, please? I didn't understand.

6 … off in the middle of the call.

a	b	c	d	e	f

5 Match the words (a–l) to their definitions (1–12).

a phone book

b engaged

c dialling tone

d reverse charge call

e roaming

f off-peak call

g wrong number

h switchboard

i extension number

j smartphone

k directory enquiries

l missed call

1 A continuous sound that means you can dial the number you want.

2 The equipment which distributes calls to the different departments and offices in a company.

3 A phone number you dial by mistake.

4 Busy – someone is using the line you want.

5 The number of each different phone in a company.

6 A call which is paid for by the person you are calling.

7 Mobile phone with Internet capabilities and touch screen.

8 A book with a list of telephone numbers.

9 A service you phone if you want to find a number.

10 When you use your mobile phone outside your local area or in another country.

11 A call someone made which you didn't answer.

12 A call made in the evening or at the weekend which has a lower charge.

a ___ b ___ c ___ d ___ e ___ f ___ g ___ h ___ i ___ j ___ k ___ l ___

Grammar

Polite questions

Direct questions	Polite questions		Differences
Where **are you** from?	Can you tell me	where **you are** from?	
How **is she**?		how **she is**?	
Where **are we** meeting?	Can you remember	where **we're meeting**?	• Word order
Where **do you live**?	Could you tell me	where **you live**?	• *if* in *Yes/No* questions
How much money **does he earn**?		how much **money he earns**?	
Does he like football?	Do you know	**if he likes** football?	
Has he got my address?		**if he has got** my address?	

Practice 1

Reorganize the words to make polite questions or statements.

a tell if got my me could you she message _____

b know be back will do when he you _____

c do long know takes you how it _____

d remember the what bus time can leaves you _____

e this know do what word you means _____

f know think he wants what you to do _____

g idea the is time I've no what _____

Practice 2

Change the direct questions into polite questions.

a What time does the meeting begin? Do you know _____?

b How much is the hotel? Could you tell me _____?

c Why is he angry? Do you know _____?

d Is there a restaurant car on the train? Can you tell me _____?

e Where can I park the car? Can you tell me _____?

f Is the office near the town centre? Can you remember _____?

Networking

Do you enjoy networking?

Learning objectives: Unit 4

People skills Making conversation with new people; Roleplay: Networking; Talking about other people
Listening Conversations with new people

1 Discuss the questions with a partner.

a When you meet someone for the first time and you are speaking your own language, how do you 'break the ice'?

b Are there any subjects which you would definitely avoid?

2 🔊 1.17 Rick Van Looy and Florent Rondele meet in a hotel bar after dinner. Listen to Conversation 1 and answer the questions.

a What does Florent do?

b What does Rick do?

c Do they know each other?

3 🔊 1.18 Now listen to Conversation 2 and answer the questions.

a Where are the speakers?

b One of the speakers asks 'Does this belong to you?' What do you think 'this' is?

c Where are the speakers going?

d Why?

4 🔊 1.17–1.18 Complete the questions from the conversations in the table below and then listen again to check your answers.

	Question words	Auxiliary	Subject	Verb	
a		Do	you	mind	if I join you?
b		Are	you		from around here, then?
c	What	_____	_____		do?
d		_____	you	_____	sports equipment?
e	How many stores	_____	_____	got?	
f	What line of business	_____	_____		in?
g		Do	_____	know	it?
h		Are	you	_____	a store here, then?
i		_____	you	_____	something to drink?
j		Does	_____	belong	_____?
k		_____	you	_____	the time?
l		Do	_____	_____	soon?
m		Do	_____	_____	Bangkok?
n		_____	this		your first trip there?

5 Write questions for the answers in bold. Use the table in 4 to help you.

a *Who do you work for?* **IBM**.

b _____ **Berlin**. Our offices are in the city centre.

c _____ **In the Royal**. It's a great hotel.

d _____ **No**, only French.

e _____ He's talking **to a client**.

f _____ I'm an **accountant**.

g _____ **Yes**, two boys aged seven and ten.

h _____ **Portugal**. I was born in Lisbon.

i _____ **Yes**, I am – in fact, this is my wife, Yuki.

j _____ **No**, I don't. There's no golf course near where I live. I play squash.

k _____ **Yes**. I met her last year at a conference in Vienna.

Answers on page 130.

6 Your company has sent you to an international meeting. It starts in five minutes. You don't know the person sitting next to you. Use the chart below and the questions in 5 to make conversation with a partner and to find out about them.

Question word	Auxiliary	Subject	Verb	
Where	do	you	live	here?
What	does	your company	work	English?
How	are	he	do	at the moment?
Why	has	she	doing	any other languages?
When	have	they	have	your job?
How many employees			got	this book?
			like	any children?
			go	to work?
			travel	much in your work?
			studying	
			speak	

Talking about other people

1 🔘 1.19 Look at the conversation below. Put the lines in the correct order. Then listen and check your answers.

- [ ] What's he like?
- [ ] Yes, isn't he Director of Business Development at Pepsico in Europe?
- [1] Do you know Jan Nowacki?
- [ ] The National Bank of Poland, that's interesting. Do you have any contact with him in your work?
- [ ] Not any longer. Now he's the Public Relations Manager at the National Bank of Poland.
- [ ] He's a nice guy. You'd like him.
- [ ] Not really, but I occasionally play golf with him.

2 Match parts of the conversation in 1 with the phrases below.

a Have you ever met   *Do you know*
b doesn't he work for   _____
c I don't anymore.   _____
d What do you think of him? _____
e You'd get on well.

3 Look at the table below, which shows the jobs five people did before and what they do now. One of them is retired. Work with a partner. Using the conversation in 1 as a model, have conversations about the people. Add comments about them using the Useful language box.

Name	Before		Now	
	Position	Company	Position	Company
Pedro Amado	Managing Director	Edwards Shipping	Sales Director	Iberica Electric
Martina Ferlan	Managing Director	Health Group	President	Biological Co.
Frank Mangliochetti	Vice-President Finance	Dynamica	Chairman & CEO	Medical Plans
Cathy Cheung	Marketing Executive	Deltaco Dental Care	Marketing Manager	Deltaco Dental Care
Dennis Sexton	President	SpeedTrackSystems		

4 Now think about some people you know and have similar conversations about them.

Useful language:
Describing people
He's/She's a nice person.
He's/She's an interesting person.
He's/She's quite reserved.
He's/She's a good laugh.
He's/She's a bit arrogant.
He's/She's a bit dull.
He/She always has the latest gossip.

pass the buck

to make someone else deal with something that you should take responsibility for

He accused ministers of trying to pass the buck on education.

Learning objectives: Workplace Scenario A

Business communication skills Discussing communication problems in the workplace; Writing a confirmation email; Roleplay: Discussing and resolving a problem
Reading Article about communication breakdown
📼 **In company in action**
A1: Passing the buck;
A2: Discussing and resolving a problem

Passing the buck

1 Read the article about communication breakdowns in the workplace and discuss the questions with a partner.

a Which of these issues do you think is the most significant cause of communication breakdowns in the workplace?

b Have you experienced any of these problems at work? How did you deal with them?

c What else can cause communication problems at work?

LET'S TALK!

Communication in the workplace is key for a productive and effective working environment. Yet breakdowns in communication at work are very common and are a frequent cause of workplace frustrations. Here are some of the issues that employees face.

1. COMMUNICATION BARRIERS
Lots of different things can cause communication barriers in the office: differences in background, experience, language and culture can all make it harder to communicate with your colleagues. The key is to find something you have in common. Then you can use that to relate to your colleagues and understand what they are talking about.

2. WORK VS PERSONAL COMMUNICATIONS
It's nice to have friends at work, but it can be dangerous to make your personal life part of your communication at work. You should avoid personal emails as much as possible; these can lead to office gossip and decreased morale. Try to stay professional at all times.

3. COMMUNICATION RULES
Relying on verbal communication can make it very hard to keep track of what you have discussed or agreed with colleagues or clients. A common policy or set of rules for company communication will help to avoid misunderstandings and disputes. For example, following up phone calls and meetings with an email gives you a useful written record of what was discussed.

4. PERSONAL ATTITUDES
It's important not to let a negative attitude interfere with how you communicate with your colleagues. Even if you dislike someone you are working with, try to maintain a positive attitude in your communication with them. Not everyone can be happy at work all of the time. But don't let a bad mood or lack of motivation affect the rest of your team.

In company in action

2 Lenz Furniture Designs is a bespoke furniture company, specializing in luxury, handmade products. They have just launched a new website but Serena Ortega, the HR Director at Lenz Furniture Designs, has noticed a problem with the site that affects her work. Watch video A1 and answer the questions.

a Where has communication broken down?
   i Between IT and HR.
   ii Between HR and Marketing.
   iii Between IT and Marketing.

b What is the issue?
   i The content of the new website.
   ii Technical problems with parts of the new site.
   iii The failure of an external supplier to deliver on time.

3 Discuss these questions with a partner.

a The conversations in the video show a situation where communication between departments has broken down. What do you think are the main problems?

b Vanessa complains to Serena that Eric is 'passing the buck'. Do you have any experience of people 'passing the buck'? How did you deal with it?

4 After her conversations with Eric and Vanessa, Serena asks her manager, Joe Walker, for advice. Read his email and answer the questions.

a What do you think of Joe's advice?

b Would you give Serena any different advice?

RE: Website problem

Good afternoon Serena,

Thanks for talking to me this morning. It's clear there has been a breakdown in communication between Marketing and IT and both sides are trying to pass the buck. It's frustrating, but I think this is an opportunity to improve communication between the departments. Vanessa is ultimately responsible for the website, so I suggest you go back and talk to her. It might also help to follow up the conversation with an email summarizing any decisions. You could also copy the email to Eric, so everyone knows who is responsible for what and that should encourage them to sort it out.

Good luck!

Joe

---

5 Following Joe's email, Serena organizes a meeting with Vanessa to resolve the problem. Work with a partner and roleplay their conversation.

Speaker A: Look at page 131.
Speaker B: Look at page 136.

6 Evaluate your performance using the form on page 132.

In company in action

7 Now watch video A2 to see what happened when Serena spoke to Vanessa. Repeat your roleplay, but this time swap roles. Use the notes from your evaluation form and as many of the useful phrases from your roleplays in 5 as you can.

8 Write an email from Serena to Vanessa to confirm their conversation. Begin like this:

Good afternoon Vanessa,
I am writing to confirm what we discussed in our meeting this morning about the website.

Then compare your email with Serena's on page 136.

05

Internet histories

Do you use apps on your mobile phone?

1 Some people think that apps are the future of the Internet. Do you think they are important in business?

2  1.20 Have you ever played the game Angry Birds™? Listen to a short history about the origins of the game and answer the questions.

a In what country was the company that developed Angry Birds based?
b When did development on the game first start?
c What were the initial development costs?
d When did the game first appear on the Apple® App Store?
e By May 2012, how many downloads of the game were there?
f Apart from downloads, how else does the game make money?

3 1.20 Complete the timeline history of Angry Birds using the words and phrases in the box. Then listen again to check your answers.

anniversary	colleagues	costs	distribution	downloads
merchandise	partnership	platforms	revenues	spin-off

With over one billion (a) _____, Angry Birds is perhaps the largest mobile app success so far. It has been praised for its successful combination of addictive games, humorous style and low price. There are versions of Angry Birds for personal computers and games consoles, a market for (b) _____ featuring its characters and even long-term plans for a feature film or television series. Here is its history.

EARLY 2009 – A designer, Jaakko Iisalo, **presents** the idea for a new game to his (c) _____ at Finnish computer game developer, Rovio Entertainment. The game featured some angry-looking birds. They **like** the basic idea, but decide to give the birds some pigs as an enemy because of an outbreak of swine flu at the time. They **estimate** the initial (d) _____ of developing the game were €100,000.

DEC 2009 – In (e) _____ with Chillingo, Rovio **publish** Angry Birds on the Apple® App Store.

MARCH 2010 – Angry Birds **achieves** top-selling app status on the USA's App Store, where it stays until October that year. Also in March they **launch** a version of the game for Facebook.

OCT 2010 – They **release** the first version of the game for Android, and experience more than one million downloads in the first 24 hours and two million in its first weekend. Throughout 2010, versions for other (f) _____ **appear**. The company **claim** (g) _____ of over $100,000 a month just for the advertising on the free version of the game.

DEC 2010 – On the (h) _____ of its first release, Rovio **announce** over 50 million downloads, including 12 million on iOS devices (Apple) and 10 million on Android.

APRIL 2011 – The UK Appy Awards **name** Angry Birds as both the 'Best Game App' and 'App of the Year'.

MAY 2012 – The different versions of the game **reach** one billion downloads.

JUNE 2012 – At the Electronic Entertainment Expo in Los Angeles, California, Rovio and (i) _____ partner Activision **reveal** plans to bring Angry Birds and two of its (j) _____ games (the Angry Birds Trilogy) to the PlayStation 3, Xbox® 360 and Nintendo 3DS systems, taking advantage of their unique features, such as glasses-free 3D visuals.

It's been quite a success story!

Learning objectives: Unit 5

Business communication skills Discussing the history of an app; Completing a quiz about the Internet; Discussing experience of the Internet; Fluency: Giving a presentation about a company's history; Asking questions about the past
Reading Timeline describing history of Angry Birds; Article about the birth of the Internet
Listening Documentaries on the history of Angry Birds and the history of the Internet
Phrase bank Talking about the past
Vocabulary Business and the Internet
Grammar Past Simple, Questions about past events

4 All the verbs in **bold** in 3 have regular forms in the Past Simple: infinitive + *-ed* / *-d*.

like → liked

release → released

The pronunciation of *-ed* can be /d/, /t/, or /ɪd/. Write the Past Simple of the verbs in **bold** in 3 in the table below, according to their pronunciation.

Group 1	Group 2	Group 3
/d/	/t/	/ɪd/
achieved	liked	presented

5 🔵 **1.20** Listen again to the history of Angry Birds. Check your answers in 4.

6 Write five questions about the history of Angry Birds. Use the Past Simple.

When did Jaakko Iisalo present the idea for the game to his colleagues?

7 Work with a partner. Ask and answer the questions you each wrote in 6. Use the Past Simple in your answers.

Who really invented the Internet?

1 Work in groups and discuss the Internet.

a When was the first time you used the Internet? What did you use it for?

b Do you think the invention of the Internet has changed your life in any way?

c What is more important for you – the Internet or your mobile phone?

2 Work with a partner and do the quiz.

THE INTERNET QUIZ

1 In which year did Leonard Kleinrock connect the first two computers?
   a 1969
   b 1975
   c 1983

2 What did the first version of the Internet connect?
   a Military installations
   b Government buildings
   c Universities

3 In which year was the first international computer connection made?
   a 1969
   b 1973
   c 1983

4 What is the 'universal language' of the Internet?
   a English
   b JavaScript
   c TCP/IP

5 What was the name of the first browser?
   a Netscape
   b Mosaic
   c Gopher

3 🔵 **1.21** Listen to a radio documentary on the history of the Internet and check your answers in 2.

4 🔘 **1.21** Listen again and put the events below in the correct order.

☐ Bob Kahn and Vincent Cerf invent software for connecting computers on the Internet.
☐ Professor Kleinrock connects two computers.
☐ Ray Tomlinson sends the first email.
☐ ARPANET links four American universities.
☐ The first Internet browser becomes available.
☐ The Advanced Research Projects Agency starts work on ARPANET.
☐ A 'universal language' of the Internet is established.

5 Complete the article with the verbs in the box in the Past Simple. Some of them are irregular.

| become | begin | call | connect (x 2) | increase | invent | launch | make | reach | send |

6 🔘 **1.21** Listen again and check your answers.

Birth of the Internet

How old is the Internet? Different experts suggest different dates. It depends on what they understand the Internet to be.

We know that in 1965, the Advanced Research Projects Agency (ARPA), under the US Department of Defence, **(a)** _____ work on a system to connect computers. They **(b)** _____ the project ARPANET.

On September 2nd, 1969, in a laboratory at the University of California, Professor Leonard Kleinrock **(c)** _____ the first two machines. For many people, that day the Internet was born. The next month they sent the first message to a computer at Stanford University.

By January 1970, ARPANET **(d)** _____ computers in four American universities, and by the following year there were 23 in the system, connecting different universities and research institutes. In 1973, Ray Tomlinson

(e) _____ the first email via ARPANET. In the same year the Net went international, connecting computers in England and Norway.

The next step was to connect different networks and to create an 'Internetwork'. In 1974, Bob Kahn and Vincent Cerf **(f)** _____ a software called TCP/IP that connected networks using different operating systems. On January 1st, 1983, this software **(g)** _____ the universal language of the Internet – many experts think that this event was the real birth of the Internet because it **(h)** _____ it possible to link different networks in one web.

More and more networks joined the system and the number of connected computers **(i)** _____

dramatically: from 10,000 in 1984 to 100,000 in 1987. By the early 1990s, the network was accessible to anyone in the world with a computer. In 1992, the number of hosts **(j)** _____ 1,000,000.

In 1993, two programmers, Marc Andreessen and Eric Bina, **(k)** _____ the first version of Mosaic – the first graphics-based browser of the type we all use today – which made the Internet an easy means to browse websites, get information and spread news.

7 With a partner, ask and answer questions about the history of the Internet using the word prompts.

a When / Professor Kleinrock / connect / first two computers?

b Where / they / send / first message?

c What / Ray Tomlinson / send / 1973?

d What / Bob Kahn and Vincent Cerf / invent?

e When / TCP/IP / become / universal language of the Internet?

f How much / the Internet / grow / between 1984 and 1987?

8 The questions in 7 use the following structure:

Question word	*did*	Subject	Infinitive	
When	did	Professor Kleinrock	connect	two computers?

When you do not know the subject, you use the following structure:

	Who/What	Verb in past simple	
~~Who did send the first email?~~	Who	sent	the first email?
~~What did happen yesterday?~~	What	happened	yesterday?

This usually only happens with *who* and *what*.

9 Look at the chart below and practise asking and answering questions like this.
Who did Sarah text? Jack. Who phoned Jack? John.

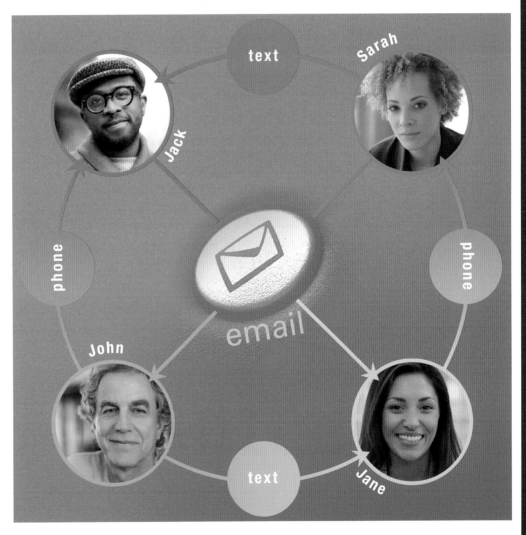

10 Work with a partner. Combine verbs and phrases in the tables below to ask questions beginning *When was the last time you ...?* Then ask follow-up questions.

A *When was the last time you sent an email?*

B *This morning.*

A *Who did you send it to?*

B *To a customer.*

A *What was it about?*

Use the phrases in the box, if you like.

| I never do / have. | I really can't remember. | It was a long time ago. | I'm not sure. |

Speaker A		Speaker B	
send	an interview	take	a car
find	a phone call	download	late for a meeting
travel	an email	deal	a plane
make	on business	negotiate	to a useful meeting
take	something useful on	go	a smartphone
go	the Internet	buy	a new program
eat	on a course	hire	with a complaint
have	sushi	arrive	a deal
	a taxi		

Company history

Prepare a short presentation about the history of your company (or one that you know about) or an invention. You may find some of the words in the box useful. Then give your presentation to the other students in the class.

| achieve | begin | develop | establish | expand | found | increase |
| launch | manufacture | produce | reach | want | | |

Include information about the following, if you know it.

- the origins of the company, who founded it and when
- key dates in its history
- the opening of new offices or factories
- important orders or contracts it obtained
- periods of important growth
- introduction of new products or services
- establishment of subsidiaries
- appointment of key personalities in its management
- significant recent events

BUSINESS PLAN

05 Internet histories

Phrase bank: Talking about the past

When did they first ...?   Who started the company?

How long ago did ...?   Who invented ...?

When was the last time ...?   What happened in ...?

Vocabulary

Business and the Internet

Complete the sentences below with an appropriate verb. The first letter has been given.

a Angry Birds™ b_____ a popular app very quickly.

b The company plans to r_____ a new version next year.

c It can take a lot of time and money to d_____ an idea into a successful product.

d They c_____ to have a turnover of over $1,000,000 a month.

e The final costs were much higher than they originally e_____.

f Our objective is to r_____ sales of $30 million this year.

g They a_____ the joint venture at the Las Vegas conference.

h Last month 3 million people d_____ the app.

i The designer p_____ an idea for a new product at the meeting.

j Did they a_____ the expected turnover last year?

Answers on page 145.

Grammar

Past Simple

Affirmative		Negative		Interrogative		
I		I			I	
You		You			you	
He		He			he	
She	worked.	She	didn't work.	Did	she	work?
It		It		Didn't	it	
We		We			we	
They		They			they	

Formation: regular verbs

- infinitive
    work – worked
- infinitive ending in *e*
    like – liked
- infinitive ending in consonant + *y*
    hurry – hurried
- one-syllable verbs ending in one vowel + one consonant
    stop – stopped
    (except verbs ending in *w* or *y*)
    play – played, show – showed
- two-syllable verbs with the stress on the second syllable
    prefER – preferred, admIT – admitted
- two-syllable words with the stress on the first syllable
    VISit – visited, ENter – entered

Formation: irregular verbs

Many of the most common verbs are irregular.

go – went, come – came

See page 128 for the Irregular verb list.

Use

You use the Past Simple to express finished actions, events or situations.

- *We **moved** to a new office last year.**
- *Before I got married I **lived** in Lisbon.*
- *In my first job, I **travelled** a lot.*

* You often use the Past Simple with expressions describing completed periods of time: *three weeks ago, last year, on Tuesday, in March, at Christmas*, etc.

Time expressions

To say when things happened in the past, you use:

- *in* + month / year – *in March, in 1987*
- *on* + day / date – *on Monday, on 5th December*
- *at* + time / special periods – *at 5.00, at Christmas*
- length of time + *ago* – *five minutes ago, a week ago*
- *when* + past situation / action – *when I was younger, when he arrived*
- *before* + past situation / action – *before I met him*

Practice 1

Write the verbs in the Past Simple.

a	work	_worked_	j	marry	_____
b	stop	_stopped_	k	plan	_____
c	live	_____	l	reach	_____
d	start	_____	m	arrive	_____
e	use	_____	n	fit	_____
f	travel	_____	o	visit	_____
g	drop	_____	p	call	_____
h	carry	_____	q	increase	_____
i	tip	_____	r	like	_____

Practice 2

Write the irregular verbs in the Past Simple.

a	tell	_told_	g	make	_____
b	say	_____	h	do	_____
c	get	_____	i	go	_____
d	give	_____	j	come	_____
e	take	_____	k	write	_____
f	put	_____	l	have	_____

Practice 3

Write questions about the missing information.

a I went to ... on my last business trip.
   Where did you go on your last business trip?

b He set up the company in ...
   When _____

c They started selling ... last year.
   _____

d At first, the product sold well because ...
   _____

e They made a profit by ...
   _____

f He worked for ICI for ... years.
   _____

g I spoke to ... at the conference.
   _____

h ... invented the mobile phone.
   _____

i ... people work in the Lille factory.
   _____

j I travelled from Munich to Berlin by ...
   _____

Practice 4

Complete the sentences with the words in the box or put 'X' when no word is necessary.

| ago | at | for | in | on | when |

a John started working here _____ Christmas but I met him for the first time ten minutes _____.

b I travelled a lot _____ last year.

c _____ Monday I had a meeting with Mr Leblanc.

d I sent them the fax _____ on 5th July.

e _____ I lived in London, I usually went away _____ the weekend.

f The delegation from Geneva arrived _____ three o'clock.

g I worked for IBM _____ three years.

h We had a really interesting business trip to Turkey _____ March.

i I had a meeting _____ 9.30 _____ the evening and eventually got to my hotel _____ two _____ the morning.

j When I woke up _____ yesterday morning, I didn't know where I was.

k Did Mr Heinkers phone _____ I was out?

Practice 5

The following facts are incorrect. Make the sentences negative. Then give the correct information.

a Steve Jobs co-founded Google.
   Steve Jobs didn't co-found Google, he co-founded Apple®.

b On 4 October 1929, the Wall Street Crash started a worldwide economic boom.
   _____

c On 25 March 1957, six European states signed the Treaty of Madrid, creating the EEC.
   _____

d On 1 January 1999, eleven member states of the European Union adopted the pound as a common currency.
   _____

e Engineers at Apple produced the Android smartphone.
   _____

f Mark Zuckerberg invented Twitter.
   _____

Answers on page 131.

06 Orders

What's the biggest mistake you've made at work?

1 🔊 **1.22** Listen to a telephone conversation about an order and answer the questions.
a Who does Elena Moretti want to speak to?
b What product does she want to order?
c What is the reference number?
d How many units does she want?
e What is the delivery date?
f Why is this order particularly important?

2 Work with a partner. Practise the conversation using the prompts.
A S-A-G / help?
B Yes / speak / John Bird?
A afraid / not / office / now // can / message?
B Oh, dear! // urgent order / we / five hydraulic pumps / 22 June
A Just / minute // tell / name please?
B sorry // Elena Moretti / Stern Hydraulics / Switzerland
A Right / take down / details / get John / contact // say five units?
B Yes / reference / SG 94321
A SG 94321 / five units
B yes / right // important thing / delivery date / 22 June
A not think / a problem
B good / for / new customer
A I see // when John comes / tell him immediately // confirm / order / by email?
B yes / course / thanks / much
A you / welcome / goodbye
B goodbye

3 Complete Elena Moretti's email confirming the order.

---

ref SG 94321

Dear John,

Further to (a) _____ with your colleague this afternoon, I wish (b) _____ our order for (c) _____ hydraulic pumps (ref SG 94321), to arrive no later than (d) _____. Please let us know about any problems processing this order. We are especially concerned about receiving the parts on time, as it is for a (e) _____ customer.

Best regards,
Elena Moretti

---

4 Later that day, John Bird phoned back. Work with a partner. Try to complete the conversation using the words and phrases in the box.

all the details	Could I speak to	good	help you	in touch	Is that	it's quite
more business	phoning	worried	worry			

John _____ Elena Moretti, please?

Elena Speaking. _____ John?

John Yes. Hello, Elena. I'm just _____ back about your order.

Elena Yes, _____ urgent; I hope you can help.

John Don't _____. I've got _____ in your email. No problem – we're happy to help.

Elena That's _____. I was quite _____ about it.

John It should be fine. Can I _____ with anything else?

Elena No, thank you. I hope we get _____ from this customer.

John Yes, of course. Okay, I'll be _____. Bye for now.

Elena Goodbye.

5 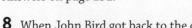 **1.23** Now listen to the conversation in 4 to check your answers.

6 Later, Elena received this email confirming her order. What is the mistake?

ORDER CONFIRMATION	
Date:	1 June
Order no:	DH010601
Received:	23 May
No. of units:	5
Delivery required:	7 July
Processed by:	John Bird

7 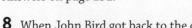 **1.24** Elena called SAG to tell John Bird about the mistake. Put the conversation in the correct order. Then listen and check.

☐ S-A-G, can I help you?

☐ No, it's not your fault. Just ask John to phone me.

☐ Right, Elena, leave it with me. I'm terribly sorry about this.

☐ Oh, hello, Elena. I'm afraid John isn't here at the moment. Can I take a message?

☐ Yes, it says 7th July, but the agreed delivery date was 22nd June. It's really important.

☐ Yes, this is Elena Moretti from Stern Hydraulics. Could I speak to John Bird, please?

☐ Oh, dear. Can you give me the details?

☐ All right, then. Bye for now.

☐ Thank you. I'm not at all happy about this. A lot depends on this order.

☐ I see. Well, I'll tell him as soon as he comes in.

☐ Yes, he sent me an order confirmation – the reference is DH010601 – but the delivery date is wrong.

☐ Goodbye.

Answers on page 131.

8 When John Bird got back to the office, he tried to phone Elena but couldn't get through. He decided to send an email. Write his email using the prompts below.

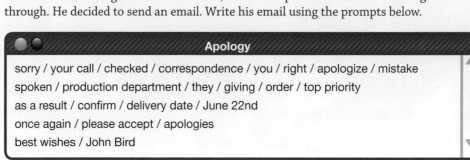

Apology
sorry / your call / checked / correspondence / you / right / apologize / mistake
spoken / production department / they / giving / order / top priority
as a result / confirm / delivery date / June 22nd
once again / please accept / apologies
best wishes / John Bird

9 On 22nd June the parts didn't arrive. They didn't arrive until 30th June. Elena phoned John again. Work with a partner and act out the conversation.

Speaker B: Look at page 145.

Speaker A: You are Elena Moretti. You are furious with John Bird. The order arrived late and as a result you will get no more orders from your new customer. SAG let you down and you think John Bird is responsible. You are also angry about the fact that he never returns your calls and always makes mistakes. Unless he offers you some compensation (such as heavy discounts on future orders), tell him you will take your business elsewhere.

Correspondence

1 Discuss these questions with a partner.

a Some people think that emails are an informal way of communication (or less formal than a traditional letter). Do you agree?

b If someone sends you a badly written email, do you find it annoying? Are you more understanding if you know they are not writing in their first language?

c Is there anything else about emails that annoys you, e.g. not using a sensible title in the subject line, not including the original message when replying, etc?

2 Read the article from a business magazine. Do you think the bosses in the survey were right? Why / Why not?

—Does— grammar matter?

According to a report published recently, standards in written English are falling. This is because people see email as an informal way of communicating where the normal rules of grammar and punctuation do not apply. In a survey by MSN, two-thirds of those aged 18–24 said that they were more concerned about the content of their emails than grammatical correctness. Of older users, one in four also admitted they were not concerned about grammatical correctness in their messages.

Surprisingly, in the same survey, most people said they were annoyed by errors in the emails they received. Annoyance with mistakes in conventional letters was an even bigger problem. In another survey, bosses said they would not do business with companies whose correspondence had mistakes in it. Unbelievably, they thought it was worse than charging too much.

3 Read the following emails from a company called CiclosCiclone to a customer, David Holmbrook.

a Rewrite the emails and correct the mistakes in punctuation and grammar. Change anything which you do not think is appropriate in style.

b Compare your emails with the versions on page 144. <u>Underline</u> any phrases which you think are useful for this type of email.

CiclosCiclone

Order Form

Customer:	David Holmbrook	
Customer order no:	15724	
Details:	1 x item GH56	£19.50
	3 x items GH98	£48.00
Shipping:		£12.40
Total:		£79.90

Re: CiclosCiclone

Dear mr Holmbrook

Thanks for the order. I just wish confirm that we have received your order details and we have started to process the order. If your item is not instock or if there are are any dispatch problems we will contact you within the next 24/36 hrs. Please contact us if you not have received you order within 7 days at orders@ciclosciclone.com so we can resolve the issues.

thankyou once again for your order.

Kind Regards.

CiclosCiclone (Despatch Team)

Re: CiclosCiclone

Hi there,

Re the modification thats not a problem the whole amount for your order will be £84.85.

I look forward to hearing from you,

Best wishes

Diego Martin

Re: CiclosCiclone

Dear dave

We apologize for the delay, but we have worked out the cost of your shipping amounts of the modified order, it is going to cost you £6.99 more.

To activate this transaction. we will need to re-take your card details by phone to process the payment manually. We will need the long number on the front of your card, the expiry date and the security code on the back of card.

Thank you for you patience and shopping with CiclosCiclone, I look forward to hearing from you,

Best wishes

Diego

Re: CiclosCiclone

ok Dave, will sort this out for you, and it shall be with you soon! Sorry again.

Best wishes

Diego

On-the-spot decisions

1 🔘 **1.25** Listen to the telephone conversation between David Holmbrook, the caller, and Jim Kutz, who answers the call. Answer the questions.

a Who does David want to speak to?
b Why?
c Why did David send a text message?
d What solution does Jim offer?
e What is Jim's email address?

2 Some situations require on-the-spot decisions. What did the speakers in 1 say? Circle the correct answers.

I'll send you I'm going to send I'm sending	a copy of the certificate.
I'll deal I'm going to deal I'm dealing	with the email straight away.

You use *will* + infinitive to show that you are making an on-the-spot decision and to promise action.

3 Complete the conversation below using *will* + infinitive of the verbs in the box.

fly   ring   send (x2)   write

A Have we got the details of the order from David Holmbrook?
B No, but don't worry, I _____ now.
A I tried – there's no answer.
B Well, I _____ him an email, then.
A You can't – our server is down.
B Never mind – I _____ him a fax.
A I don't think he has a fax machine.
B Well, in that case, I _____ him a letter before I leave the office.
A Oh, come on, that'll take far too long.
B So, we _____ out to see him!
A Oh, that's a bit expensive …

4 🔘 **1.26** Listen and check your answers.

5 Work with a partner.

Speaker A: Look at the chart on page 141.
Speaker B: Choose a problem from the table and tell Speaker A. Begin *I've got a problem* …
Speaker A will offer a solution and then tell you about a problem. React using one of the solutions below. Say *Don't worry, I'll* …

A *I've got a problem, the battery in my mobile's flat.*
B *Don't worry, I'll lend you mine.*

Problems	Solutions
I've got a headache.	I'll take you to the airport.
We didn't get your text.	I'll scan the details to you instead.
This report has lots of errors in it.	I'll show you how it works.
I can't remember his phone number.	I'll explain them to you.
I haven't booked my flight to Berlin.	I'll call the IT technician.
I need three copies of this proposal.	I'll phone you this afternoon.
I don't know anything about this company.	I'll change the ink cartridge.

Answers on page 146.

06 Orders

Phrase bank: Dealing with orders

Thank you for …
Please accept my apologies for …
I apologize for …
I'll deal with it …
Please contact us / let us know if …
Let me take down the details …
Regarding …
I'm not at all happy about this.
I wish to / would like to confirm our order.

Business communication

1 Match the sentence beginnings (a–h) with the endings (1–8).

a There is a message …		**1**	… in writing last week.
b There is a mistake …		**2**	… in the letter you sent me.
c I asked him to phone …		**3**	… to your order.
d I sent you an email …		**4**	… about this problem last week.
e We confirmed the date of the meeting …		**5**	… back this afternoon.
f I will send you the packet …		**6**	… for what happened.
g I'd like to apologize …		**7**	… by courier this afternoon.
h We are giving top priority …		**8**	… from Dave Cartwright for you.

a	b	c	d	e	f	g	h

2 The following emails have no punctuation or capital letters and the tone is incorrect. Correct the emails so that they make sense.

a dear mr gonzalez thank you for contacting lexington technical support unfortunately I do not understand the nature of the problem you are having or in fact even the product you are using can you please write back with as much information as you can about what product you are using what you are trying to do what problem you are having etc best regards kamal bouaissi technical support engineer

b dear richard tennant thank you for registering your lexington product your new customer number is 55563500 when calling technical support (925–253–3050) or lexington customer service (800–225–4880) please have your customer number ready we recommend writing your customer number in your lexington manual keeping it with our phone numbers and filing this email for future reference thank you for your interest in lexington if there is anything we can do for you please let us know we will be happy to help you regards lexington customer service

3 Complete the crossword using the words in brackets as clues.

Across

1 The _____ date for this order is 26th June. (when the order is supposed to arrive with the customer)

6 We'd like a _____ reply. ('quick' or 'fast')

8 People see emails as an _____ way of communicating. (the opposite of 'formal')

9 I'm sorry, I can't read his _____. (He wrote it with a pen.)

10 Machine used to send documents by telephone. (not a modem)

13 We hope to do more _____ with them in the future. (buy or sell things or services)

15 I need to look at the _____ again. (the noun of 'correspond')

19 To make sure something is correct.

21 Sometimes it's difficult to make a _____. (the noun of 'decide')

22 Could I leave a _____, please? (what you leave when someone is not there)

24 I'm really _____ he hasn't phoned me. (irritated)

28 'Thank you.' 'You're _____.'

29 Could I take _____ the details? (the opposite of 'up')

30 Could you _____ that you have received this email? (the verb of 'confirmation')

Down

2 Please do it _____. (at once)

3 The opposite of 'cheap'.

4 The name written at the bottom of a document or email.

5 Could you confirm the _____ in writing, please? (bits of information)

7 A service which picks up and delivers documents. (like UPS)

11 I'd like to _____ for the mistake. (say sorry)

12 I'm still waiting for a _____ from John to my letter.

14 Nowadays I use it for all my research and for sending emails.

16 I'm very _____ about this. (the adjective of 'worry')

17 I'm _____ about the order. (calling)

18 Error.

20 'Hello, is _____ John?' 'Yes, speaking.'

23 Bad writing _____ cost companies a lot of money. (abilities)

25 I want to place an _____ for 300 units.

26 Can you _____ it to me by email?

27 How much will it _____ us to send it?

Answers on page 138.

Grammar

will for unplanned decisions

You use *will* + infinitive to show you are making an on-the-spot or new decision.

Practice 1

When would you say the following sentences? Match the decisions (a–g) to the situations (1–7).

a   I'll open the door for you.
b   I'll take a taxi.
c   I'll catch an earlier train.
d   I'll lend it to you, if you like.
e   I'll have a look on the Internet.
f   I'll speak to the boss about it.
g   I'll have another look at the figures.

1   A customer asks if you can give him a better discount.
2   Your boss asks you if you can start work before the usual time.
3   A colleague reminds you about a meeting with a client on the other side of town in ten minutes.
4   Someone asks you where you can get a new battery for a laptop computer.
5   A colleague is carrying a lot of files and documents and has both hands occupied.
6   Your wife/husband asks if you can take a day off work.
7   A colleague admires a new CD you are listening to.

  a   b   c   d   e   f   g

Practice 2

What would you say in these situations? Reply using the word in brackets.

a   Someone offers you something to drink. You can have tea or coffee. (coffee)

b   You are ordering a meal in a restaurant. You can have either soup or salad for a starter. (salad)

c   You go out with some friends. You decide to pay for the drinks. (pay)

d   A colleague is having problems with a new computer program you are familiar with. (help)

e   Someone reminds you that you are taking a flight at 10.30 am. It is now 9 am. (taxi)

f   A colleague has heard on the radio that the buses are on strike and now they can't get home. You have your car. (lift)

07 Hotels

What is the best hotel you have ever stayed in? And the worst?

Learning objectives: Unit 7

Business communication skills Discussing hotel features; Making comparisons; Making and responding to special requests; Discussing world records; Fluency: Discussing the pros and cons of different office locations
Reading Posts on a forum about hotels; Article about YOTEL
Listening Conversation at airport check-in; Conversation at hotel reception
Phrase bank Travel and accommodation
Vocabulary Hotel services
Grammar Comparatives and superlatives
In company interviews Units 5–7

1 How often do you stay in hotels? Have you had any of the problems which frustrated travellers in the survey quoted on the left? What things about hotels do you like?

2 🔵 **1.27** Listen to a conversation and answer the questions.

a Where does the conversation take place?

b What does the customer want?

c What is the customer going to do?

3 🔵 **1.27** Complete the dialogue using the phrases in the box. Then listen again to check your answers.

> booked on the next flight   Can you recommend   could try the Travel Inn
> like me to phone for you, sir   there's nothing before   was delayed, so I've missed

A Hello. My connecting flight, IB621, (a) _____ the flight to Caracas.

B Yes, sir. I'm sorry about that. You're (b) _____.

A Yes, but it's not until eleven tonight, right?

B Yes. I'm afraid (c) _____.

A That's nearly eight hours to wait. (d) _____ a hotel I could try?

B You (e) _____. It's not far from the terminal building.

A Thanks. I really need somewhere to sleep.

B Would you (f) _____?

A No, that's okay. I need to stretch my legs anyway. Thanks very much.

4 Have you ever been in this situation? What did you do?

5 🔵 **1.28** Listen to another conversation and answer the questions.

a Where does the conversation take place?

b What special request does the guest make? Does he get what he wants?

c What would the guest like sent to his room?

d Does the room have Internet access?

6 🔘 **1.28** Write questions using the prompts. Then listen again to check your answers.

a have / room / available ? *Do you have any rooms available?*

b is / just / tonight ? _____

c is / possible / pay / room / hour ? _____

d could / see / passport ? _____

e would / like / anything / send up / room ? _____

f Internet access / available ? _____

7 With a partner, act out the dialogue. Use the questions in 6 to help you.

Time to kill

1 What do you expect a good hotel to provide? Tick the features you like to have. Add your own ideas to the list.

☐	widescreen television	☐	minibar
☐	bar	☐	24-hour room service
☐	Wi-Fi connection	☐	air conditioning
☐	restaurant	☐	massage service
☐	convenient location	☐	beautiful surroundings
☐	swimming pool	☐	gym
☐	parking	☐	sauna
☐	fitness rooms	☐	meeting rooms

2 Read these comments by business travellers about a type of hotel. What kind of hotel is it? Where do you think the hotel is?

HOME	Hotels	Flights	Restaurants	Things to do	More	Write a review

Author	Topic
Chris Roberts, Boston, USA	*posted – 14.02.14* Before my flight home I had a few hours to kill and I checked in using the automatic service. The price was very reasonable and I was very impressed with the stylish interior of the rooms. I would recommend it to anyone who finds themselves waiting for a flight and doesn't have a problem with small spaces.
Stephanie, New Jersey, USA	*posted – 11.01.14* Incredible what they can fit into seven square metres! A chance to shower and sleep off the jet lag after my overnight flight from New York. And good the other way, too. Many short-hop flights from continental Europe arrive in the UK late in the afternoon, leaving you stranded until the next day's flight to the US.
Sally Chatterley, Las Vegas, USA	*posted – 29.08.13* This is great for airports where passengers have to change planes and perhaps wait for eight hours. It's certainly more comfortable than stretching out on a couch in the departure lounge. No windows but it's quiet and private, and within walking distance of the terminal building.

3 Find words and phrases in the comments in 2 which mean the same as the following:

a had nothing to do for a few hours *had a few hours to kill*

b not expensive _____

c the opposite of 'long-haul flights' _____

d to be stuck somewhere _____

e lying down _____

4 Read the article about a hotel chain called YOTEL and decide whether the statements below are true or false.

a	YOTEL rooms are standard three-star hotel rooms.	true ☐	false ☐
b	You can't sit down in a YOTEL room.	true ☐	false ☐
c	YOTEL aims to provide a service for office workers.	true ☐	false ☐
d	Only the premium YOTEL rooms have natural light.	true ☐	false ☐
e	Check-in is automated but there is room service available.	true ☐	false ☐
f	YOTEL hopes that in any 24-hour period, more guests will stay in the hotel than there are rooms.	true ☐	false ☐
g	You can rent YOTEL rooms by the hour.	true ☐	false ☐
h	The creator of YOTEL thinks that travellers like having reduced space.	true ☐	false ☐

The 46 rooms at YOTEL Gatwick manage to squeeze a bed, a pull-up desk, closet space, a shower and a flat-screen TV into just seven square metres (or ten square metres for the 'premium' class). The rooms have all the best features of first-class air cabins. The result is clean and stylish, like the interior of a luxury yacht.

The philosophy of YOTEL is to provide luxury, but at an affordable price. To reduce costs, they use many of the features of budget flights such as online-only booking, self-service check-in and a pricing policy which encourages early booking. The concept is really a Western adaptation of the Japanese 'capsule' hotel – ultra-cheap accommodation for office workers who sleep in coffin-like plastic modules stacked on top of each other. This is ideal for sites where space is limited, like airports and city centres.

Of course, YOTEL's rooms are bigger than the Japanese capsules. They are also more luxurious than the average three-star hotel room. Each soundproof cabin contains a sofa that converts into a double bed and leaves space for your suitcase underneath. A soft white-and-grey colour scheme and lots of glass and mirrors gives an impression of light and airiness. On the other hand, there is no natural light as the Premium 'cabins' have only a window onto the corridor and in Standard class there is no window at all.

YOTEL want to become the iPod of the hotel industry. They are hoping that techie travellers won't mind booking into a small but well-designed box filled with electronic gadgets. There are 60 TV channels, 80 radio channels and 5,000 music tracks, as well as wireless Internet to keep you entertained if you find it difficult to get to sleep. You can order food through the TV, and it is delivered promptly by the 'cabin crew' in takeaway boxes with wooden cutlery.

Any hotel in the world aims for 100% occupancy, but YOTEL aims for better than 200% occupancy. There are travellers who stay the night, another group who check in for four or five hours' rest in the morning and finally the afternoon guests looking for a more comfortable place than the airport terminal to have a siesta. The standard room costs £55 for the night or £25 for a four-hour slot (the minimum). Premium costs £40 for four hours, £80 overnight.

If you have an early morning flight, a long wait between flights or an unexpected delay, YOTEL offers an attractive option. At first sight it may seem a little claustrophobic but its creator, Simon Woodroffe, believes that this is compensated for by the quality of the product. 'Ask a focus group if they would like to sleep in a ten-square-metre room with no natural light and you won't get many takers – walk into a YOTEL room and you want it,' he says. YOTEL has plans to open more YOTELs at airports around the world.

GOODBYE MINIBAR,
HELLO MINIROOM

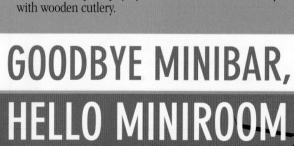

5 Look at the floor plan of the YOTEL rooms. There is a mistake in the article. What is it?

Standard cabin

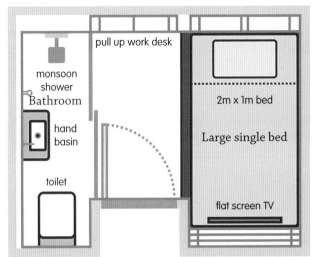

Room dimensions: 3.02m x 2m

Premium cabin

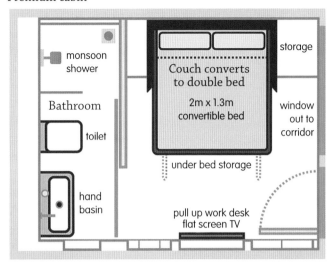

Room dimensions: 3.47m x 2.55m

6 Do you think you would want to stay in a YOTEL room? Why / Why not?

7 Look at this sentence from the article.

Of course, YOTEL's rooms are bigger than the Japanese capsules.

Underline any other sentences in the article where things are compared.

8 Make as many sentences as you can comparing a Japanese capsule room, a YOTEL room and an average three-star hotel room using the adjectives in the circle.

A YOTEL room is smaller than a normal hotel room.

A capsule is more claustrophobic than a YOTEL room.

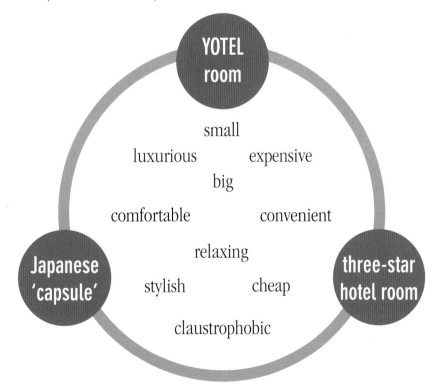

9 Now work with a partner and compare the following:

a three cities you both know

b three different cars

Room service

1 🔊 **1.29** It is ten o'clock at night. A guest calls room service to ask for something. Complete the conversation below. Then listen and compare your answers.

Room service Room service. My name is Johan. Can I help you?

Guest Yes, this is room 301. (a) _____ an early morning call, please?

Room service Certainly, sir. What time (b) _____ the call?

Guest At **half past six**.

Room service **Six thirty**. No problem. (c) _____ breakfast sent up to your room?

Guest No, thanks. I (d) _____ it in the dining room.

Room service The dining room doesn't open for breakfast until **seven thirty**.

Guest Oh, in that case I (e) _____ in my room. **Just coffee and a croissant.**

Room service **Coffee and a croissant.** (f) _____?

Guest No, that's all.

Room service Okay. (g) _____, sir.

Guest Thank you. Good night.

2 Change the phrases in **bold** in 1 to make a new conversation and practise with a partner.

3 Work with a partner to roleplay different conversations with room service.

Speaker A: You are the room service clerk.

Speaker B: Call room service to make requests for:

- something to eat
- someone to fix the air conditioning
- tomorrow's weather forecast
- someone to dry-clean a tie or a skirt
- help with Wi-Fi connection
- (your own request).

Now change roles.

Speaker B: You are the room service clerk.

Speaker A: See page 131.

World records

1 Use the adjectives in the box to say how the hotels below are world record breakers.

The Palazzo Resort and Casino in Las Vegas is the largest hotel in the world. It has 8,108 rooms.

expensive   high   large   old   tall

Hotel	Location	Detail
The Palazzo Resort and Casino	Las Vegas, USA	8,108 rooms
Burj Al Arab	Dubai, UAE	321 metres
Royal Villa at Grand Resort Lagonissi	Athens, Greece	$50,000 room/night
Hotel Everest View	Nepal	3,800 metres above sea level
Hoshi Ryokan	Awazu, Japan	Opened in 717

Answers on page 139.

2 Work with a partner. Do you know any new record-breaking hotels?

3 The room prices of four hotel chains vary from country to country. Work with a partner to complete the information in the tables, and discuss the hotel prices.

In Frankfurt, the most expensive chain is First Class Hotels. The cheapest chain of the four is Executive International. The second most expensive is Royal Inn and the third in the list is Travel Express.

Speaker A: Look at the information below.

Speaker B: Look at the information on page 141.

City	Chain	Price	City	Chain	Price
Amsterdam		272	London	Executive International	476
		238		Royal Inn	408
		195		First Class Hotels	329
		178		Travel Express	188
Frankfurt	First Class Hotels	494	New York		584
	Royal Inn	330			457
	Travel Express	157			268
	Executive International	152			260
Geneva		394	Paris	First Class Hotels	420
		357		Executive International	381
		260		Royal Inn	361
		148		Travel Express	254

Locating an office

Your company is planning to open a European office and needs to choose the best location. Look at the information below and decide which cities are the most suitable.

Talk about the following:

- high / low population
- near to / far from an international airport
- high / low taxi fares
- high / low / expensive / cheap office rents
- expensive / cheap hotel rooms
- high / low / expensive / cheap apartment rents
- high / low cost of living
- expensive / cheap place to live

In company interviews
Units 5–7

DATA	CITY A	CITY B	CITY C	CITY D
Population	642,811	185,028	495,781	1,031,925
Distance – city centre to airport (km)	12	4	10	14
Average taxi fare to airport (€)	24–29	27–31	17–20	40–44
International conferences per year	27	161	42	189
City centre office rents (€/sq m)	630	540	936	447
Hotel rooms (€ mid range/top range)	110/270	140/360	140/290	110/230
Three-room apartment rents (€/month)	1,431	1,430	2,545	1,367

07 Hotels

Vocabulary

Hotel services

1 Put the dialogue in the correct order.

Receptionist

☐ Yes, sir. What would you like?

☐ Room service. Katherine speaking. Can I help you?

☐ Of course, that's no problem. Would you like it with some toast?

☐ You're welcome, sir. Goodbye.

☐ Yes. Sparkling or still?

☐ Right, sir. It will be with you in fifteen minutes.

Guest

☐ Hello, Katherine. This is room 208 here. I'm feeling a bit hungry. I'd like to order a snack.

☐ Thank you, Katherine.

☐ Oh, sparkling, please, and nicely chilled.

☐ Oh, I don't know. Perhaps a little smoked salmon?

☐ Yes, please. And I'd also like some mineral water.

2 Complete the sentences using the correct form of the words in brackets.

a It can be difficult to find a decent hotel room at an _____ price. (afford)

b If you call room service, they will _____ meals to your room. (delivery)

c Although the room was small, it was perfectly _____. (comfort)

d A lot of our revenue comes from food and drink, but our rooms are more _____. (profit)

e Hotel guests from the USA _____ a standard room layout. (preference)

f You can _____ old buildings into hotels, but there is a limit to what you can do. (conversion)

g We have to meet our customers' _____. (expect)

h Multinational companies often expand by taking over smaller _____. (operate)

Grammar

Comparatives and superlatives

Adjective type	Adjective	Comparative	Superlative
one syllable	rich cheap	rich**er** cheap**er**	**the** rich**est** **the** cheap**est**
one syllable with one vowel + consonant	hot big	hot**ter** big**ger**	**the** hot**test** **the** big**gest**
two syllables ending in –y	early heavy	earl**ier** heav**ier**	**the** earl**iest** **the** heav**iest**
two syllables or more	economical	**more** economical	**the most** economical
	interesting	**more** interesting	**the most** interesting

You can often use the comparative form of adjectives with *than* to compare people, places and things.
- *Life is **easier than** in the past.*
- *The company is **more profitable than** its competitors.*

You can use *much, a lot, a bit* and *a little* to show if the differences are big or small.
- *Mexico City is **a lot bigger** than Rome.*
- *London is **much more expensive** than Madrid.*

You can also use *not as … as* to show differences.
- *Travelling by train is **not as expensive as** by plane.*

You use the article *the* with the superlative form of the adjective.
- *Taking important decisions is **the hardest** part of management.*
- ***The most useful** aspect of the Internet is communication.*

You can use *second, third* etc with superlatives.
- *Locally we are **the second largest** provider of Internet services.*

You can also use *less … than* and *the least* to show differences.
- *Life in the past was **less comfortable than** it is now.*
- *His company is **the least profitable** on the stock exchange.*

Practice 1

Rewrite the sentences using the opposite adjective.

a The Internet is faster than the post.
The post *is slower than the Internet.*

b Hotels are more expensive than motels.
Motels _____

c English is easier to learn than Mandarin.
Mandarin _____

d Trains are more comfortable than buses.
Buses _____

e People think that marketing is more interesting than accounting.
People think that accounting _____
_____

f Flying is safer than driving.
Driving _____

g Small meetings are more efficient than large ones.
Large meetings _____

h This job is better paid than my last one.
My last job _____

i The economic situation is worse than it was four years ago.
Four years ago the economic situation _____

Practice 2

Complete the sentences with *as* or *than*.

a The job isn't as interesting _____ I hoped.

b The meal was more expensive _____ I expected.

c This office has more space _____ the old one.

d I'm feeling more tired _____ yesterday.

e Fords aren't as good _____ Audis.

Practice 3

Complete the second sentence so that it means the same as the first sentence.

a It's easier to build hotels in the USA than it is in Europe.
It's not as difficult to build hotels in the USA as it is in Europe.

b A Maserati GT is more powerful than a Chevrolet.
A Chevrolet isn't _____
_____

c Profitability is more important than turnover.
Turnover isn't _____
_____

d Sales aren't as good as last year.
Sales are _____
_____

e It isn't as hot as yesterday.
Yesterday _____
_____

Practice 4

Which are the most populated countries in the world today? Look at the table and complete the sentences.
Do you know the population of your country? Discuss with a partner.

2002	2012	Country	Total population 2002 (millions)	Total population 2012 (millions)	Population growth rate 2012 (%)	Continent
1	1	China	1,281	**1,350**	0.48	Asia
2	2	India	1,050	**1,260**	1.31	Asia
3	3	United States of America	287	**314**	0.90	North America
4	4	Indonesia	217	**241**	1.04	Asia
5	5	Brazil	174	**194**	1.10	South America
7	6	Pakistan	144	**180**	1.55	Asia
8	7	Nigeria	130	**170**	2.55	Africa
9	8	Bangladesh	134	**153**	1.58	Asia
6	9	Russia	144	**143**	−0.48	Europe
10	10	Japan	127	**128**	0.08	Asia

In 2002, ...

a China had the _____ population in the world.

b Russia's population was _____ Nigeria's.

c The _____ heavily populated continent was Asia.

d Indonesia had a _____ population than India.

e Only one country had a _____ population in 2002 than in 2012.

In 2012, ...

a India had the second _____ population in the world.

b Russia had the _____ growth rate of all these countries.

c Brazil's population wasn't _____ as China's.

d Nigeria had the _____ growth rate of all these countries.

e China still had the _____ population in the world.

Telling stories

What do you think are the key features of a good story or anecdote?

anecdote /ˈænɪkdəʊt/
noun a story that you tell people about something interesting or funny that has happened to you

Learning objectives: Unit 8

People skills Telling an anecdote; Asking questions of encouragement; Fluency: Telling interesting stories **Listening** An anecdote about a journey

1 1.30 Complete the anecdote below with suitable words. Then listen and compare your answers.

A Look at that car!

B Yes, very nice. It's a Porsche 911.

A Did I ever tell you about the time I had a (a) _____ in a Porsche?

B No, I don't think so.

A It was when I (b) _____ a student. I was (c) _____ in Europe and a man in a Porsche stopped. He took me all the way across Austria. We (d) _____ about 220 kilometres an hour all the way.

B What about the (e) _____?

A Well, they (f) _____ us about four times, but this chap just showed them some identity card and they waved us on.

B Was he someone (g) _____, then?

A I don't know, I didn't ask. I (h) _____ he was some sort of high-ranking official. Anyway, it was the fastest I've ever been in a car.

2 1.31 Look at these sentences from the anecdote in 1.

It was when I was a student.
I was hitchhiking in Europe.

Make similar sentences using the prompts below. There are several alternatives. Then listen and compare your answers.

a	while / live / Italy	g	look / job
b	before / start / work / here	h	do / Masters / the States
c	after / leave / university	i	study / at Cambridge
d	when / work / ICL	j	work / small company / north
e	before / get / married	k	travel / Asia
f	just after / children / born	l	stay / Continental Hotel / Prague

3 ⊙ 1.32 You can encourage other people to tell you about their experiences by asking *Have you ever …?* or *Did you ever …?* Match the questions (a–h) with the answers (1–8). Then listen and check your answers.

a Did you ever hitchhike when you were a student?
b Have you ever had a car accident?
c Have you ever been to Rome?
d Have you ever lost any money on the stock exchange?
e Did you ever fail an exam at school?
f Have you ever been camping?
g Have you ever played a video game in 3D?
h Have you ever done anything illegal?

1 No, I'm glad to say. I nearly had one this morning!
2 Yes, lots of times. Actually, we bought a camper van last year.
3 No, but I'd love to see the Coliseum one day.
4 Yes, but it was a long time ago, and I hated waiting in the rain.
5 I didn't know you could. I've seen films with it though.
6 Not unless you count speeding and parking fines.
7 Not at school but I did at university.
8 No and I've never made any either.

a	b	c	d	e	f	g	h

Useful language:
Telling stories
Have you ever …?
Did you ever …?
I'll never forget the time I …
It was when I was at …
I … at the time.
Then what happened?
How did you feel about that?

4 Work with a partner and each tell two anecdotes based on the questions below. Help your partner by asking more questions. Use the useful language to help you.

Speaker A

Have you ever been stopped by the police when you were driving? Where were you going? Why did they stop you? Were they right or wrong? What was the outcome? Did it change your attitude either to driving or to the police, or did it confirm what you already thought?

Speaker B

Who was your least favourite teacher at school or lecturer at university? Why didn't you like them? Can you remember an incident that was typical of that person? Who was involved? What happened? What was the outcome? Did it change your point of view in any way or did it confirm what you already thought?

Speaker A

What was the best holiday you ever had? Where did you go? Who did you go with? Did you do anything unusual? Have you been back to the same place again?

Speaker B

What was the worst holiday you ever had? Where did you go? Who did you go with? Did you do anything unusual? Have you been back to the same place again?

In my shoes

in someone's shoes

imagining yourself in the situation that someone else is in

I'm having trouble with my boss. What would you do if you were in my shoes?

Learning objectives: Workplace Scenario B

Business communication skills Discussing complaints; Identifying strategies for dealing with complaints; Roleplay: Expressing concern and dealing with complaints
Reading Website about complaints
📹 **In company in action**
B1: An unsuccessful complaint; B2: Expressing concern and dealing with complaints

1 Read the business advice below and discuss the questions with a partner.

a When was the last time that you complained about something? What happened and how was your complaint dealt with? Were you happy with the outcome?

b Do you ever have to deal with complaints from customers or colleagues? What kind of things do people in your company complain about?

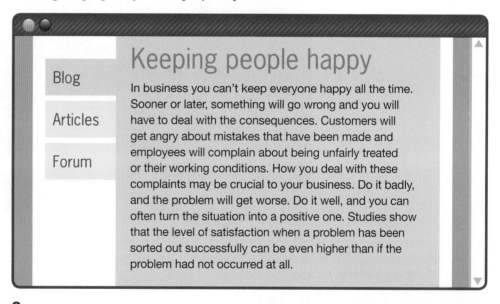

Keeping people happy

Blog

Articles

Forum

In business you can't keep everyone happy all the time. Sooner or later, something will go wrong and you will have to deal with the consequences. Customers will get angry about mistakes that have been made and employees will complain about being unfairly treated or their working conditions. How you deal with these complaints may be crucial to your business. Do it badly, and the problem will get worse. Do it well, and you can often turn the situation into a positive one. Studies show that the level of satisfaction when a problem has been sorted out successfully can be even higher than if the problem had not occurred at all.

In company in action 📹

2 Claudia López works in Marketing at Lenz Furniture Designs. She is having trouble with her computer and complains to the IT helpdesk. Watch video B1 and answer the questions.

a What is the complaint about?

b Eric, the IT technician, does not deal with the complaint successfully. What does he do wrong?

c Have you experienced similar problems with a different department in your company?

3 Read the advice opposite from the website about how to handle complaints and answer the questions.

a Do you think the four-step approach for dealing with complaints is an effective strategy?

b Do you think it helps to have a prepared strategy in these situations? Do you have any similar strategies?

c How important is it to 'put yourself in the shoes' of the person complaining?

Blog

Articles

Forum

The following four-step strategy will help you to take the heat out of a difficult situation and deal with a complaint effectively.

1. Listen with an open mind
Hear what the person has to say. Let the person speak without interruption. Listen carefully so you fully understand what has happened and why the person is upset.

2. Repeat the problem back
Once you see what the complaint is about, repeat it back in your own words to check that you have understood correctly. Ask questions if you are unsure of anything.

3. Be sympathetic and fair
Try to put yourself in the other person's shoes and be sympathetic. Reassure them that something will be done. Don't blame anyone, but show understanding and be fair and reasonable – this will help the person you are dealing with feel their complaint is being handled effectively.

4. Follow up promptly
As soon as possible, follow up with a report on what went wrong and the steps you plan to take to overcome the problem and stop it from happening again.

4   Here are some useful phrases for dealing with complaints. Match each phrase to the correct step in the strategy above. Add more phrases of your own if you can.

> Are you referring to …?   Can you describe the problem you had?
>
> Could you give me your mobile number / email address so I can get back to you?
>
> Do you mean that …?   Have I understood that correctly?
>
> I can see there may have been a misunderstanding. Let me see what I can do.
>
> I'll get back to you by the end of the week.
>
> I'm really sorry to hear that you have had a problem. Can you tell me what happened?
>
> I'll look into this and get back to you as soon as possible.   So, you are saying that …
>
> Tell me what happened.   The way you've described this, I can see why you are unhappy.

Dealing with complaints	Useful phrases
1 Listen with an open mind	
2 Repeat the problem back	
3 Be sympathetic and fair	
4 Follow up promptly	

5   When Claudia does not get a satisfactory solution to her IT problems, she decides to speak to David McCann, the Production and Operations Manager. Work with a partner and roleplay their conversation.

Speaker A: Look at page 135.
Speaker B: Look at page 130.

6   Evaluate your performance using the form on page 143.

In company in action

7   Now watch video B2 to see what happened when Claudia spoke to David. Repeat your roleplay, but this time swap roles. Use the notes from your evaluation form and as many of the useful phrases from 4 as you can.

8   With a partner, think of three other situations where you would make a complaint or use the examples below. Roleplay the conversations, taking turns to complain and using the four-step strategy and the phrases from 5.

- You are away on business and you overslept because you didn't get your wake-up call from the hotel. You missed an important meeting.
- You receive a telephone bill and you have been overcharged.
- You just got your payslip and you think you have been paid incorrectly for the second month in a row.
- The e-book which you just bought online has downloaded, but you cannot access it.

B IN MY SHOES   **55**

Spirit of enterprise

How important do you think it is in business to look ahead and think about the future?

Learning objectives: Unit 9

Business communication skills Exchanging information about a company; Discussing entrepreneurs; Describing change in a country or company
Writing Completing a report about a company
Reading Articles about two successful companies
Listening Radio programme about entrepreneurs; Company profile: Inditex
Phrase bank Talking about business developments
Vocabulary Language to describe change
Grammar Present Perfect

1 Work with a partner. Student A reads text A and Student B reads text B. Complete the chart below with information from your text.

	A blackcircles.com	B Dreams
First job of founder	*He worked in a garage.*	
Age when he started the company		*He was 35.*
First business premises		
Main product		
Distribution network		
Customer services		
Recent developments		

2 Ask your partner questions to complete the table for the company you didn't read about.

3 Read the other text. Underline the examples of the Present Perfect in both texts.

A

blackcircles.com

Michael Welch left school at 16 and started work in a garage as a car tyre fitter. He quickly learnt about the car tyre business and decided to set up his own mail-order company. He advertised in motoring magazines and sold high performance specialist tyres. He knew very little about running a business, so he took a college course to study aspects like financial management.

His next step was to get a job with the tyre company Kwik-Fit, where he got some experience and was able to study his future competition. After a year there and still only 20, he decided it was time to go it alone.

Welch set up a company called blackcircles.com, which allows customers to order tyres on the Internet and get them fitted within a day at one of its 1,300 affiliated garages. He started in an office with furniture from a rubbish tip. His first priority was to find reliable independent garages to fit the tyres and at the beginning he spent a lot of his time approaching and checking fitters across the country. After six months, he took on his first employee to help and the business began to grow, despite some problems with his investing partners.

Since those early days, blackcircles.com has built up a network of over 900 franchises. The company clearly thinks that it is successful partly because it listens to its customers, and the website encourages them to give feedback on the service by emailing Welch directly. As it says, 'Since 2001 we have supplied and fitted tyres for thousands of satisfied customers, many of whom have bought tyres from blackcircles.com again and again.'

After a year of negotiations and discussions, the company's impressive track record led to the recent launch of tesco-tyres.com, in partnership with Britain's leading retailer. This joint venture has meant access to Tesco's massive nationwide customer base – including 13 million Clubcard holders. As a result of the Tesco Tyres deal, the company has achieved an estimated annual turnover of around £30 million.

When Mike Clare left school at 18 with a basic business diploma, he started working in the beds department of a furniture shop. He became a manager, but when he was 35, after 12 years working for someone else, he decided it was time to start his own business. He got a small loan, sold his car to raise some money, and found a small shop, which was in a bad state but was cheap. He started the Sofabed Company in 1985 and within two years he had three stores. After a while he decided to concentrate on beds because they take up less space and are easy to store. He also found that people are less concerned about the look of a bed than a sofa, so beds are easier to sell. He then changed the name of the company to Dreams.

Dreams has built its business on four main selling points: Choice, Price, Delivery and Comfort. Distribution has been the company's biggest challenge

and it now has a fleet of over 100 vans. Dreams has also given a lot of special attention to customer service. When a Dreams driver delivers a bed he puts on a special pair of slippers to avoid making a mess. 'The slippers cost us virtually nothing, but after a delivery it's all the customers can talk about,' explains Clare.

The company has grown very quickly and in 2008 opened the 200th store – doubling its size in just five years. These days Dreams is still the UK's fastest growing retailer and it has branched out into the international market through franchising. In the last couple of years, with the increasing importance of social media in marketing strategies, it has launched a Dreams YouTube channel and is on Facebook.

DREAMS

entrepreneur

/ˌɒntrəprəˈnɜː/

noun someone who uses money to start businesses and make business deals

4 Michael Welch and Mike Clare are both entrepreneurs. Read the extracts below and discuss the questions which follow.

I've always felt that going to business school was a substitute for being an entrepreneur, not a complement. Those who can, sell. Those who can't, sit in class.

Business consultant and writer Arnold Kling on http://gondwanaland.com/mlog/2005/11/23/learning-by-selling/

Born entrepreneurs can be taught how to become better businesspeople. But businesspeople cannot be taught how to become entrepreneurs.

Wil Schroter's Blog http://www.gobignetwork.com/wil/

Entrepreneurs are people who imagine things as they might be, not as they are, and have the drive to change the world. Those are qualities that business schools do not teach.

Founder of The Body Shop, Anita Roddick

a What is the word for 'entrepreneur' in your language? Give some examples of entrepreneurs who are famous in your country.
b Is it possible to teach someone to be an entrepreneur?
c What kind of skills and qualities do you think entrepreneurs need?
d Is it an advantage to go to university before you start a business? Which opinion above do you agree with most?

5 🔘 **1.33** Listen to a radio programme that discusses a book about entrepreneurs. Answer the questions.

a Which of the opinions in 4 does the author most agree with?

b How many examples does he give of successful businesses?

c Which of the following does he say the entrepreneurs have in common?

☐ an MBA

☐ working for someone else before setting up a business

☐ hiring good employees

☐ luck

☐ taking risks

☐ providing excellent customer service

☐ intelligence

☐ using television advertising

☐ setting up efficient distribution networks

☐ hard work

6 🔘 **1.33** Listen again and complete the phrases.

a Mike Clare, the founder of Dreams, and Michael Welch of blackcircles.com are both good examples of people who _____ work when they _____ school.

b They _____ knowledge and skills while they _____ for someone else, but each _____ that his real mission in life was to be an entrepreneur.

c Both _____ customer service a major selling point.

d _____ successful at building up their networks.

e They _____ incredibly hard to get where they are today.

7 Which of the sentences in 6 are examples of the following:

• the Past Simple _____

• the Present Perfect _____

• an event or stage in someone's life which is completely finished _____

• an achievement or event which is part of an ongoing situation _____

Change

1 Label each graph with two verbs from the box which describe change.

fall   go up   go down   not change   increase   remain stable

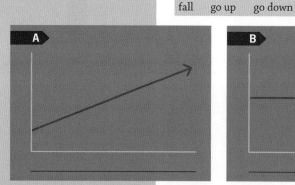 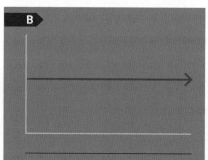 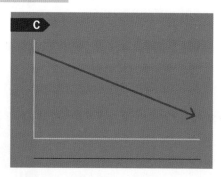

2 Work in groups. Using the verbs in 1, describe what has happened recently in your country or region, and in the company you work for. Use the topics below to help you.

*Interest rates **have fallen** in the last six months.*

*The number of people working in my team at work **has increased** recently.*

in your country or region

• house prices

• rate of inflation

• unemployment

• economic growth

• taxes

• interest rates

• population

• traffic

in your company

• profits

• revenues

• number of staff

• amount of work

Has anything else important happened in your country, region or company?

3 🔘 **1.34** You are going to hear an extract from a radio programme about Inditex, one of the world's biggest clothes manufacturers. Before you listen, try to match the names in the box to their descriptions below.

| Arteixo, Spain | H&M | La Coruña, Spain | Massimo Dutti | Middle East | Pablo Isla | Zara |

a competitor   _____

b CEO   _____

c flagship store   _____

d location of first store   _____

e location of majority of manufacturing   _____

f Inditex retailer   _____

g location for expansion   _____

Now listen and check your answers.

4 🔘 **1.34** Listen again and answer these questions.

a How many stores and employees does Inditex have?

b What are the four 'key factors' in Inditex's business model?

c Why does Zara only make 'small batches of each product'?

d What does Zara use its IT system for?

e What were Inditex's sales in 2012?

f What are the potential problems of expansion?

g What is the advantage of having a strong online presence?

h What do you think is meant by the term 'fast fashion'?

5 Match the sentence beginnings (a–e) with the endings (1–5).

a In 1963, Ortega …

b Ortega believes in …

c 60% of production …

d Zara believes communication with …

e Inditex is a company which …

1 … takes place at Inditex's headquarters in Spain.

2 … its customers is extremely important.

3 … began his career in the clothing industry.

4 … is constantly moving forward.

5 … inexpensive and fashionable clothing.

6 Complete the report using information from 3 and 4 and the verbs in the box in either the Past Simple or Present Perfect.

> add   give   grow   increase   open (x2)

Inditex is a tremendous success story. Since its first store (a) _____ in (b) _____ in 1975, it (c) _____ enormously. It now has (d) _____ employees and (e) _____ over 5,000 stores around the world. Over the years, Inditex (f) _____ retailers such as Uterqüe, Bershka and (g) _____ to its collection of brands. This (h) _____ the company a strong presence on the high street and, in 2012, net revenues (turnover) (i) _____ to an amazing (j)_____.

7 Write a similar report describing the changes in a company you know about. You should mention:

- any new development in commercial activity
- increase/decrease in turnover and net profits
- number of employees
- percentage domestic and export sales
- market trends (areas of growth or decline).

09 Spirit of enterprise

Phrase bank: Talking about business developments

He left school (at 16).
Eventually he became a manager.
They picked up skills and knowledge.
He was still only (twenty) when he set up the business.
One thing they have in common is a capacity for hard work.
The company is still growing.
The level of profits has remained stable.
Turnover has doubled in (five) years.
Customer service is a major selling point.

Word-building

Complete the table below with the appropriate form.

Verb	Noun	Adjective
acquire	acquisition	acquired
reject	_____	rejected
grow	_____	growing
_____	success	_____
_____	_____	beneficial
innovate	_____	_____
_____	_____	flexible
_____	operation	operating
_____	_____	profitable
_____	increase	_____
_____	fall	fallen/falling
install	_____	installed

Present Perfect

Affirmative

I You We They	've (have)	finished the report.
He She	's has	

Negative

I You We They	haven't	finished the report.
He She	hasn't	

Interrogative

Have Haven't	I you we they	finished the report?
Has Hasn't	he she	

Short answers

Have you seen John?
Yes, I have. / No, I haven't.
Has Jane sent the letter?
Yes, she has. / No, she hasn't.

The past participle of regular verbs is the same as the Past Simple, but with many common irregular verbs it is different:

- *go – went – gone*
- *come – came – come*
- *eat – ate – eaten*

The tense you use to talk about past events depends on how you see them.

If you see actions and situations as part of a sequence of finished past events and situations (e.g. stages in your life, events in history, events in a narrative, etc) you use the **Past Simple**.

- *I studied economics at university.*
- *His first wife was Argentinian.*
- *Her last job was with an engineering firm.*
- *Bill Gates founded Microsoft with a friend.*
- *Some people made a lot of money in the war.*
- *Suddenly he stopped talking and left the room.*

If past actions or situations are not related to other past events or time periods (they simply happened before now), you use the **Present Perfect**. Often it is because you are referring to recent events, or to contrast a present situation with the past.

- *I've had a fantastic idea!*
- *We've developed a new product for our range.*
- *Our turnover has grown by 10%.*
- *The photocopier has broken down.*

There is one important exception:

- *What did you say?* NOT ~~What have you said?~~

See the Irregular verb list on p128.

Practice 1

Write the past participles of the verbs below.

a see _____   i write _____
b buy _____   j break _____
c sell _____   k set _____
d do _____   l read _____
e find _____   m fall _____
f come _____   n rise _____
g put _____   o meet _____
h take _____   p think _____

Practice 2

Reorganize the words to make sentences in the Present Perfect.

a lost   glasses   I   have   my

_____

b gone   by   3%   prices   have   up

_____

c has   stable   economic   remained   growth

_____

d prices   last   years   have   in   fallen   five   the

_____

e has   2,000 workers   sacked   Molinex

_____

f company   has   the   Mr Rodriguez   left

_____

g not   a   John   week   I   have   for   seen

_____

Practice 3

Write a sentence using the verbs in the box and the Present Perfect for the situations below.

| arrive   be   break   change   give   lose   move   stop |

a Half an hour ago, it was raining and now it isn't.
   It's stopped raining.

b The photocopier doesn't work. Half an hour ago, it did.
   _____ down.

c Ten minutes ago, you called for a taxi. It's now outside the office.
   The taxi _____.

d Last year, your company was based on a site outside town. Now its offices are located in the centre of town.
   _____ into the centre of town.

e You can't find your notes for a presentation.
   _____ notes.

f You're giving a presentation. You did the same presentation last week and the week before.
   This is the third time _____.

g Philip Windish works for a company. A week ago, he worked for a different company.

   _____.

h A friend comments that nowadays he never sees you.
   _____ very busy lately.

Practice 4

Match the questions (a–g) to the answers (1–7).

a Where is my pen?
b Why are you looking so pleased with yourself?
c How is the new product line doing?
d Why are you looking for a new car?
e What's our share price today?
f Why are you looking so tired?
g Where's Jeremy?

1 It's gone up by four cents.
2 I've achieved my sales target for this month.
3 Because I've sold my old one.
4 It's been a really long day.
5 It's been very successful so far.
6 He's gone to Sydney for the week.
7 I don't know. I haven't seen it.

a	b	c	d	e	f	g

Practice 5

Complete the text with the verbs in the box, using either the Past Simple or the Present Perfect.

| acquire   add   be   create   finish   increase   launch |
| open   reach   start   turn |

The Inditex group consists of almost a hundred companies dealing with textile design, production and distribution. Its unique management techniques and its successes (a) _____ Inditex into one of the world's largest fashion groups.

The first Zara shop (b) _____ in 1975 in La Coruňa in northern Spain. Over the years, the group (c) _____ other chains to the original Zara, each covering a different market sector. In 1991, the group (d) _____ Pull & Bear, and in 1995, (e) _____ 100% of Massimo Dutti. Bershka (f) _____ its activity in 1998, followed by the acquisition of Stradivarius in 1999. Two years later, Inditex (g) _____ Oysho, a chain specializing in fashionable lingerie and underwear. More recent additions (h) _____ Zara Home, a home decoration store, and Uterqüe, which focuses on fashion accessories.

In the last four years, the number of shops in the group (i) _____ a figure of over 5,000, and the group now has operations in 82 countries worldwide. In the same period, sales (j) _____ by 46% and net profits by 54%.

Despite its size, the group still controls its activities from a logistical centre in Arteixo, a village in the north-west of Spain, but in 2003 it (k) _____ work on 'Plataforma Europa', a new distribution centre in Zaragoza.

Answers on page 130.

10 Stressed to the limit

> *Pressure is part and parcel of all work and helps to keep us motivated. But excessive pressure can lead to stress, which undermines performance, is costly to employers and can make people ill.*
>
> UK Health and Safety Executive

Do you work well under pressure?

Learning objectives: Unit 10

Business communication skills Discussing the causes of stress; Comparing different jobs; Asking about someone's responsibilities and duties at work; Roleplay: A management consultant's interview; Writing a consultant's report on a company

Reading Article about stress at work

Listening People talking about stress at work

Phrase bank Talking about stress

Vocabulary Stress at work

Grammar *have to / don't have to, should / shouldn't*

1 Work with a partner. Which of these factors produce the most stress? Add your own ideas.

being promoted	looking after children
being responsible for people's lives	making phone calls
dealing with big sums of money	meeting deadlines
dealing with the public	travelling
doing boring, repetitive tasks	waiting for other people to do things
learning to use new technology	working long hours

2 🔘 **1.35–1.38** An interviewer for the radio programme *Work Today* spoke to four people in the street about stress. Listen to the interviews and answer the questions.

		Interview 1	Interview 2	Interview 3	Interview 4
a	What does the speaker do?				
b	Does the speaker suffer from stress?				
c	What causes the stress, according to the speaker?				
d	Does the speaker mention any of the reasons in 1? Which?				

3 The last speaker says that stress 'is more a problem of mental attitude than what you do'. Do you agree? Why / Why not?

4 In your opinion, what are the three most stressful jobs? Use the list below to help you.

accountant	air traffic controller	airline pilot	architect	computer programmer
corporate executive	doctor	event co-ordinator	factory worker	firefighter	journalist
lawyer	military general	pilot	police officer	public relations executive	secretary
soldier	stockbroker	taxi driver	teacher	telephonist	waiter

Now compare your ideas with the list on page 132. Are you surprised? What do you think are the least stressful jobs?

5 For each set of prompts (a–h), make at least two sentences with *has to, have to, doesn't have to* or *don't have to*.

a air traffic controller   factory worker   take decisions   be creative
   An air traffic controller has to take decisions very quickly. (It's necessary)
   A factory worker doesn't have to be creative. (It's not necessary)

b lawyer   secretary   wear a suit   type letters

c middle managers   chief executives   solve day-to-day problems   take strategic decisions

d shop assistant   computer programmer   deal with the public
   know computer languages

e lorry driver   taxi driver   drive long distances   memorize street maps

f nurse   factory worker   wear special clothes   work at night

g accountant   telephonist   use a computer   be honest

h teacher   engineer   tell people what to do   wear a tie

Make sentences about the other jobs in 4.

6 Now interview your partner about their job like this:

A *In your job do you have to ...?*

B *No, but I have to ... / Yes, and I also have to ...*

7 Match the words and phrases (a–g) to the definitions (1–7). These all appear in an article you are going to read about stress.

a	linked to	**1**	doing too much work
b	root cause of	**2**	is good for the company
c	overwork	**3**	principal reason for
d	performance-related pay	**4**	connected to
e	staff turnover	**5**	money for getting better results
f	makes business sense	**6**	people joining and leaving a company
g	morale	**7**	positive or negative attitude

a ☐ 4   **b** ☐   **c** ☐   **d** ☐   **e** ☐   **f** ☐   **g** ☐

8 In your opinion, are the sentences below true or false? Discuss with a partner.

a	Stress is always a bad thing.	true ☐	false ☐
b	Work-related stress can cause health problems.	true ☐	false ☐
c	Bad management is the main cause of stress.	true ☐	false ☐
d	Reducing stress costs companies money.	true ☐	false ☐
e	It's easy for companies to reduce stress.	true ☐	false ☐

9 Now read this article about stress. Does the writer agree with your opinions in 8?

Stressed to the limit

Deborah Houlding of BMG online magazine explores the problem of work-related stress and examines ways in which it can be avoided.

Stress is not an illness or a negative condition. A certain amount of pressure brings out the best in our work. In the initial stages of stress, there is a sensation of excitement and increased mental concentration.

However, too much stress is negative. It is bad for the individual. It is also bad for the employing organization. In the UK, for example, stress-related illness is the cause of half of lost working days.

The negative impact of stress is linked to heart disease, alcoholism, nervous breakdowns, job dissatisfaction, certain forms of cancer, migraines, asthma, hay fever, insomnia, depression, eczema and many other medical and social problems.

Many surveys confirm the root cause of work-related stress to be bad management and overwork. Too much pressure, long hours and poor communication are the main factors. Reports and studies have identified the principal cause of stress as 'new management techniques' designed to 'improve performance'. Policies such as 'performance-related pay' increase stress and demotivate a workforce.

Many legal and medical experts are advising companies to consider the costs and legal implications of stress-related illness. They emphasize the benefits of reducing stress as:
- better health
- reduced sickness absence
- increased performance and output
- better relationships with clients and colleagues
- lower staff turnover.

Taking the decision to reduce stress makes sound business sense. It's better for profits and better for staff morale.

Managers should learn to motivate but not exhaust employees. There is a balance between obtaining maximum efficiency, and a worker's need to rest and recuperate their creative energies.

10 Complete the chart with the correct form of the word.

Noun	Verb	Adjective
stress	stress	_____, stressed
motivation	_____	motivating, _____
creativity	create	_____
_____	excite	_____, excited

11 Complete the sentences with the words from 10.

a Working 14 hours a day can be very _____.

b When the new boss arrived, staff morale was very low and nobody was very _____.

c I'm a graphic designer so my job requires a lot of _____.

d I don't find the new project very _____; the tasks are very repetitive.

12 Make similar sentences about your own company.

13 Look at these sentences.

*Managers **should** recognize their mistakes.* (It's a good idea.)
*Employees **shouldn't** work under unnecessary pressure.* (It's not a good idea.)

Make sentences that are true for you using *should/shouldn't* and the prompts below.

a work well / have a certain amount of pressure
  To work well, you should have a certain amount of pressure.
b companies / try / reduce the level of stress
c workers / work very long hours
d managers / communicate / ideas
e companies / invest money / improve conditions
f managers / learn / motivate workers
g workers / have time / rest

14 Make sentences about your company like this:

In my company ... should / shouldn't ... but often / in fact they / he / she / we ...

Include the ideas below and add your own.

- distribution of work
- communications
- performance-related pay
- sufficient training
- new technology

The consultant's report

You are going to write a report on a company with problems. Follow steps 1–4 below.

Work with a partner. Create your own company.

▶▶ **Step 1**

a What line of business is the company in?

b What's the name of the company?

c Where is it located?

d Is it an old-fashioned or a modern company?

e How long has it existed?

▶▶ **Step 2**

You are going to perform a roleplay with a new partner. First, with your original partner, decide who is the employee and who is the consultant. Then find a new partner who is playing a different role to you.

Employee: You work for the company you invented. You are completely negative about every aspect of your job and company. Criticize everything and everybody.

Consultant: You are a management consultant hired to interview the staff of the employee's company to assess the levels of stress and morale. Interview the employee and note down the answers. Ask questions about:

- working hours
- company organization
- internal communication
- pay
- training provided
- holidays
- your own ideas.

▶▶ **Step 3**

Work with your original partner from Step 1. Write a report of the management consultant's interview.

Use the framework below or adapt it to suit the interview.

- According to ... the main cause/s of stress in his/her work is/are ...
- Communications in the company are ...
- The system of payment is ...
- With regard to training, the situation is ...
- Other causes of problems are ...
- To reduce the level of stress the company should ...
- In conclusion, ...

▶▶ **Step 4**

Work with your partner from Step 2 again. Check that the report of your interview is accurate.

MQSC consulting

Interview report

Company:

_____

_____

Name of interviewee:

_____

Interviewer:

_____

Date:

_____

10 Stressed to the limit

Phrase bank: Talking about stress

My job is very stressful.
Too much pressure and long hours are the main factors.
Work-related stress can cause health problems.
I find being at home more stressful than being at work.
I get a bit on edge at times.
Stress is linked to heart disease.
It's easy for companies to reduce stress.

Vocabulary

Stress at work

1 Complete the sentences with the correct form of the word in brackets.

a An air traffic controller has a very _____ job. (stress)

b A _____ has to defend their clients in court. (law)

c His work involves a lot of different _____. (responsible)

d Our boss is always shouting at us. I don't find it very _____. (motivate)

e Too much stress is bad for the workers, and it's also bad for the _____. (employ)

f Stress-related _____ is the cause of half of lost working days. (ill)

g It's a problem of _____ – we never know what's happening in the company. (communicate)

h Nobody knows how to use the new machine – we need urgent _____. (train)

i Employees shouldn't work under _____ pressure. (necessary)

j You should _____ your mistakes and correct them. (recognition)

k One of the benefits of reducing stress is better _____ with clients and colleagues. (relate)

l Workers need to rest and recuperate their _____ energies. (create)

m The experts say that bad _____ is the main cause of stress. (manage)

n Policies such as _____-related pay demotivate a work force. (perform)

2 Complete the second sentence so that it means the same as the first.

a Does your work cause you stress?
Do you find *your work stressful?*

b My boss makes life difficult.
My boss doesn't make life _____

c My husband isn't very helpful.
My husband doesn't _____

d At times I get nervous.
At times I get a bit on _____

e 75% of visits to the doctor are because of stress.
75% of visits to the doctor are the _____ of stress.

f People don't think that teaching is a difficult job.
Everyone thinks that teaching is an _____

g I hope things improve for you.
I hope things get _____ for you.

h Worrying about things doesn't help you.
There's _____ in worrying about things.

i I don't work for anyone. I'm self-employed.
I work for _____

Grammar

have to and should

have to

I You We They		have to don't have to	work at night.
He She		has to doesn't have to	work at night.
Do **Does**	I/you/we/they he/she	have to	work at night?

should

I You He/She We They		should shouldn't	do that job for free.

You use *has to* or *have to* to show that it is necessary to do something.

• *Everyone **has to** pay taxes.*

• *We all **have to** use the same computer programs.*

When you want to show that it isn't necessary to do something, you can use *doesn't have to* or *don't have to*.

• *He **doesn't have to** travel much in his job.*

• *We **don't have to** dress formally for work.*

You use *should* or *shouldn't* to show that it is a good or bad idea to do something.

• *You **should** use the Internet for getting new ideas.*

• *You **shouldn't** work so hard if you want to live to an old age.*

Practice 1

Complete the sentences with *has to, have to, doesn't have to* or *don't have to* and the verbs in the box.

come	do	finish	get	get up	go	make	show
sign	wear	work					

a All visitors to the factory _____ a register.

b Our company has a 'casual Friday' policy, which means you _____ formal clothes in the office on Fridays.

c 'Why are you working so late?' 'Because I _____ this report for tomorrow.'

d To get to work on time, he _____ at 5.30 am.

e Every Monday morning, we _____ to a departmental meeting.

f I like holidays because you _____ anything.

g If you want to see Mr Smith, you _____ an appointment. He's a very busy man.

h You _____ if you don't want to. We can do it without you.

i You _____ a visa if you travel to certain countries.

j When you cross an international border, you usually _____ your passport.

k He's so rich he _____, but he still does. He's a workaholic.

Practice 2

Reorganize the words to make questions.

a finish this do have I today to

_____

b dress do have work for to you formally

_____

c year abroad how to go many you times a do have

_____

d complete when have order we the to do

_____

e do English go this have year classes we to to

_____

f your have drive do in you job to much

_____

Practice 3

Give appropriate advice using *should* or *shouldn't* and the verbs in the box.

go (x 2)	have	leave	set up	spend	work

a I can't get a job because I don't speak any foreign languages.
You should go to English classes.

b I don't know how to use this new accountancy program.
_____ on a course.

c I keep getting these headaches.
_____ so much time staring at figures.

d My plane is at 2.30.
_____ now or you'll miss it.

e I have a constant pain in my chest.
_____ a check-up at the doctor.

f My family is complaining they never see me.
_____ so late.

g I don't like working for someone else.
_____ your own business.

Practice 4

Complete the sentences using a form of *have to, don't have to, should* or *shouldn't*. Sometimes there are two possible answers.

a The doctor says I _____ take things easy.

b You _____ spend so much time in front of a computer – it's bad for your eyes.

c Managers _____ be good communicators.

d You _____ just give people orders, you _____ motivate them to do a good job.

e I _____ do this job even if it is stressful – I need the money.

f I'm going home now because I _____ get up early tomorrow to catch my plane.

g If you need travel information, you _____ look it up on the Internet.

h You _____ speak to the boss like that.

i If you want to know more about the company, you _____ visit them.

j You _____ come with me. I can do the presentation on my own.

11

Top jobs

1 Discuss these questions with a partner.

a How many different types of media can you name?

b What kind of people do you think work in the media industry? In what ways do you think media is different from any other business?

c How do you think the Internet has changed the world of media?

2 Read the extract from an article about a successful media executive and answer the questions.

a Where did Dan Gibson grow up?

b Why did he decide to stop acting?

c Does Dan regret his decision?

d Dan Gibson says 'It's pretty simple. If the ratings are up, my bosses love me; if they're down, I lose my job!' Why do you think this is? What kind of person do you think he is?

What are the top five skills needed to be a good leader?

Learning objectives: Unit 11

Business communication skills Discussing the media industry; Talking about someone's experiences; Writing: A report

Reading Article about a media executive; Article about MercadoLibre

Listening Documentary about MercadoLibre; Telephone call from a headhunter

Phrase bank Describing a company's development

Vocabulary Company news

Grammar Present Perfect for unfinished past, *for* and *since*

🖥 **In company interviews** Units 9–11

'It's pretty simple. If the ratings are up, my bosses love me; if they're down, I lose my job!'

When Destiny Calls

Dan Gibson has worked in the TV industry for over 20 years. The chances are you will have seen at least one of the many TV shows which he has helped to produce.

At the age of 17, his first experience in the world of TV and film was as a struggling actor. 'I was born and grew up in LA, so I figured it was my destiny. There was one problem though – I was no good!'

After five years of auditions, with only a handful of acting jobs to show for it, Dan decided to look for work on the other side of the camera. Starting as a junior researcher on *Breakfast AM* for DPS Entertainment, he secured a job as one of the show's associate producers just three years later, and became its executive producer soon after that.

Gibson spent his 30s moving around the major TV networks, helping to produce several successful series, including *Yours Truly* and *On Campus* (and a couple of unsuccessful ones too!). He finally settled at USC Universal where he was offered the role of President of its Television Group.

'When I was younger, I always wanted to be on the other side of the camera but I think it all worked out in the end; *this* is my destiny'.

3 Look at the information about Dan Gibson above and on page 71 and complete the sentences using the verbs in the box.

is not	joined	has been	has worked	started working	still works

a Dan Gibson _____ in the TV industry over 20 years ago.

b He _____ in the TV industry for over 20 years.

c He _____ in the TV industry.

d He _____ the Board of Directors at DPS Entertainment in 2000.

e He _____ a member of the Board of Directors since 2000.

f He _____ an actor anymore.

DAN GIBSON

President of Television Group
USC Universal
2012–present day

Vice President
USC Universal
Controller: Drama and mini series
2010–2012

Co-chief Operating Officer
Broadcast House
Controller: Drama
2008–2010

Studio Manager
E-Net
Worked on *Katie Rocks!*, *Outsiders*, *The Blood Line*
2005–2008

Operational Manager
NEC News Network
News and Current Affairs
2004–2005

Supervising Producer
Live Wire Network TV
Worked on *Comedy Kicks*, *In session with …*
2002–2003

Joined Board of Directors at DPS Entertainment
2000–present

Executive Producer
DPS Entertainment
AM scheduling
1999–2002

Associate Producer
DPS Entertainment
Worked on *Breakfast AM*
1997–1999

Line Producer
DPS Entertainment
Worked on *Breakfast AM*
1995–1997

Researcher
DPS Entertainment
Worked on *Breakfast AM*, *Kitchen AM*
1994–1995

4 Match the sentences in 3 to the verb forms below.

Past Simple ☐ ☐
Present Simple ☐ ☐
Present Perfect ☐ ☐

5 Put the time expressions in the correct column.

| 1945 | 20 years | 5 o'clock | a couple of days | a few years | a long time | five minutes |
| he arrived | I was born | last year | months | this morning | yesterday | |

since	for

6 Write six sentences which are true for you. Use the Present Perfect with *since* and *for*.
I've been in my present job for two years. *I've had* this smartphone since April.

7 Make questions with *you* using the prompts. Use the Present Simple, Past Simple and Present Perfect, as appropriate.

a What kind of car / have? How long / have / it? Why / choose it?
b have / a mobile phone? How long / have / it? use it / a lot?
c Where / live? How long / live / there?
d Who / work for? How long / work / there? What / job?
e How long / have / present job? Like / it?
f know
g be interested in

8 Work with a partner. Ask and answer the questions in 7. Try to get more information about each subject, if you can.

9 Change partners. Tell each other about your previous partner.
Lucien lives just outside Toulouse. He has lived there for three years.
He works as a research scientist at the university. He's worked there since last June.

Entrepreneur of the year

1 🔘 **2.01** These words and phrases are from a radio programme about a business personality. Listen to the extract and number the words and phrases in the order you hear them.

1	online auction site
☐	mobile devices
☐	online commerce platform
☐	Latin American eBay™
☐	John Muse
☐	1.2 million transactions
☐	Stanford

2 🔘 **2.01** Read the article while listening to the extract again. Correct eight mistakes in the article. Then look at the script on page 152 and check your answers.

3 <u>Underline</u> four examples of the Present Perfect in the article which tell us when a present situation started.

In July 2012, Marcos Galperin, founder and CEO of MercadoLibre, was named as an 'Ernst and Young World Entrepreneur of the Year'. His company is the world's largest online auction site. Since September 2001, it has been a partner company of the US auctioneer, eBay™, which acquired 5% of MercadoLibre in exchange for its Brazilian subsidiary, Ibazar.com.br.

Galperin grew up in Buenos Aires, but went to college in the United States. After graduating, he returned home and worked for three and a half years at the largest gas company in Argentina. He then went back to the United States to do an MBA at Stanford. While Galperin was there, he pitched his ideas for an Internet company to John Muse, the founder of a private equity fund. Muse thought the ideas showed potential and agreed to invest.

Galperin has known the co-founder of MercadoLibre, Hernan Kazar, since they were students together at Stanford. In fact, after creating the business plan and securing financing, Galperin recruited several teachers there to help manage the business. Since its creation in 1999, MercadoLibre has grown dramatically to become the largest online commerce platform in North America, with sites across nine countries including Brazil, Argentina and Mexico.

Back in the 1990s, there were many start-up companies trying to become the Latin American eBay. Galperin was different to the others in that he focused more on IT and getting investment and less on marketing or PR. As a result, his company flourished while the rest went bankrupt. Following the rise of smartphones and tablet computers, it modified its original technology so it could run its services on mobile devices and allow external developers to build applications.

Company sales grew 37% between 2007 and 2011 and MercadoLibre is the tenth highest-ranked retail site for traffic in the world. During 2011, there were almost 53 million products sold, an increase of 35% from 2010. Every month the company manages more than 1.2 million transactions, attracting 75,000 buyers, and business has more than doubled every year for the last five years.

4 How much of the story can you remember without looking? Use the words and phrases in 1 to summarize the story with a partner.

5 Find words and phrases in the article which mean the same as the following:

a Enterprising person who sets up businesses _____

b A company wholly or partly owned by another company _____

c To attend university _____

d To present your plan for a company or business _____

e A formal statement of a set of business goals and the strategy for achieving them
_____

f When a business fails because it can't pay its debts _____

g A website where people can buy products online _____

6 Use the words and phrases in 5 in the correct form to complete the following sentences.

a I would prefer to be an _____ and be my own boss than work for someone else.

b In my country you can _____ and then make a clean start with a new business.

c In my own language I am confident about _____ ideas to colleagues or customers.

d I know how to write a _____ which I could present to a bank or an investor.

e I often do my shopping online _____.

f It's essential to _____ if you later want to be successful in business.

g I work for the _____ of a large multinational company.

7 Are the sentences in 6 true for you? Write your own sentences using the words and phrases in 5.

headhunter

/hed,ˈhʌntə/

noun a person or company who searches for good staff and tries to persuade them to leave their jobs and go to work for another company

Headhunters

1 🔘 **2.02** Peter Davis is in the office when he receives an unexpected call from John Lindsay. Listen to the conversation and answer the questions.

a Why does John Lindsay call Peter Davis?

b When did Peter Davis start working for Blueprint International?

c What did he do before that?

d How long has he been in charge of the International Division?

e When did he get married?

f Has he got any children?

g Is he interested in what the caller has to say?

2 Discuss the following questions with a partner.

a What type of management consultants does John Lindsay work for?

b Do you think what he does is ethical?

c How would you react in this situation?

3 Read the report for *People Search* about Peter Davis.

People Search

Report

Peter Davis has worked for Blueprint International since 2006, where he has been head of their International Division for one year. Before Blueprint International he was at Navigate for three years. This was his first job after university, where he studied engineering. He graduated from Nottingham University in 2002. He has been married for two years and has one child.

4 Now write a similar report about your partner. Ask questions about his/her career history to help you to write the report. Use the phrases in the box.

How long have you ...?   When / Where did you ... before?
When did you start / leave / finish ...?

In company interviews
Units 9–11

11 Top jobs

Phrase bank: Describing a company's development

He pitched his ideas for (an Internet company).

They created a business plan and secured funding.

Company sales grew (37) per cent between (2007) and (2011).

His company is the world's (second-) largest (online auction site).

It's the (tenth) highest-ranked (retail site) in the world.

We don't get a bonus at the end of the year.

Vocabulary

Company news

Match the sentence beginnings (a–j) with the endings (1–10).

a Dan Colman graduated from York University in 1980 with ...

b He and some student friends founded ...

c In 1998 they moved ...

d At the beginning it was a small firm which produced components ...

e The company quickly expanded and set ...

f Recently, it has launched ...

g The engineers responsible ...

h It has also entered the ...

i Dan Colman has held ...

j The company has recently celebrated ...

1 ... for other manufacturers.

2 ... mobile phone market.

3 ... the top position since it was founded.

4 ... a degree in electronic engineering.

5 ... a range of computer accessories, which is doing very well.

6 ... its thirtieth anniversary.

7 ... up new divisions.

8 ... its headquarters to Milton Keynes.

9 ... for this success have become directors of the company.

10 ... the company ALTS in 1982.

a	b	c	d	e	f	g	h	i	j

Grammar

Present Perfect – the unfinished past

You use the Present Perfect to say when present situations began.

Past Simple: *I started working here 25 years ago.*

Present Simple: *I work here now.*

Present Perfect: *I've worked here for 25 years.*

(NOT ~~I am working here for 25 years.~~)*

Past Simple: *I met John for the first time in 1997.*

Present Simple: *I still know him.*

Present Perfect: *I've known John since 1997.*

(NOT ~~I know John since 1985.~~)*

* In many languages, you use a present tense to express this idea so these are very common mistakes. In English you can only use the Present Perfect.

To say when the action began, you use *since* or *for*. You use *since* with a point in time and *for* with a period of time.

since	for
eight o'clock	two years
2001	a month
August	a few minutes
last week	half an hour
I was born	ages
he arrived	hundreds of years

*Things **have been** better since we changed offices.*

*He **has lived** here for ten years.*

(NOT ... ~~since ten years ago.~~)

You can also use *for* with the Past Simple. Compare the sentences below.

Present Perfect: *I've lived in Manchester **for** three years / **since** 1998.* (I still live in Manchester.)

Past Simple: *I lived in Manchester **for** three years / **from** 1995 to 1998.* (Now I live somewhere else.)

Practice 1

Complete the sentences with *since* or *for*.

a Mr Bianchi has been out of the office _____ last Thursday.

b We haven't had a holiday _____ the summer.

c They have been friends _____ they were at university together.

d He's had his own business _____ a few years now.

e I haven't seen you _____ a while. How are things going?

f I've known Pete _____ we met at a trade fair nearly ten years ago.

g They've had that old car _____ years.

h Mr González has been here _____ 9.30. He's waiting for you in reception.

i _____ his wife had a baby, he's spent more time at home.

j He's waited for this promotion _____ months.

Practice 2

Write questions with *How long ...?* and the Present Perfect.

a you / work / here
How long have you worked here?

b he / know / about this problem

c she / be / a director of the company

d you / want / change jobs

e they / have / their website

f he / be / interested / in working for us

g he / have / a company car

h she / be / responsible for that account

Practice 3

Rewrite the following sentences using the Present Perfect.

a He works here – he started work in January.
He's worked here since January.

b He lives in Paris – he was born there.

c He's a computer programmer – he became a programmer when he left university.

d They make furniture – they started making furniture over a hundred years ago.

e She owns a business – she set it up five years ago.

f They lead the market – they became market leaders in 1998.

Practice 4

Rewrite the following sentences using the Present Perfect.

a I met him at university.
I've known him since university.

b Mr Jones arrived here hours ago.

c When did you buy your car?

d I got this job in January.

e They told me about the problem yesterday.

f They got divorced two years ago.

Practice 5

Read the biographical details of James Rodgers. Then use the prompts to write sentences using either the Present Perfect or the Past Simple and *for*, *since*, or *from ... to*.

James Rodgers

1984	started running marathons
1986	went to university to study engineering
1989	graduated with a degree in engineering
1990	got a job with Rolls Royce as an aeronautical engineer
1991	became interested in boats
1992	got married
1993	bought his first yacht
1995	got a job with P & W in Canada and moved to Montreal
2001	moved back to the UK and went to work at the P & W factory in Manchester
2003	ran his tenth marathon
2006	moved to a new job in the P & W offices in Portsmouth

a be / an aeronautical engineer
He's been an aeronautical engineer since 1990.

b marathon

c study engineering / university

d be / interested / boats

e be / married

f work / Rolls Royce

g have / yacht

h live / Canada

i live / the UK

j have / job / Portsmouth

k work / for P & W

l ten marathons

Conversation gambits

What's your favourite way to start a conversation with someone you don't know?

gambit /ˈgæmbɪt/
noun something that you say or do in an attempt to gain an advantage

Learning objectives: Unit 12

People skills Introducing yourself and starting conversations; Choosing safe topics of conversation; Ending a conversation; Roleplay: A successful conversation
Reading Conversation strategies
Listening People meeting by chance

1 You are at a conference where you don't know any of the other delegates. Discuss with a partner which of the following strategies you might use to create the opportunity to introduce yourself.

a Go up to someone and just say 'Hello', then tell them your name and ask them theirs.

b Ask someone for help or information – where you need to go to register or what is on the conference programme.

c Make a comment about the weather – 'It's a lovely day, isn't it?'

d Make a comment about the conference hall – 'It's an amazing building, isn't it?' or 'It's freezing in here, I hope it warms up a bit.'

e Ask someone for their opinion about something – 'What did you think of the last talk?' or 'It's a long programme, isn't it?'

f Make a remark about something the other person is wearing or carrying – 'That's a great tie, where did you get it?' or 'I see you've got the new iPhone. Are you happy with it?'

2 2.03–2.06 Listen to four conversations which take place at a conference. Which strategies in 1 do the speakers use?

3 2.03–2.06 Complete the conversations and then listen again to check your answers.

1 **A** Excuse me, _____ the ITM conference?
  B Yes, that's right.
  A Me too. _____?
  B I think it's over there.
  A Oh, yes, right. I'm Paulo, _____.
  B Hello, Paulo, I'm Kate. _____.

2 **A** Phew! Is it me, or _____?
  B Yes, they always seem to have the heating on full.
  A So, it's not _____?
  B No, it's my fourth time here.
  A Oh, right, so _____. I'm Boris.
  B David. _____.

3 **A** Is it _____, or is there some problem with coverage here?
  B Oh, _____. No, mine seems _____ okay.
  A Typical – flat batteries and nowhere to charge up.
  B _____?
  A Oh, _____, but I was expecting a call on this number.
  B I see.
  A _____ Nadine, by the way. From Xanadu Electronics.
  B Pleased to meet you. I'm Miko.

4 **A** Excuse me, do you know _____?
  B No, I'm sorry, I don't.
  A I can't find _____.
  B Oh, here. _____.
  A Thanks. By the way, I'm Bill Smart from Silicon Technologies.
  B Right, _____?
    I'm Kazuo Yamada from Lexico.

4 When you meet someone for the first time, some topics are more suitable than others. For example, sport is a 'safe' topic. What other topics are safe? Which should you avoid? Circle the safe topics.

art   business   cars   local attractions   money and personal finance   music
personal life   politics and the state of the world   religion   the opposite sex
the stock exchange   the weather

5 2.07 Two businessmen have just finished dinner in a Belfast hotel. Listen to their conversation and answer the questions.

a   What strategy does Allan Vilkas use to start a conversation?

b   What topic of conversation does he introduce?

6 Work with a partner. Look at the headlines below. Imagine you borrowed your partner's newspaper and you are now giving it back. Start a conversation about one of the headlines. Maintain the conversation as long as possible. Begin: *Thank you for the newspaper. Have you seen this article about …?*

Prime Minister says economic situation 'hopeless'

UK to drive on right

DOG WINS LOTTERY

Scientists discover link between video games and intelligence

MOBILES BANNED ON PUBLIC TRANSPORT

Life found on the surface of Mars

First genetically modified human being

US PRESIDENT CONSULTS PRIVATE ASTROLOGER

7 When they are getting to know each other, people often ask some of the following questions. Reorganize the words to make questions. Then match them to the answers (1–10). There are two possible answers for each question.

a   you where are from
   Where are you from?

b   been have long you how here
   _____

c   long staying how are you
   _____

d   think what you Belfast do of
   _____

e   business here you on are
   _____

1   I'm from Turkey.
2   Until Friday.
3   Another four or five days.
4   It seems very nice.
5   I've been here for a couple of days now.
6   Yes. I'm visiting some customers.
7   I come from South Africa.
8   It's a bit cold for me.
9   Since Saturday.
10   Yes. I'm here to buy some machinery.

a ☐☐   b ☐☐   c ☐☐   d ☐☐   e ☐☐

8 2.08 Listen to the conversation. Which of the questions and answers in 7 do the speakers use?

9 Sean O'Malley ends the conversation by saying 'It's getting late. I have to be off.' Match the sentence beginnings (a–e) with the endings (1–5) to make other ways to end a conversation.

a   Excuse me, but I've just …
b   I think they're going …
c   Excuse me, but I think …
d   Hang on a minute, but I think I have …
e   Sorry to cut you off, but I arranged …

1   … a call on my mobile. I'll catch you later.
2   … someone is trying to catch my attention.
3   … seen someone I have to talk to.
4   … to start. I'll see you later.
5   … to meet someone at the bar five minutes ago.

Useful language:
Conversation
Excuse me. Could I have a look …?
Did you read that article about …?
I can't believe that …
Would you like …?
Are you busy or …?

10 Now work with a partner and roleplay a complete conversation.

a   Ask to borrow a newspaper and then make a comment on something in it.

b   Offer to buy a coffee or drink for the other person.

c   Make conversation with questions from 7, e.g. *What do you think of …?*, *How long are you staying …?*

d   End the conversation with one of the phrases from 9.

Stick to your guns

stick to your guns
to refuse to change what you are saying or doing even if other people disagree

They tried to persuade me my proposal was a bad idea, but I stuck to my guns.

Learning objectives: Workplace Scenario C

Business communication skills Discussing staff satisfaction surveys; Roleplay: Expressing opinions, defending ideas and making suggestions; Presenting a survey

Reading Article about staff satisfaction

In company in action
C1: Staff dissatisfaction;
C2: Sticking to your guns

---

1 Read the extract from a business blog and discuss the questions with a partner.

a Have you ever done this type of survey? Did you find it useful? What sort of results did it show?

b Do you think carrying out a staff satisfaction survey is beneficial for a company? How?

c Which of the questions below do you think are the most useful and why?

ARE YOU SATISFIED?

Many companies use staff satisfaction surveys to measure staff morale. A satisfaction survey is usually a series of questions that employees answer on how they feel about their job or what they think of their work environment and culture. The questionnaire usually asks employees to give a score for a particular area of the work environment. Sometimes they are also asked to answer open-ended questions that allow them to express opinions. When a staff satisfaction survey is repeated, for example, every year, the employer can track employee satisfaction over time to look for trends and to see if staff morale is improving. Here is an example of the kind of questions a survey might include.

On a scale of 1–5, where 1 means 'I strongly disagree' and 5 means 'I completely agree', give each of these statements a score.

I have a good understanding of the mission and the goals of this organization.
1 ○ 2 ○ 3 ○ 4 ○ 5 ○

I understand how my work directly contributes to the overall success of the organization.
1 ○ 2 ○ 3 ○ 4 ○ 5 ○

Our senior managers demonstrate strong leadership skills.
1 ○ 2 ○ 3 ○ 4 ○ 5 ○

I have the resources I need to do my job well.
1 ○ 2 ○ 3 ○ 4 ○ 5 ○

The information systems I need are in place and help me to get my job done.
1 ○ 2 ○ 3 ○ 4 ○ 5 ○

My manager supports and recognizes my contribution.
1 ○ 2 ○ 3 ○ 4 ○ 5 ○

I have been provided with the training and support I need to perform my job effectively.
1 ○ 2 ○ 3 ○ 4 ○ 5 ○

In company
in action

2 Lenz Furniture Designs is planning to do a staff satisfaction survey. Vanessa, the Sales and Marketing Manager, discusses the survey with Ralph, a Sales Executive in her team. Watch video C1 and answer the questions.

a Which of the following issues do Vanessa and Ralph discuss:
  i anonymity.
  ii what happens to the results of the survey.
  iii being honest when answering the questions.
  iv the type of questions in the survey.
  v who has to do the survey.
b Do they both feel the same about the survey?
c Can you think of any other objections staff members might have to the survey?

3 Lenz CEO Joe sends Serena, the HR Director, an email. Read his email and answer the questions.
a Why does he want to meet Serena?
b What does the phrase 'open-ended questions' mean?

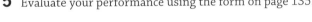

RE: Satisfaction survey

Good morning Serena,

Hope you had a good weekend. Now that you have some feedback on the trial survey we did with the sample group, there are a few things I would like to discuss before we launch the process with the whole company:

– General feedback from the Sales and Marketing team.

– Cost (use external consultant vs internal process).

– Anonymity.

– Type of survey (paper or online).

– Type of questions (scoring from 1 to 5 or open-ended questions).

– Follow up with focus groups.

– What we do with the results (publish? action to be taken?).

How about this afternoon at 14.00?

Best wishes,

Joe

4 Following Joe's email, Serena and Joe meet that afternoon. Work with a partner and roleplay their conversation.

Speaker A: Look at page 134.
Speaker B: Look at page 131.

5 Evaluate your performance using the form on page 135.

In company
in action

6 Now watch video C2 to see what happened when Serena spoke to Joe. Repeat your roleplay, but this time swap roles. Use the notes from your evaluation form and as many of the useful phrases from your roleplays in 4 as you can.

7 Serena arranges a staff briefing meeting to introduce the staff satisfaction survey. With a partner, prepare a short presentation that introduces the survey. Try to anticipate any objections using the list in Joe's email to help you.

8 Give your presentation to another pair and answer their questions. Stick to your guns!

13 Air travel

Which is the best low-cost airline you've flown with? And the worst?

Learning objectives: Unit 13

Business communication skills Discussing experiences of flying; Discussing the dos and don'ts of business travel; Roleplay: A negotiation game
Reading Article about comfortable air travel; Article about cut-price travel
Listening Conversations at check-in
Phrase bank Air travel
Vocabulary Air travel, Negotiating
Grammar Conditionals with *will*

1 Discuss the following questions with the rest of the class.

a How often do you fly?

b What things can go wrong when you travel by air?

c Have you had any bad flying experiences?

2 2.09–2.10 Listen to the conversations. Someone is checking in at the airport. What goes wrong in each case?

3 2.09–2.10 Complete the conversations using the words in the box. Listen again and check your answers.

check in	excess baggage	long queue	look it up	main desk	passport	queue up
reference number	straight to the front	suitcase	£30			

Conversation 1

A Good morning. Is this where I (a) _____ for flight RA 264?

B Yes. Can you give me your (b) _____, please?

A I'm afraid I've lost the paper I had it on, but here's my (c) _____.

B I'm sorry, but if you haven't got the reference number, I can't check you in. You'll have to go to the (d) _____ over there. They'll give it to you.

A But can't you (e) _____? You've got my name.

B I'm afraid not, sir.

A Do I have to (f) _____ again?

B No. Just come to the front.

A Okay.

B Next, please.

Conversation 2

A Can I have your reference number and passport, please?

B Here you are.

A You've just got one (g) _____ to check in?

B Yes, this one.

A I'm afraid it's over 15 kilos. You'll have to pay (h) _____.

B It's only just over, isn't it?

A Actually it's 17 kilos.

B Are you sure? How much will it cost me?

A It'll be (i) _____, but you have to pay over there at the main desk.

B What, over there? There's a really (j) _____. Can't I pay here?

A No, I'm sorry. But come (k) _____ when you come back.

B Okay. Thanks.

Battle of the armrests

1 Work in groups. Make a list of five dos and five don'ts for business air travellers.

Do: *Allow a lot of time for checking in and security controls.*

Don't: *Book your flight at the last minute.*

2 Read the introduction to an article on avoiding a travel problem. What do you think the 'strategies' might be?

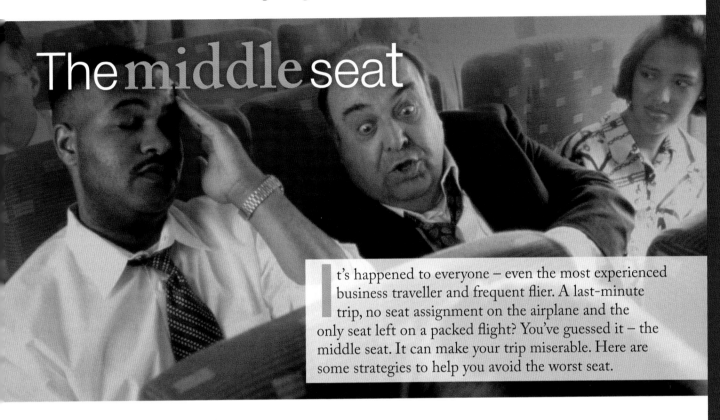

The middle seat

It's happened to everyone – even the most experienced business traveller and frequent flier. A last-minute trip, no seat assignment on the airplane and the only seat left on a packed flight? You've guessed it – the middle seat. It can make your trip miserable. Here are some strategies to help you avoid the worst seat.

3 Look at these First Conditional sentences.

Condition	Consequences
If + present	*will* + infinitive

If you check in early, you'll be able to choose your seat.

or

You'll be able to choose your seat if you check in early.

Match the conditions (a–j) to the consequences (1–10). Make as many logical combinations as possible.

a If you book months in advance,
b If you sit at the front,
c If you check in late,
d If you're polite to the check-in attendant,
e If you pretend to be ill or pregnant,
f If you trust your instincts,
g If you dominate the armrests,
h If you use your laptop,
i If you drink too much,
j If you get up during the flight,

1 you'll get on and off the plane faster.
2 you'll be too early for a seat assignment.
3 you'll have to go to the toilet a lot.
4 you'll be able to stretch your legs.
5 you'll sometimes be able to change seat.
6 you'll get more personal space.
7 you'll pay for it with an uncomfortable seat.
8 you'll choose better seatmates.
9 you'll feel claustrophobic.
10 you'll feel guilty the entire flight.

a 2, 5, 6   **c** _____   **e** _____   **g** _____   **i** _____

b _____   **d** _____   **f** _____   **h** _____   **j** _____

4 🔘 **2.11** Listen to someone giving advice about getting a good seat. Circle the combinations in 3 which correspond to what the speaker says. Do you agree with the advice?

Buying an airline ticket

1 Read the article and answer the questions.

a Why won't you have anyone to blame if you get a bad deal on your airline ticket?

b If more than nine seats are empty, why will easyJet not be happy?

c If you ask Ryanair about their prices, what will they say?

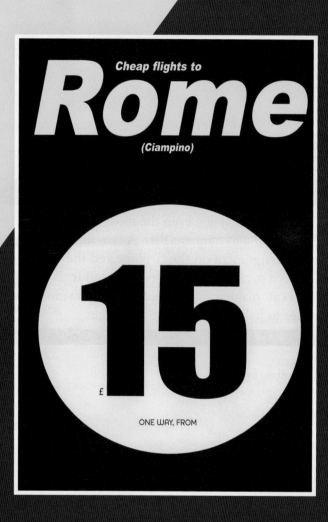

Cheap flights to

Rome

(Ciampino)

£ **15**

ONE WAY, FROM

Cut-price travel

How is it possible that two passengers sitting shoulder to shoulder in the same plane can pay such different prices for their tickets? Buying an air ticket has become a test of skill and timing, where the customer is responsible for getting the best deal possible. With the online reservation systems of cut-price airlines it is your fault if you get a bad deal, because there is no travel agent to blame.

Nowadays, all airlines have a 'pricing' department which is responsible for 'yield management'. In other words, their job is to adjust the price of tickets in order to get the maximum possible profit for each seat on the flight. Ticket prices vary according to supply and demand and depend on how full the flight is, and when you make your reservation. The result is a tremendous difference in prices. In one investigation, *Le Monde* newspaper made enquiries at different times about Air France tickets on the same flight from Paris to New York in economy class. They were quoted 17 different prices, ranging from €467 to €3,228.

Airlines justify these variable pricing policies on the extremely narrow profit margins of the business. To illustrate this, easyJet use a graphic which shows the seating plan of a plane with 155 seats. They need to sell 39 of these seats to cover airport costs. 37 seats go in fuel costs and 15 to pay the pilots and crew. That leaves just 9 seats for profit.

Another airline, Ryanair, blames special extra fees for pushing up the prices. For example, each passenger pays extra for the wheelchair that the plane is obliged to carry and, since the attack on the twin towers in 2001, an extra amount for insurance against the risk of terrorism. However, it is also true that if your luggage is just over the allowed weight, or you have an extra piece of luggage, they will charge you a fortune for 'excess baggage'. At the same time, you can't claim a refund if a flight is delayed, but if you're five minutes late for check-in, they won't let you through and you'll miss your flight.

2 Complete the sentences based on the information in the article.

a If you book your ticket at a different time to another passenger, the price of your tickets _____.

b If there isn't much demand for seats on a flight, the price _____.

c You will only have yourself to blame if you _____ deal.

d If they only sell 91 seats, _____ profit.

e easyJet don't make a profit on a flight if _____ seats left.

f If you have an extra bag, _____.

g They won't let you get on your flight if _____.

3 What is your experience of cut-price travel? Discuss with the class.

4 The verbs in the four lists below often collocate with the nouns on the right. One verb in each list is wrong. Delete the verbs which are wrong.

get buy offer see negotiate	... a good deal	cover estimate reduce increase delete	... costs	cost do pay make charge	... a fortune	adjust increase reserve lower reduce	... the price

5 Use the verb + noun combinations in 4 to complete the sentences below.

a It is difficult to _____ without customers changing to suppliers who are cheaper.

b Nowadays if you need to fly somewhere, you can always _____ on the Internet.

c Companies use computers to _____, but in fact they often create more work and are expensive.

d It is not possible to _____ without hard work and good luck.

e Low-cost airlines _____ if you book just before you travel, so you should make your reservation well in advance.

f Some cut-price airlines _____ on their website, but often there are a lot of hidden charges, so flights aren't as cheap as they seem.

g Airlines say that extra costs which they can't control _____ of an air ticket.

The negotiation game

1 Think of situations where it is necessary to negotiate at work and at home. Work with a partner and discuss these questions for each situation.

a Are you a good negotiator?

b Is it always possible to negotiate?

2 2.12 You are going to play a game in which you have to negotiate the price, quantity, delivery time, payment terms and guarantee period of a product to gain points. Before you play, listen to two people playing the game as an example.

3 Work with a partner. First of all, decide what the product is.

Speaker A: You are the buyer. Look at the instructions and chart on page 133.

Speaker B: You are the seller. Look at the instructions and chart on page 139.

13 Air travel

Phrase bank: Air travel

Is this where I check in for flight (RA 264)?

Is it okay if I take this bag on as hand luggage?

Could you show me where the available seats are?

I'd really like an aisle / a window seat if possible, please.

Did you pack your bag yourself?

The flight will be boarding at gate number (23) in (20) minutes.

Have a good flight.

Vocabulary

Air travel

1 Imagine you are flying from Europe to the USA. Put the following events in a logical order.

a ☐ Book your flight over the Internet or by phoning the airline.

b ☐ Check in at least 45 minutes before your flight.

c ☐ Go through the metal detector and wait for your flight to be announced.

d ☐ Fasten your seat belt and take off.

e ☐ Show your boarding pass at the boarding gate and get on the plane.

f ☐ Check the details of your reservation and seat assignment.

g ☐ Dominate the armrests!

h ☐ Go through customs.

i ☐ Take a taxi to your hotel.

j ☐ Land at JFK airport and get off the plane.

k ☐ Go through passport control and pick up your luggage in baggage reclaim.

2 Match the sentence beginnings (a–f) with the endings (1–6).

a You should ask for the seat you want when you book ...

b It's important to be polite ...

c There was a traffic jam and I missed ...

d The flight was overbooked, so they offered me ...

e If you don't get a good deal on your ticket, ...

f If your flight is delayed, ...

1 ... your flight.

2 ... my flight.

3 ... to the check-in attendant.

4 ... you can only blame yourself.

5 ... you can't claim a refund.

6 ... a refund or a later flight.

a	b	c	d	e	f

Negotiating

3 Complete the dialogue with the words in the box.

10%	accept	business	deal	deliver	discount	do
more	order	payment	price	up		

A Okay, we want to do (a) _____ with you, but we need to talk about the (b) _____.

B Well, the catalogue price is $30.25.

A I know, but we're talking about a big (c) _____ here. If we order 100 units, for example, what (d) _____ will you give me?

B If you order (e) _____ than 100 units, I'll give you a discount of (f) _____.

A Ten per cent. And for 150 units?

B For 150 units, I'll go (g) _____ to twelve per cent.

A Twelve per cent. That sounds good. What about (h) _____?

B Payment is within 60 days.

A Er, if you let us pay within 90 days, I'll (i) _____ a lower discount ... say ten per cent on 150 units.

B So, you're saying that if I offer a discount of ten per cent on the catalogue price for an order of 150 units, with payment within 90 days, we'll have a (j) _____?

A Yes, we'll have a deal ... if you can (k) _____ in two weeks.

B All right, then. I think we can (l) _____ that. It's a deal!

4 Complete the dialogue with the phrases below.

if I can finish this report	if I can get a room
If there's nothing on Tuesday	I'll ask him to take me
I'll ask you to take me	I'll just take a taxi then
I'll take the new metro	What will you do

A Have you got your trip next week organized?

B More or less. I haven't actually booked anything yet.

A You know it's a long weekend. There'll be a lot of people travelling on Tuesday. (a) _____ if you can't get a flight?

B (b) _____, I'll go on Wednesday and re-schedule a couple of meetings.

A What about getting to the airport?

B If Derek is free, (c) _____.

A And if he isn't?

B Well, if you're available, (d) _____.

A Sorry, I can't.

B (e) _____.

A How are you getting into town?

B Unless I'm pushed for time, (f) _____. It's very convenient because there's a stop near the hotel.

A Oh, will you stay at The Majestic again?

B I will (g) _____. It might be difficult with the conference on.

A You'd better get on and make some reservations.

B Yes, (h) _____, I'll get on the Internet or give them a ring before I go to lunch.

Grammar

Conditionals with *will*

If + Present Simple, *will* / *won't* + infinitive
- *If I **have** time, I'**ll finish** the figures this afternoon.*
- *If they **don't offer** me more money, I **won't accept** the job.*

will / *won't* + infinitive + *if* + Present Simple
- *He **won't wait** if you **arrive** late.*
- *I'**ll phone** you if my mobile **works** there.*

You can use conditionals with *will* to talk about future events which depend on other things happening.

Practice 1

Match the sentence beginnings (a–j) with the endings (1–10).

a	If you don't leave now, …	**1**	… they won't be able to get on the plane.
b	You'll be late …	**2**	… if I go to so many business lunches.
c	If I get a promotion, …	**3**	… you'll miss your flight.
d	I'll buy a better car …	**4**	… if you don't keep interrupting them.
e	If people are rude to the ground staff, …	**5**	… if you don't call a taxi now.
f	If we make a good offer, …	**6**	… if we coincide with the rush hour.
g	It'll take longer to get to the airport …	**7**	… I'll earn more money.
h	I'll put on weight …	**8**	… if they increase my salary.
i	If you don't have any plans for tonight, …	**9**	… will you have dinner with me?
j	They'll get more work done …	**10**	… we'll get the contract.

a	b	c	d	e	f	g	h	i	j

Practice 2

Complete the sentences with the verbs in the box in the correct form.

adopt	be	find	have	improve	lose	need	pay
phone	tell						

a If I see John, I _____ him what you said.

b If anyone _____ to contact me, tell them I'll be back at four.

c We _____ able to get the 10.14 am train if we hurry.

d If you _____ my keys, will you let me know?

e Your English _____ if you spend some time in the USA.

f I _____ you if there's any news.

g If we _____ within 30 days, will you drop the price?

h If BA's policy on rude passengers is a success, other airlines _____ it.

i If he checks in late, he _____ his seat assignment.

j You _____ to hurry if you want to catch your flight.

Practice 3

Write a sentence using a conditional with *will* based on each piece of advice.

a You should confirm your booking or you won't get a good seat.
If you confirm your booking, you'll get a good seat.

b You should pretend you're not interested in buying from them or they won't drop the price.

_____

c You should apologize to the boss or you will have problems.

_____

d You shouldn't drink too much on the flight or you'll have to keep going to the toilet.

_____

e You should leave for the airport now or you'll miss your flight.

_____

f You shouldn't be rude to airport ground staff or they won't let you on the plane.

_____

g You should study something practical or you won't get a job.

_____

h You shouldn't work too hard or you'll get ill.

_____

i You should take the client out to lunch or you won't get his business.

_____

14 Hiring and firing

Have you ever had to fire someone? What happened?

Learning objectives: Unit 14

Business communication skills Discussing when sacking is justified; Writing a letter of application; Asking for clarification; Roleplay: A CV and an interview; Discussing labour laws and industrial action
Reading Article about someone being fired; A CV
Listening People talking about applying for a new job; Job interview
Phrase bank Job interviews
Vocabulary Procedures
Grammar The passive

1 Look at the headline below. What do you think the article is about?

2 Read the article to see if you are correct. Then answer the questions.
a Do you think the sacking was justified?
b Would this be possible in your company or in your country?
c What advice would you give to Nicola?

IBIZA PHONE-IN PRIZE WINNER FIRED

Nicola Williams, a 31-year-old single mother from Newbridge in South Wales, couldn't believe her luck when she was told she was the winner of a Mediterranean holiday for herself and her six-year-old daughter.

The week's break on the sunshine island of Ibiza was the prize in a radio phone-in competition. She told reporter Hefina Rendle on BBC Wales television that she was 'totally over the moon, really excited'. However, only minutes later, she was laid off. Nicola, an electronic parts worker, who phoned the radio station from work using her own mobile phone, was unaware that her boss was standing nearby. He asked her to hang up, took her into his office and told her she was sacked. She was ordered to leave the factory immediately.

This was her first job since the birth of her daughter, and she was fired by the same manager who originally hired her.

But the story may have a happy ending. The commercial radio station which ran the competition is now trying to find her another job. A spokesman for the station said that

people should be allowed to take part in competitions from work, as they are in general life. He said it was sad that the manager couldn't see the good side and just congratulate Nicola on her good luck.

Skytronics, Nicola's former employer, refused to be interviewed by the BBC, and later issued a statement supporting the action of their manager.

3 Find two verbs in the article that are similar in meaning to 'sack'. Which verb is more formal?

4 Find sentences in the article that are similar in meaning to the following:
a They laid her off. _____
b They ordered her to leave the factory immediately. _____

5 Compare the two pairs of sentences in 4.
a Which are active and which are passive?
b Who is mentioned first in the active sentences?
c Who is mentioned first in the passive sentences?
d Who is the story about?
e What is the advantage of using the passive sentences?
f The agent in the active sentences is _they_. What happens to it in the passive sentences? Why?

6 Read the manager's report of the incident in 2. He uses the passive to sound more objective and formal in style. Complete the report using the verbs below in the passive.

ask   give (x 2)   inform (x 2)   note   warn

RE: Nicola Williams

On two occasions in November, Ms Nicola Williams, an employee in the assembly plant, (a) _____ that using a mobile phone in work hours was against the company rules. Both these warnings (b) _____ by another supervisor, and (c) _____ in her file. Then, in December, on a further occasion, she (d) _____ a written warning. Finally, on Friday 12 January at 10.30, I (e) _____ of a problem on the factory floor. When I arrived there, I found a lot of noise and shouting going on. Ms Williams was using her mobile phone to participate in a radio phone-in programme. Apparently she had won a prize. I asked her to put the phone down immediately, and to come in to my office. I decided to terminate her employment, and in the presence of Ms Jones, my deputy, Ms Williams was told that she was being dismissed. She became hysterical and abusive, and (f) _____ to leave the factory immediately. She (g) _____ that her possessions would be forwarded to her by post.

---

7 In what way are the details about the incident different in the newspaper article and the report?

8 Make these short texts more formal by changing one verb to the passive in each text.

a They have laid off over 35,000 people in the last five years, unemployment is rising, and there are social problems in the region.

35,000 people have been laid off in the last five years, unemployment is rising, and there are social problems in the region.

b The business is a great success. They are hiring new staff and it is expanding fast.

c As there was a recession and the number of orders decreased, they closed one of the factories.

d To improve margins, it is making the new model in Hungary, where labour costs are lower.

e Ford™ has several plants in Europe. One of them is in Valencia and it produces the Escort there.

f They have announced plans for the new industrial estate. It will cover ten hectares and create space for over 15 business ventures.

9 Work in groups. In what situations do you think sacking is justified? Discuss your opinions and think about the points in the box.

dishonesty   disrespect to superiors   inappropriate dress   industrial action (going on strike)
not meeting objectives or achieving results   punctuality   revealing company secrets   violence

Add your own ideas, if you like.

Applying for a job

1 🔘 **2.13–2.16** Listen to four people talking about their approach to applying for a job. Take notes and match the speakers (1–4) to the summaries (a–d).

a 'I'm looking for a chance to develop and demonstrate my true potential.' ☐

b 'My qualifications and experience speak for themselves.' ☐

c 'I'm so brilliant at whatever I do, they would be lucky to have me working in their company.' ☐

d 'There may be people with better qualifications and experience, but no one is more enthusiastic or hard-working than me.' ☐

2 Which speaker(s) do you agree with? What approach did you use to get your present job? Does the approach you use depend on the job?

3 Read the following extracts from letters of application. Match them to the summaries in 1.

> **i** I am very keen to work for your company because of its excellent reputation. I do not have the specific qualifications or experience referred to in your advertisement. However, I am applying because I feel I am able to make up for this through hard work and willingness to learn. ☐

> **ii** If you believe in the pursuit of excellence, then I am interested in joining your company. I set high standards for myself and expect them from others, especially the organizations that I work for. I look forward to an opportunity to add to the list of already outstanding achievements, which are outlined in my CV. ☐

> **iii** From my CV, you will see that five years at a chemicals multinational have given me a solid business background. I am responsible for my department's logistical planning, which has developed my organizational skills. However, I am now looking for opportunities for further development and responsibility, which my present employer cannot offer. ☐

> **iv** As a commercially aware and linguistically trained university graduate, I have a broad range of employment experience at blue-chip companies in both the USA and Europe. I am dynamic and creative, with a strong team spirit and leadership qualities. I have a proven record of working with individuals at all levels through highly developed interpersonal and communication skills. ☐

4 Read the extracts in 3 again. There are certain formal phrases people use in letters of application to talk about their qualities and achievements. <u>Underline</u> phrases which mean the following:

a I'd really like to work for you because you're such a great company.

b If you think doing things well is important, I'd like to work for you.

c I don't really have the profile of the ideal candidate.

d I've worked with many different, important companies.

e I've shown I can work with all kinds of people and get on with everyone.

f I look after the practical day-to-day aspects of department organization.

g I want a new job because my company probably won't be able to promote me.

h I have five years of international business experience working for a chemicals company.

5 Use some of the phrases in 3 to write a paragraph introducing your own CV.

A job interview

1 Read the job advert and CV. Why do you think Sara applied for the job?

CURRICULUM VITAE

Name Sara Verkade

Address 58, Stoppard Drive, London SW16

Telephone Tel: 353 865 344872

Email sara.verkade@gmz.net

Date & place of birth 23.7.78, Maassluis, The Netherlands

Marital status Single

Nationality Dutch

Qualifications September 1996 – July 1999 BComm, Marketing Management, Haagse Hogeschool, The Hague

Employment history

June 2000 – present Management Team Co-ordinator, Helena Rubinstein, L'Oréal Organizing meetings, events and conferences. Analyzing sales figures and producing relevant reports and charts. Customer relations and responding to complaints and queries.

June 1999 – June 2000 SPC Professional, Sales Productivity Centre, IBM Sales team support. Research, pricing and proposal-writing on million-dollar bids.

Languages Dutch, English, German, Spanish

IT Skills Proficient user of Microsoft Office® suite

2 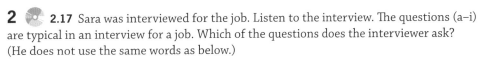 **2.17** Sara was interviewed for the job. Listen to the interview. The questions (a–i) are typical in an interview for a job. Which of the questions does the interviewer ask? (He does not use the same words as below.)

a Why did you apply for this job?

b Why should we employ you?

c When are you free to start?

d Does your present employer know that you want to leave?

e Have you ever done anything like this before?

f How do feel about travelling?

g How good are your computer skills?

h What are your language skills like?

i Do you have any questions?

3 Do you think the interviewer was fair in the interview? Do you think Sara got the job?

4 🔘 **2.17** Listen again and complete the phrases below.

a How much managerial experience do you have ? It's _____ your CV.

b Yes. _____ you're the leader of the team?

c Oh, I see. _____ of personal assistant?

d But _____ a manager?

e _____ in your previous position you were 'an SPC professional'. What _____?

f _____ you were directly involved in sales?

g So, _____ involve?

h Can _____ specific, please?

5 Write a brief CV for yourself and give it to your partner. Then take it in turns to interview each other for the job Sara wanted or another job. Ask for clarification of the details of the CV.

What about the workers?

1 What is happening in the photo on this page? How do you think this situation relates to employment and staffing?

2 Work with a partner. You will each read an article relating to the employment situation in a country and do three exercises. When you have finished, turn back to this page.

Speaker A: Look at page 133.
Speaker B: Look at page 134.

3 Which country do you think the article you read is about? Could it be your country? Why / Why not? Discuss with your partner.

14 Hiring and firing

Phrase bank: Job interviews

Now, can we just check out some details?

Does that mean ...?

But do / are you ...?

It says on your CV / in your email that ... What exactly does that mean?

What does ... involve?

Could you be a bit more specific about ..., please?

I'd like to work for you because ...

In the past, I've ...

At my last job, I ...

I'm responsible for ...

I have (five) years of experience in ...

Vocabulary

Procedures

1 Match the sentence beginnings (a–j) with the endings (1–10).

a She was employed ...

b The incident was reported ...

c John was consulted ...

d The staff have been informed ...

e She was sacked ...

f The conditions were agreed ...

g He didn't accept the offers which were put ...

h The worker was injured ...

i The flight was delayed ...

j The passive is used ...

1 ... on a temporary basis.

2 ... about the decision.

3 ... for writing reports.

4 ... for stealing office stationery.

5 ... to him by the employment office.

6 ... by the bad weather.

7 ... to the supervisor.

8 ... at a company wide level.

9 ... of the new working hours.

10 ... by an explosion in the chemical plant.

a	b	c	d	e	f	g	h	i	j

2 Combine one word from column A with one word from column B to complete each sentence below.

A	B
electronics	application
written	secrets
job	position
company	rights
workers'	needs
job	security
previous	workers
skilled	warning
temporary	staff
unemployment	benefits
staffing	industry

a For young people _____ is not usually as important as a good salary.

b We gave the employee a _____ for arriving late to work two days running.

c In the summer there is more work so we have to take on more people to meet our _____.

d He was accused of revealing _____ to a competitor.

e A hundred years ago _____ didn't exist because there were no unions.

f You always have to include a CV in your _____.

g Education is important because industry needs a supply of _____.

h Was your _____ a full-time post?

i In many countries there are no _____ for people who have no work.

j At Christmas, shops take on _____ because it's a busy time of year.

k The _____ is an important sector of the local economy.

3 Reorganize the letters to form words to complete the sentences.

kasc	veritwine	girinf	dalifof	revbal	nowd

a Two hundred workers at the factory have been _____ because of the bad financial situation.

b I asked her to put the phone _____ and come into my office.

c They can't _____ you without giving you at least two warnings in writing.

d _____ someone is one of the most difficult things a manager has to do.

e The first thing you have to do is give the employee a _____ warning.

f How did your _____ go? Did you get the job?

The passive

The object in active sentences becomes the subject in passive sentences.

Active	Passive (*to be* + past participle)
Someone **services** the machine every year.	The machine **is serviced** every year.
They **have closed** five factories.	Five factories **have been closed**.
They **decorated** the offices last year.	The offices **were decorated** last year.
They **are encouraging** her to apply for the job.	She **is being encouraged** to apply for the job.
They **don't clean** the office on Friday.	The **office isn't cleaned** on Friday.

You often use the passive to put the important information at the beginning of a sentence. The passive can be more impersonal than the active. For this reason, you can use it in formal documents such as reports.

You can use *by* to emphasize *who* or *what* performed an action.
- *The book was written **by** Peter Hudson.*
- *The equipment is damaged **by** prolonged exposure to sunlight.*

Practice 1

Reorganize the words to make correct sentences.

a June was at the contract the signed end of

_____

b sacked slowly Sheila was working too for

_____

c damaged fire the the in was office

_____

d workers accident injured were the in some

_____

e measures announced the have new been

_____

f staff employed new no year this be will

_____

g redesigned corporate is image being our

_____

h salaries increased year have this been our

_____

Practice 2

Rewrite the sentences in the passive.

a They have cancelled the order.
   The order has been cancelled.

b They haven't finished the new building.

_____

c Someone told him about the meeting.

_____

d Someone stole the plans for the new engine.

_____

e Someone will pick you up at the airport.

_____

f They didn't ask him if he wanted the job.

_____

g Did anyone tell you about what happened at the meeting?

_____

h They hold a sales conference every year.

_____

Practice 3

Answer the questions using a sentence in the passive and *by*.

a Who was the inventor of the light bulb?
   The light bulb was invented by Thomas Edison.

b What currency was the replacement for the peseta, franc and lira in 2002?

_____

c How many countries form the United Kingdom?

_____

d Who is the author of this book?

_____

e Who is the owner of this book?

_____

f What type of heating have you got in your office – oil, gas or electric?

_____

g Who was the director of the film *Avatar*?

_____

h Which company was the original manufacturer of the PC?

_____

Answers below.

Answers (Practice 3)
b euro c four d Simon Clarke
g James Cameron h IBM

15 Time

What time management skills do you use?

Learning objectives: Unit 15

Business communication skills
Discussing time management; Fluency: Talking about decisions and plans; Asking and answering questions about time management techniques

Reading Article about wasting time at work; Article about working without clocks

Listening A conversation about a delayed project; A talk on time management

Phrase bank Talking about time

Vocabulary Time collocations, Working conditions

Grammar *going to, going to* vs *will*

In company interviews Units 13–15

1 Add vowels to make collocations with *money* and *time*.

```
s p _ n d   |
s _ v _     |
w _ s t _   |   money / time
h _ v _     |
_ n v _ s t |
```

2 Complete the sentences using words from 1. Are they true for you?

a At work, I _____ a lot of time on the phone and answering emails.

b I plan my day carefully. If you prepare things well, you can _____ a lot of time.

c I don't _____ much time for myself, but when I do, I like to get some exercise.

d Computers should make you more efficient, but they can also make you _____ time.

3 Discuss the following questions with a partner.

a Some people say 'Time is money'. Do you agree?

b What do you think of Stefan Töpfer's basic rules of time management? Are there any you disagree with?

c How aware do you need to be of time in your job? Do you have the same routine every day?

d Could you work without a watch or clocks?

4 Read the article and answer these questions.

a How did AOL try life without time?

b What was the aim of the experiment?

c Why do companies use time as a measure of productivity?

d Why is the normal working timetable (nine to five) inefficient?

e What was the result of the experiment?

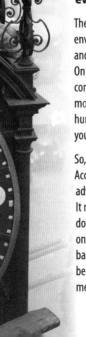

Life without time

How dependent are we on time? Is life without clocks less stressful? One company decided to find out. At AOL, they removed all the clocks from their UK headquarters. Then everybody carried on working as usual.

They wanted to investigate how pressure of time can lead to stress, and to see how an environment without clocks would affect productivity. They say that time is money, and most companies use time to control their activities because it is easy to measure. On the other hand, humans have a biological clock which doesn't necessarily correspond to the standard eight-hour working day. We are more productive in the morning, and then our efficiency tends to drop off after lunch. So, if you're feeling hungry, why not have something to eat instead of waiting for the lunch break? Or, if you've finished your work, don't hang on until it's time to clock off, just go home.

So, what happens when you rely on your own body clock instead of artificial deadlines? According to one worker, 'Most people carried on as normal, although some took advantage of the opportunity to have an early lunch.' Another said 'This is great. It makes sense to be able to work when you need to and leave the office when you don't.' On the other hand, one secretary found the experience 'disorientating'. However, one office manager was in no doubt: 'Thank goodness we are going to bring the clocks back tomorrow. Make no mistake, a clockless office leads to chaos. Some people may be less stressed without clocks, but you need to know where people are and when, and meetings, for example, can last forever if you don't have a time limit.'

5 Find words and phrases in the article in 4 which mean the same as the following:

a continue   _____

b result in   _____

c quantify   _____

d fall quickly   _____

e wait   _____

6 Complete the sentences with the words and phrases in 5.

a Time management methods _____ unnecessary stress.

b In some businesses, it is difficult to _____ efficiency.

c When you have to make a decision, it's best to _____ until the last minute.

d If you _____ in the same job for a long time, you lose interest.

e The amount of activity in an office _____ on a Friday afternoon.

7 Which of the sentences in 6 do you agree with? Discuss with a partner.

8 Look at this sentence from the article in 4 and answer the questions.

Thank goodness we are going to bring the clocks back tomorrow.

a Does the sentence refer to the past, present or future?

b Which of the following is closest in meaning to *we are going to bring the clocks back*?

We would like to bring the clocks back …

We intend to bring the clocks back …

We have to bring the clocks back …

9 Plan how you are going to spend your next working day. Then explain your plans to your partner like this.

At 9.00, when I arrive at work, I'm going to check my email. Then …

The new database

1 Match the words and phrases (a–d) with the definitions (1–4).

a	deadline	**1**	late
b	delay	**2**	point in time by which something must be done
c	behind schedule	**3**	a hold-up
d	time frame	**4**	period in which something is expected to happen

2 2.18 Listen to the conversation and answer the questions.

a What problem is the conversation about?

b When was the system supposed to be online?

c When is it going to be ready now?

d What do you think of the IT technician's attitude?

3 2.18 Listen again and complete the phrases with one word for each gap. Contractions count as one word.

a We're worried because it's _____ _____.

b Well, yes, I'm sorry about _____ _____, but there have been some problems …

c … the system was supposed to be online last October. You _____ _____ _____ _____, and it's now February.

d … not compatible with the new design. That means we have a _____ _____ _____.

e What do you mean? How _____ _____ _____ _____ _____ _____?

f Are you saying that _____ _____ for all this is now next October?

g Can you guarantee that you're giving us priority on this? Will _____ _____ _____ _____?

4 Complete the phrases so they are true for you. Then compare your ideas with a partner.

a It takes me _____ to get to work in the morning.

b I _____ meet my deadlines.

c In my company we _____ time frames for getting things done.

d When people are not on time for meetings _____.

e IT projects _____ behind schedule.

f At work the schedules for projects are _____.

g When things are delayed I _____.

h In my country, _____ on time.

Wasting time

1 Match the words to make four common collocations.

a	bottom	**1**	balance
b	delicate	**2**	caught
c	get	**3**	time
d	waste	**4**	line

2 Use the collocations in 1 to complete the introduction to an article.

Wasting time at work

Lots of people are so afraid of getting caught, they never (a) _____ at work. They work the entire eight hours. They are right to be afraid. There is a (b) _____ between not doing any work and doing too much. The (c) _____ is you must get your work done. If you start wasting hours at a time, you'll (d) _____. To be an effective time waster, you have to find small ways to eat up time. Remember, you can't waste the company's time if you don't work for the company. However, with a little effort, no one will ever know how little you do.

3 Here are the headings from the rest of the article. What tips do you think the author gives under each heading?

- Be sloppy
- The Internet
- Meetings
- The computer
- Office conversations

4 Look at page 142 to see what the author recommends.

5 Complete the sentences with words or phrases from the text on page 142 that mean the same as the words in brackets.

a 'Your papers are _____.' 'Yes, but I know where everything is, so don't touch anything.' (untidy)

b Before making an important call, you should _____ time to prepare for it. (reserve)

c I only use the Internet to get specific information. I don't have time to _____ the Web. (move around from link to link with no particular aim)

d My job requires a lot of _____, so I need a good Internet connection. (information searching)

e People who always _____ and agree with everything are no use at all. (move head up and down)

Dealing with problems

1 🔘 **2.19–2.21** Complete the following conversations using the verb in brackets with either *going to* or *will*. Then listen and check your answers.

Conversation 1

A Where are you going?

B Well, I've finished everything I had to do, so I (a) _____ (leave) early.

A What about the sales predictions for next month?

B Oh, I'd forgotten about that. I (b) _____ (start) on them tomorrow first thing. I've arranged to meet someone at five.

Conversation 2

C Have you planned Mr Logan's visit? What about lunch tomorrow?

D I (c) _____ (take) him to The Redwing.

C I seem to remember he's a vegetarian.

D Is he? In that case, I (d) _____ (phone) to check they have a vegetarian menu.

Conversation 3

E Is everything confirmed for your trip to San Sebastián?

F Yes, the plane goes to Bilbao. I (e) _____ (take) the train from there.

E No, don't do that – it takes forever. The bus is much faster.

F Is it? Well, I (f) _____ (take) the bus, then.

2 Read the conversations again and look at how *will* and *going to* are used. <u>Underline</u> the correct option in the following sentences.

You can use *will* or *going to* to talk about decisions and plans:

a Using *will / going to* shows that you are making a decision now.

b Using *will / going to* shows that you made the decision earlier.

3 Work with a partner. Have similar conversations as in 1 using the prompts below and following this pattern:

A Say what you are going to do: *I'm going to walk to the station.*

B Mention a problem with the plan: *But it's raining.*

A React with an alternative plan using *will*: *Oh, in that case, I'll take a taxi.*

Plan	Problem	Alternative
walk to the station	it's raining	?
attend Japanese classes	you're too busy – you'll miss classes	?
buy a bargain computer	it's an old model – it'll be obsolete very soon	?
get an easier job	you'll earn less money	?
take a taxi to the airport	the taxi drivers are on strike	?
take up roller skating	it's dangerous – there are lots of accidents	?

The myth of time management

1 2.22 Listen to a talk on the topic of time management. Put the topics in the correct order.

| 1 | Introduction – does time management work? |
| Prioritizing |
| Dealing with interruptions |
| Defined tasks versus problem-solving |
| Factors beyond our control |

2 2.22 Complete the sentences with the words in the box. Then listen again to check your answers.

efficient   expectations   intelligence   ~~online~~   operators   problem   tasks   voicemail

a There are thousands of books and _online_ courses on the market which are designed to help people be better managers of their time.

b They recommend making 'to do' lists, prioritizing and not answering the phone as ways to make us more time _____.

c As a result, you can be a very efficient user of your time – disciplined, organized and choosing the right moment to do vital _____ – yet still feel stressed and overworked.

d One of the recommended techniques is to close your door at certain times, or leave your _____ to deal with calls.

e I think most people of average _____ can normally see the difference between activity which is useful and activity which is a waste of time.

f Machine _____, for example, don't have to worry much about managing their time because the pace of work is imposed from outside.

g If you are faced with a task which involves creativity or _____-solving, how exactly to perform the task may not be clear.

h Above all, it is about having a positive attitude towards your work, combined with reasonable _____ about how much you can do.

3 Is the speaker for or against time management techniques? Do you agree? Why / Why not?

4 How well do you manage your time? Complete the 'You' column with approximate percentages for the time you spend on the different activities. Add other activities, if necessary. Then complete the 'Your partner' column by asking *How much time do you spend on ...?*

Activity	You	Your partner
planning and delegating		
meetings		
correspondence		
telephoning		
reading		
dealing with problems		
_____		
	100%	100%

5 What differences are there in the way you and your partner manage your time? Why do you think this is?

In company interviews
Units 13–15

15 Time

Vocabulary

Working conditions

1 Match one word from A with its collocation from B to complete the sentences.

A	B
realistic	planning
eight-hour	deadline
long	forecasts
sales	line
forward	hours
bottom	day

a Monday is too soon for us; next Friday is a more

_____.

b The traditional _____ does not suit our natural daily rhythm.

c According to our _____ we are going to sell over 20% more next year.

d In any business the _____ is that you have to make enough money to survive.

e You should give priority to important tasks such as _____ and problem analysis.

f In the UK, people work _____ but their productivity is not as high as in France or Germany.

2 Complete the sentences using the correct form of the words in brackets.

a Most people _____ better in the morning. (performance)

b A psychologist is going to _____ the staff to see how they work. (observation)

c Time management _____ will not be impressed by the results of the experiment. (specialize)

d We are not so _____ after a good lunch. (production)

e They _____ to reduce the working week to 35 hours in some countries. (intention)

f Have you _____ what to do about the situation? (decision)

g The _____ went on for hours and the meeting ended very late. (discuss)

Grammar

be + going to + infinitive

Affirmative/Negative

I	am 'm not	going to apply for the job.
You We They	are aren't	
He She	is isn't	

Interrogative

Are(n't)	you they we	going to phone later?
Is(n't)	he she	

You can use *going to* to talk about intentions and decisions you have made about the future before the moment of speaking.

- *We're going to open a new office in Berlin.*
- *I'm going to ask for an application form for the new post.*

going to or will?

You use *will* to show you are making a decision at the moment of speaking.

A *Could I speak to Mr Gomez, please?*

B *I'm afraid he's out at the moment. Can I take a message?*

A *No thanks, I'll phone later.*

Practice 1

Write sentences using *going to* and the words below.

a this evening / meet / friends / a drink
This evening, I'm going to meet some friends for a drink.

b they / employ / more staff / deal with the new order
_____

c you / meet / me / airport?
_____

d what / you / say / at / meeting?
_____

e next year / I / study / German
_____

f he / look for / new job
_____

g she / not / accept / our offer
_____

h we / take / train / bus?
_____

Practice 2

Read the sentences and make responses with *will* and an idea from the box.

> ask her for her business card
> call the IT department
> call the office and apologize
> switch it off
> ~~take the team out for lunch~~
> take a taxi back to the office to collect them
> take an aspirin and go home

a Your sales team has met its targets for this month.
I'll take the team out for lunch.

b You're at a meeting and your phone rings.
_____

c Your computer has just crashed.
_____

d You've forgotten some important documents for a meeting.
_____

e You suddenly have a terrible headache and feel sick.
_____

f You see an important client at a conference and you can't remember her name.
_____

g You've overslept and you're going to be late.
_____

Practice 3

Complete the responses with the verb in brackets using either *going to* or *will*.

a We've run out of toner for the photocopier.
Have we? I _____ (order) some more.

b What are your plans for the weekend?
We _____ (visit) some friends in the country. Do you want to come?

c Did you remember to book the hotel?
No, I forgot! I _____ (phone) them now. I hope they still have some room.

d You should consult George about the production problems.
I've already mentioned it to him. We _____ (discuss) it this afternoon.

e Have you seen their offices? They're miles from anywhere in this really old building.
Yes, I know. But they _____ (move) to a new place next year.

f I'm dying for a cup of coffee.
All right, I _____ (make) you one now. Do you take sugar?

g Why are you working so hard?
Because I _____ (leave) on time today, for a change, and I want to finish this before I go.

h I have to go to the airport and my car won't start.
Don't worry. I _____ (lend) you mine.

Practice 4

Complete the conversation with the words in the box.

> do   easier   information   learn   someone   start
> strategy   time   urgent

A What are you doing?
B I'm putting this customer (a) _____ into the database.
A Why don't you get (b) _____ else in your team to do it?
B Well, it's (c) _____ if I just do it myself.
A Yes, but if you do it yourself, they'll never (d) _____.
B Yes, you're probably right. I'll (e) _____ that next time.
A Anyway, have you finished the marketing (f) _____ for the new product launch?
B No, I'm going to (g) _____ that this afternoon.
A Oh, come on! It's really (h) _____. We're all waiting for it.
B I know, but I haven't had (i) _____.

Getting things done

1 🔘 **2.23–2.24** Complete the extracts from two conversations which take place in an office. Then listen and compare your answers.

Extract 1

A I _____ go to the Post Office to pick something up and it's _____. _____ lend me your umbrella?

B Of course. As long as _____.

Extract 2

A The thing is that I need _____ where we won't be interrupted. _____ use your office?

B All right, as long as _____. I've got a meeting myself.

What's the difference between *Could I …?* and *Could you …?*

2 Work with a partner. Act out conversations using the prompts below. Use the conversations in 1 as a model. Then think of two more of your own problems and ask for help.

Problem	Request	As long as …
phone home / mobile batteries flat	use / your mobile	just a short call
send an email / computer not working	use / computer	not take too long
be at airport at five / taxi services not answering	give / lift	get back before six
post a letter / can't leave the office	post it on your way home	have it ready by five o'clock
translate this letter / no dictionary	borrow yours	get it back by this afternoon
take notes / no pen	lend me one	give it back later
make copies / photocopier not working	take / photocopy shop	answer the phone while I'm out

3 🔘 **2.25** It is important to say *No* to a request tactfully, otherwise you can create problems for the future. Listen to the conversation and answer the questions.

a What favour does the speaker ask Richard?

b How does Richard react?

4 Use the phrases in the box to rewrite the conversation in 3 so that it sounds more polite. Then act out the more tactful version with a partner.

I'd take my own, of course, but it's being repaired.   Nothing serious, I hope.
What's the problem?   Well, actually, I'm not very keen on the idea.
It's just that I don't feel happy about other people driving my car.
Oh, all right. Not to worry.

5 2.26 Put the conversation in the correct order. Then listen and check your answers.

Jeff

a ☐ ... but on the other hand, if you do it, I'll see it as a personal favour.

b ☐ I know, but you can take the time later on.

c ☐ No, there isn't. Look, I know it's inconvenient, but I can't think of any other solution.

d ☐ 1 Sandra, we need someone to answer the phone from 2.00 till 4.00 while Julia is off sick. Could you do it?

e ☐ Yes, in principle, yes. But you never know. Your contract is up for renewal next month. Enough said?

f ☐ No, it isn't, and obviously I can't force you to do it, but ...

g ☐ 7 Not really. It creates such a bad impression. Listen, I'd do it myself, but I've got to be somewhere else.

Sandra

h ☐ From 2.00 to 4.00? It's not my hours.

i ☐ Well, can't we just put the answering machine on for a couple of hours?

j ☐ 14 Yeah, enough said.

k ☐ It's not the time. I'll have to get someone to pick the kids up from school. Isn't there anyone else?

l ☐ I see. I don't really have much choice, do I? I hope it's just this time ...

m ☐ But?

n ☐ I'm sure you would, but it's not my problem, is it?

6 Identify phrases in 5 for the following:

a a request _____

b a suggestion _____

c emotional blackmail _____

d a threat _____

Useful language:
Being polite

I was wondering ...

I'd really appreciate it if ...

I'm sorry to put you to any trouble.

Do you think you could ...?

Would you mind ...?

Upgrade

1 Have you ever asked for, or been given, an upgrade on a flight? Discuss with a partner.

2 2.27 A passenger is checking in for a flight. Listen to Conversation 1 and answer the questions.

a Do you think the passenger really expects to pay for the upgrade?

b Is the passenger polite? Does he get what he wants?

3 Underline the phrases in the conversation which the passenger uses to sound polite.

A Good afternoon, sir.

B Hello. I'm on flight IB 603. I was wondering if there's any chance of an upgrade to business class?

A Well, I don't know. It depends how crowded the flight is.

B Yes, I quite understand, but I'd really appreciate it if you could have a look. I don't mind paying the extra. It's just that I've had a really hard day, and it'd be really nice to have a bit more space and comfort.

A Just a minute, sir.

B I'm sorry to put you to any trouble.

A No, that's okay. Oh, yes, there's lots of space in business class. I think we can do it.

B Oh, fantastic. How much is that?

A That's all right, sir. Don't worry.

B Oh, thank you ever so much.

A You're welcome. Have a good flight.

4 2.28 A guest is checking in to a hotel. Listen to Conversation 2 and answer the questions.

a Do you think the guest's request is reasonable?

b Is the guest polite? Does he get what he wants?

5 Work with a partner. Find Conversation 2 on page 155 and act it out. This time the guest is polite. Use the phrases you underlined in Conversation 1. If you are the receptionist, decide what to do.

change for the better

a situation that begins to improve

Despite the initial objections, the merger soon proved to be a change for the better.

Learning objectives: Workplace Scenario D

Business communication skills Discussing health and safety; Understanding strategies for leading change; Roleplay: Leading change

Reading Health and safety in the workplace

📹 **In company in action**
D1: Poor leadership;
D2: Change for the better

Change for the better

1 Look at the health and safety signs below and match them to the correct instructions in the box.

Caution overhead load	Danger construction work	Respiratory equipment must be worn
Eye protection must be worn	Foot protection must be worn	Hand protection must be worn
Head protection must be worn	Safety harness must be worn	Danger electric shock risk

_____ _____ _____ _____ _____

_____ _____ _____ _____

2 Work with a partner and discuss these questions.

a What is the main difference between the blue signs and the yellow signs?

b Have you seen any of these signs in your workplace?

c Are you affected by health and safety regulations in your work? Have any new regulations been introduced recently?

In company in action

3 Lenz Furniture Designs needs to make some changes to its health and safety regulations. Joe, the CEO, explains the changes to David, the Operations Manager, and asks him to inform the factory staff. Watch Video D1 and answer the questions.

a Why does Lenz Furniture Designs need to change its health and safety regulations?

  i Because Joe wants the staff to do more overtime.

  ii Because there will be a health and safety audit soon.

  iii Because the number of accidents has gone down.

b Which two changes does Joe explain to David?

  i All office staff must wear a mask.

  ii No overtime is allowed for factory staff.

  iii All factory staff must wear a mask.

  iv All staff must wear a mask when they do overtime.

4 Work with a partner and discuss these questions.

a Joe describes the new rules as 'changes for the better'. Do you think they are a good idea?

b David is not happy about telling Felix and the other factory workers. Why do you think Felix and his team will not like the new changes?

5 Following his conversation with Joe, David receives an email from Serena, the HR Director, with some advice on leading change. Read Serena's email and answer the questions.

a What does the phrase 'pros and cons' mean? Give examples of pros and cons in this situation.

b Do you think Serena's advice will be helpful for David?

c Have you ever had to lead a change that was unpopular?

Health and safety

Good morning David,

I understand that Joe has just spoken to you about the new health and safety regulations and that you are concerned about Felix and his team's reactions. Here are some tips on leading change:

1. Communicate the vision clearly, giving as much information as you can.
2. Involve those that are affected in the planning/implementation of the change.
3. Explain the impact of the change for the individual, not the organization.
4. Be honest about both the pros and cons but in the end confirm that this is a change for the better.
5. Ask for and listen to feedback.

I hope this helps. Good luck for your meeting with Felix.

Best wishes,
Serena

---

6 With a partner, use Serena's tips to brainstorm some ideas for how David might present the change to Felix.

7 The next day, David meets with Felix to tell him about the new health and safety regulations. Work with a partner and roleplay their conversation.

Speaker A: Look at page 143.

Speaker B: Look at page 137.

8 Evaluate your performance using the form on page 144.

In company in action

9 Now watch video D2 to see what happened when David and Felix discussed the changes. Repeat your roleplay, but this time swap roles. Use the notes from your evaluation form and as many of the useful phrases from your roleplays in 7 as you can.

10 Choose a scenario from the list below. Use Serena's advice to decide how you would lead this change. Then work with a partner to roleplay the situation.

Speaker A: convince your partner that this is a change for the better.

Speaker B: try to resist the change.

- The company has decided to make the working day one hour longer.
- The company has decided to relocate to another town, 60 kilometres away.
- The company has decided to outsource 50% of its manufacturing to a factory in Asia.
- The company has decided to change its brand name and logo.
- The company has decided to stop supplying a major customer because of repeated problems with payments.
- Your own ideas.

Office gossip

Do you think it's important for employees to have communal areas where they can share information and build relations?

Learning objectives: Unit 17

Business communication skills Reporting gossip; Discussing the pros and cons of gossip at work; Fluency: Discussing office policy about gossip

Reading Article about a company banning gossip; Posts on a forum about office gossip

Listening Conversation about company gossip; Radio interview about gossip at work

Phrase bank Social conversations

Vocabulary Relationships at work

Grammar Reported speech, *say* and *tell*

1 2.29 Listen to the conversation and answer the questions.

a   Why has Trixy been out of the office?
b   What is the news which she hasn't heard?
c   Is Gary their boss or a colleague?
d   Why are they worried?
e   Why don't they think that Maureen will be worried?
f   The expression 'There's no smoke without fire' means that when people gossip about something, there's usually some truth in what they say. Do you have an equivalent saying in your language? Do you think it's true?

2 2.29 Look at this sentence from the conversation in 1.

... he said that we were overstaffed.

The original statement was 'You are overstaffed'.

Listen to the conversation again and complete the reported statements.

a   'You will have to let some people go.'
    This consultant _____ have to let some people go.
b   'How many people does it involve?'
    Gary _____ it involved.
c   'It depends on individual performance and attitude.'
    He _____ on individual performance and attitude.
d   'I often see them in the Café Au Lait.'
    I'm not saying who, but someone _____ them in Café Au Lait.
e   'Will you stay behind to work on this report?'
    The other day he _____ stay behind to work on a report.

3 Complete the sentences with *said* or *told*.

a   He _____ we were overstaffed.
b   He _____ me we were overstaffed.

What is the main difference between *say* and *tell*?

4 What words are missing from the following sentences?

a   'Where are you going?' He asked me _____ I was going.
b   'When are you going?' He asked me _____ I was going.
c   'Are you going?' He asked me _____ I was going.

When reporting questions, when do you use the word *if*?

5 Complete the sentences below.

a 'I'm busy.' He said he _____ busy.

b 'I'll start straight away.' He said he _____ straight away.

What changes do you make to the Present Simple in reported speech? What changes do you make to *will* in reported speech?

6 2.30–2.33 Look at the conversations below. Complete them with words and phrases which make sense. Then listen and compare your answers.

Conversation 1

A Jeff, (a) _____ last month's production figures?

B No, Jane, I'm (b) _____. Can I give them to you this afternoon?

A It's no good being sorry. There's always some (c) _____. If they're not on my desk by four o'clock, I'll have to (d) _____ Mr Bradley.

B Yes, Jane. I'll start (e) _____.

Conversation 2

C David, have you got (f) _____? There's something I want to (g) _____ with you … in my office.

D What's it about?

C Oh, well, we're missing a laptop (h) _____ from the store.

D What has that got to do with me?

C Well, you are the only other person with a (i) _____ to the store and …

Conversation 3

E Marie, the figures you need are (j) _____.

F Thanks, Pedro. Is everything (k) _____?

E Yes, no problems. Would you like to (l) _____ them with me?

F Yes, but I'm a bit (m) _____ this afternoon.

E Me too. Er, do (n) _____ that new café they've just opened? It's nice and (o) _____. We can go through them there after (p) _____.

F Oh, I (q) _____ so, but I won't be able to stay for long.

E Great. (r) _____ there at about six, then?

F Yes, all right. See you there.

Conversation 4

G Hi, Monica.

H Oh, hello, Jim. (s) _____ things going?

G Great. In fact, you can be the first to congratulate me.

H Yes, you look very (t) _____ with yourself. What's up?

G I'm the new (u) _____ of the eastern sales team.

H Oh, really? What salary are you on now, then?

G (v) _____ a year.

H I can't believe it. Sixty thousand!

G And they're giving me a new (w) _____.

H Oh, really? Congratulations, then. The (x) _____ are on you. See you later.

G Yes. Bye.

7 You are at the coffee machine having a gossip with a colleague. You have overheard the conversations in 6. Use the frameworks in the box to tell your partner what you heard. It is not necessary to report everything.

> I heard ... talking to ...   ... said that ...   ... told ... that ...   ... asked ...

Time to talk

1 Read the news article and answer the questions.

a What is the new law?

b Do you think it's a good idea? Why / Why not?

12   VIEWS

City Council gags workers

Municipal employees in the Brazilian city of Cascavel have been banned from gossiping during working hours. Under a new law approved by the city council, public employees who spread rumours or gossip about their colleagues face the sack. The city says civil servants have the right to work in a professional environment and claim the new law will promote integrity in public offices.

2 Underline words and phrases in the text which mean the following:

a ordered not to do something

b pass on information which is not official and may not be true

c be in a position where you can be dismissed

3 Discuss the following questions with other people in the class.

a How do you define 'gossip'?

b Is it always a bad thing?

c Is it possible to ban it?

d Does your company have a policy on gossip? Have you ever heard of a company that does?

4 The comments below were made on a website for office workers. Read them and classify them in the table. Then compare your answers with a partner.

Gossip is good	Mixed feelings	Gossip is bad

OFFICE WORKERS' FORUM ▶

HOME | REGISTER | LOGIN | FAQ

A Posted by Matthew Hart, England	A friendly and chatty work environment makes employees happy. This results in a better level of work from employees, which means the company makes more money. Any employer who bans office gossip will lose money by making the workforce less productive. If the workplace is friendly and employees can chat, they are happy. Happy employees work harder, so the company makes more money. An employer that bans gossip will make its workforce less productive and will lose money!	
B Posted by Janet Jones, Wales	In my office, the only way to find out anything about the company strategy is through gossip. The management refuse to talk to most of the staff.	
C Posted by Luke McCarthy, Australia	There's nothing worse than gossip – and it's especially bad when it is done by people who have nothing better to do than talk about other people.	
D Posted by Nicole Martin, France	I don't think gossip is a bad thing. It's the best way to learn about office politics. It's healthy to chat at work and it's just part of working in an office.	
E Posted by Pieter Groot, Netherlands	Gossip is just information that someone, somewhere, doesn't want you to find out about. It can be great – unless you are the one being gossiped about. But it's definitely not a sackable offence.	
F Posted by Sanjay Patel, India	I started a new job a year ago, and I try to avoid gossip. If I'm in a group who start to gossip I walk away. It can really damage your career and your relationship with your colleagues.	
G Posted by Claudia Weber, Germany	Freedom of speech is a basic human right. But harmless remarks can easily become hurtful remarks. I think it's up to each person to decide which is which.	
H Posted by John Mason, Scotland	I've found solutions to some of my biggest work problems while chatting by the coffee machine. Having a quick chat about completely unrelated topics can actually increase productivity as it helps to break up the day a little.	

5 The phrases below are from the comments above. Complete the sentences with your own words and ideas.

a In my office, _____.

b An employer that _____ will _____.

c There's nothing worse than _____.

d I don't think _____ is a bad thing.

e I try to avoid _____.

6 You are going to listen to an interview about office gossip from a radio programme. Match the words and phrases from the interview (a–f) to the definitions (1–6).

a	drive for efficiency	**1**	talking informally
b	scrapped	**2**	mobile refreshments service
c	human resources	**3**	effort to get more work done
d	encouraged	**4**	seen as positive
e	chatting	**5**	not continued with
f	tea trolley	**6**	organization and management of company staff

a ☐　　b ☐　　c ☐　　　d ☐　　　e ☐　　　f ☐

7 Before you listen, decide if you agree with the following statements. Why / Why not?

a Companies who provide an opportunity for their workers to socialize are making a mistake.

b Today, people have less time to talk to each other and socialize than they did before.

c The differences between a good job and a bad job are the social parts.

d Employees are more productive when they are happy.

e When employees share information and knowledge, the company benefits.

f Companies should take measures to encourage gossip.

8 🔘 **2.34** Listen to the interview to see if the speaker agrees with you.

9 Work with a partner and perform the following roleplay about office policy on coffee breaks and gossiping.

Speaker A: Look at the instructions on page 140.

Speaker B: You are one of the management consultants who prepared the study mentioned in the interview in 8. In a client's company you see the notice below next to the coffee machine. Say why you think some 'gossip' is a good thing and try to persuade the client to change the policy.

Company Notice

- **Employees may take up to three coffee breaks per day.**
- **Maximum time at coffee machine: four minutes.**
- **All 'gossip' or discussion of non-work related matters is prohibited.**

10 Based on your discussions in 9, complete the memo below.

FROM:　Personnel Manager
TO:　　Managing Director

With regard to the company policy on coffee breaks, _____
_____
In my opinion, _____.
According to a report by the Industrial Society, _____
_____
In the report the author says that _____.
It is a question of balance, but _____.
In conclusion, _____.

17 Office gossip

Phrase bank: Social conversations

How's it going?
Where have you been?
Have you heard the news? What news?
I can't believe it!
Really! Is it official?
Apparently they are going to …
That's awful/terrible/wonderful/incredible.
Catch you later.
See you there at about six.
Congratulations!

Vocabulary

Relationships at work

1 Combine one word from A with one word from B to complete the sentences below.

A	B
coffee	consultant
company	room
human	policy
meeting	resources
management	machine

a People have the best ideas in conversations around the _____.

b The company has hired a _____ to give advice on improving internal communications.

c What do you think about this idea of removing the chairs from the _____ so we don't spend so long talking about things?

d What is the _____ on taking coffee or tea breaks?

e Nowadays people say _____ instead of 'personnel'.

2 Complete the puzzle using the clues below. Sometimes the first letter has been given.

1 Having communal areas benefits relations in the w_____.

2 We are having a _____ for efficiency. (You also _____ a car.)

3 The topic of this unit.

4 Let's make an _____ not to waste time.

5 It's not a good idea to _____ rumours.

6 Have you heard the _____?

7 There's no _____ without fire.

8 We have banned smoking in the o_____.

9 They don't a_____ of people taking long tea breaks.

10 Let's go out for a d_____ on Friday night.

11 We should encourage employees to _____ their ideas.

12 What has happened to the tea _____?

				P			
1							
			2	R			
			3	O			
		4		F			
	5			E			
	6			S			
		7		S			
	8			I			
9				O			
	10			N			
		11		A			
	12			L			

Grammar

Reported speech

say and tell
You can use *say* or *tell* to report what someone said.

say + something
• He **says** (that) he is happy in his new job.

tell + somebody + something
• He **tells** everyone (that) he is the company boss.

Tense
When we use the past forms *said* or *told*, we usually change the verbs in the original.

Present → Past
• 'I **like** working on my own.' →
He said he **liked** working on his own.

Past → Past perfect
• 'I **worked** there for ten years.' →
'He said he **had worked** there for ten years.'

will → would:
• 'I'll help you.' →
He said he **would** help me.

No change of tense
When the situation is still true or there is no chance of confusion, we don't change the tense in the original sentence.
'I **enjoy** working there.' → He said he **enjoys** working there.
'Sales **are rising**'. → Marta says that sales **are rising**.

Pronouns

I	→	*he/she*
me	→	*him/her*
my	→	*his/her*
your	→	*my*

• 'I speak to **your** secretary every day.' →
He told me he speaks to **my** secretary every day.

Adverbs of time and place

now	→	then/at that moment
today	→	that day
here	→	there
tomorrow	→	the next day/the following day
yesterday	→	the day before/the previous day

- I'll see you **here tomorrow**. →
  He said he would see me **there the next day**.

Most of these changes are logical and natural and often similar in other languages. They depend on the differences in time, place and people between the original conversation and the reported conversation.

asked

For reported questions you can use *asked* + *what/when/*etc
- What do you want? →
  He **asked** me **what** I wanted.

or *asked* + *if* for reporting yes/no questions.
- Is it official? →
  He **asked** me **if** it was official.

Practice 1

Complete the reported sentences using the correct tense.

a We're going to have a phone conference.
   He said that they _____ going to have a phone conference.

b I spent hours on that proposal.
   She said she _____ hours on that proposal.

c I'll post the letter in the morning.
   He said he _____ post the letter in the morning.

d It's too early to check in for the flight.
   I told her it _____ too early to check in for the flight.

e We worked until ten o'clock to get everything done.
   She said they _____ until ten o'clock to get everything done.

f Can I use the photocopier?
   He asked if he _____ use the photocopier.

g Sales are at an all-time high.
   She said sales _____ at an all-time high.

h She will be home early on Thursday.
   She said she _____ be home early on Thursday.

Practice 2

Complete the second sentence to report the first one.

a I'm really enjoying my job at the moment.
   She says she's really enjoying her job at the moment.

b It's too late to cancel the meeting.
   I said _____.

c We are having a lot of problems with the production department today.
   He told me _____.

d What time is Mr Keegan going to arrive?
   He asked _____.

e We should buy a new computer system.
   He keeps telling me _____.

f Is Mr Merchant available?
   She asked _____.

g The fixed costs include the office rent and equipment hire.
   She said _____.

h Where do you work now?
   They asked me _____.

i I'll meet you at the airport at eight o'clock.
   She said _____.

j I want to see you about the arrangements for tomorrow.
   He told me _____.

k Does the office open on Saturdays?
   He asked me _____.

l When will the documents be ready?
   She asked _____.

m I'm the best salesman in the company.
   He keeps saying _____.

n Can I make a phone call?
   He asked if _____.

o What do you think of the new website?
   He asked me _____.

Practice 3

Complete the sentences with *say/says/said*, *tell/told* or *ask/asked*.

a Why didn't you _____ me you weren't happy with your job?

b What will people _____ if we try to ban office gossip?

c Did he _____ what time you had to be there?

d The boss always _____ that I should keep my desk more organized.

e He _____ me he was having second thoughts about applying for the job.

f Will you _____ him if he's going to come?

g I can't read the small print on this. What does it _____?

h Every time I visit them they _____ me how you are.

i I'll _____ you if you promise not to _____ anything to anybody else.

18 E-commerce

As a result of websites like Amazon and eBay™, consumers now have access to every kind of product and service imaginable, yet this is only the tip of the iceberg. Over the coming months and years, new technologies will continue to revolutionize the consumer shopping experience and drive even more dollars into online sales. The day is not far off when the online shopping experience will surpass any service or offering that is available in a store.

How much shopping do you do online?

Learning objectives: Unit 18

Business communication skills
Discussing purchase decisions;
Discussing advantages and disadvantages;
Roleplay: Marketing e-commerce to the over-60s;
Discussing the future of the Internet; Making predictions
Reading Survey about the future of the Internet
Listening Radio interview about the pros and cons of e-commerce
Phrase bank Discussing advantages and disadvantages
Vocabulary Shopping and the Internet
Grammar *will* for future predictions

1 Complete the sentences using the phrases in the box. Then compare them with those on page 136. Do you agree?

> you're interested in quality   who cares   you're interested in price
> you're interested in quality and price

a When you buy something for yourself with your own money, _____.
b When you buy something for someone else with your own money, _____.
c When you buy something for yourself with someone else's money, _____.
d When you buy something for someone else with someone else's money, _____?

2 Work with a partner. Ask each other the following questions.

a When was the last time you bought something for:
- yourself?
- somebody else?
- a customer or client?
- your company?

b What did you buy?
c What factors influenced your decisions?
d What kind of shopping do you like/dislike?
e How often do you buy things on the Internet?

3 E-commerce has advantages and disadvantages. Work with a partner. Decide if the features on the left are positive factors or negative factors for the seller (*S*) or the customer (*C*). Add your own ideas.

	+	−
open for business 24x7x365		
competitive pricing		
no need for physical premises		
low selling costs		
updated stock information in real time		
credit card payment		
fast communication (email / phone) with client		
cost and time of delivery		
collection of marketing data		
uncertainty about delivery		
difficulty of returning goods		
not good for perishable goods		
online information limited to text and photos		

4 🔊 **2.35** Listen to a radio programme where experts discuss e-commerce. Which of the ideas in 3 do they mention? Are their ideas the same as yours?

5 🔊 **2.35** Listen again and complete the phrases. There is one word for each gap.

a Paul, how do you see the future _____ _____? _____
_____ _____ _____ _____ _____?

b The advantages _____ _____ _____ _____
_____: access to products that may not be available locally.

c Yes, for the customer _____ _____ _____ _____ –
convenience and lower prices.

d That's absolutely right, but _____ _____ _____
_____ as well.

e After-sales service is _____ _____ _____ _____.

f On the _____ _____, the seller can deal directly with the
manufacturer ...

g For me, security is _____ _____ _____ _____ in
people's minds.

h Yes, and buying online makes the groceries more expensive, so what's the point?
Actually, _____ _____ _____ _____.

i Not _____ _____, _____ when you go to a shop and pick
something up, you choose what to look at and how to look at it.

j There's _____ _____ _____. Because payment is by credit card,
very small or very large transactions tend not to be conducted online.

6 Look at this phrase from the discussion.

Books and DVDs are one thing, but fruit and vegetables are another.

Make similar sentences using the following prompts.

a the right qualifications / have experience
   The right qualifications for a job are one thing, but having experience is another.

b a high turnover / make good profits
   _____

c have a good idea / put into practice
   _____

d high productivity / improve staff motivation
   _____

e create a good product / sell it
   _____

🔊 **2.36** Now listen and compare your answers.

7 Work with a partner. Brainstorm and discuss the advantages and disadvantages of the following. Use similar phrases to those in 6.

a Working for a company and working for yourself.
b Living in the country and living in a town.
c Having children and not having children.
d Going to university and starting work straight after school.

8 Work in groups of three. You all work for a marketing company. Market studies have shown that retired people spend a significant amount of their free time surfing the Internet. You have formed a focus group to explore the possibility of marketing to the over-sixties using the Internet. Make notes about what you are going to say.
Use some of the expressions in 5 and 6 in your discussion.

Speaker A: You think this is a fantastic idea. Think of
arguments to support it.

Speaker B: You think this is a ridiculous idea. Think of
arguments against it.

Speaker C: You are the focus group leader. You are not
sure about this idea. Lead the discussion, listen to
the others and ask questions.

The future of the Internet

1 The words and phrases (a–h) are from a survey on the future of the Internet. Match them to the explanations (1–8).

a	copyrighted content	**1**	Open to and respectful of other people's opinions and ideas
b	tolerant	**2**	The ability of a computer device to 'understand' what we say
c	privacy	**3**	Music, video or text which is illegal to reproduce because it belongs to someone
d	augmented reality	**4**	It works without fail and won't let you down
e	portable		
f	voice-recognition	**5**	Where our experience of the real world is combined with computer generated sound, video, graphics or GPS data
g	reliable		
h	virtual office	**6**	The freedom to do things without other people watching you
		7	Not a physical place of work, but one where all the work is done with computers and where people work together online
		8	Small enough to carry around easily

2 In the survey, technology experts and social analysts made predictions about the state of the Internet and its influence on our lives in in the future. Work with a partner and say if you agree (✓) or disagree (✗) with each prediction.

	Agree or disagree?
The mobile phone (or smartphone) will be the primary Internet connection and the only one for the majority of people across the world, providing information in a portable, well-connected form at a low price.	
People will be more tolerant than they are today, because the Internet and other information and communication technologies will help them to learn about other people. There will be less violence and fewer wars.	
There will be strict controls on copyrighted content thanks to new laws and the efforts of the technology industry and media companies. People who use copyrighted materials will automatically pay the content owners, and Internet service providers will notify authorities when they identify clients who illegally share music and films.	
People will be more open to sharing personal information, opinions and emotions than they are now. The concept of privacy will change and as their lives become more transparent, people will become more responsible for their own actions.	
Virtual worlds and augmented reality will be popular thanks to the rapid evolution of technology. Most well-equipped Internet users will spend some of their day – at work and at play – linked to augmentations of the real world or alternate worlds. It will be more difficult to distinguish between virtual reality and 'real life'.	
As all phones, tablets and computers will have built-in voice-recognition, it will be completely normal to hear people talking in public to their computing devices. In addition, these devices will allow you to display a full-size virtual keyboard on any flat surface and it will be common to see people 'air-typing' on a projected keyboard only they can see.	
The Internet will still have its original architecture and won't be replaced by a totally new system. It will be more reliable and secure, but unfortunately those who want to commit crimes and cause problems will still be able to do so.	
The separation between work hours and personal time will disappear. People won't depend on fixed timetables for work and play. They will perform both their professional and personal duties from wherever they happen to be – home, the gym, the mall or from work, which will often be a virtual office.	

3 Compare your answers to what the experts thought on page 137.

4 Complete the sentences below with the words and phrases (a–h) in 1.

a The problem with tablets is that they aren't _____ and you need a bag to carry them.

b The right to _____ is more important than free speech.

c Young people are too _____ of illegal downloading of music and films.

d _____ in a digital format is almost impossible to protect.

e Nowadays computers are much more _____ than in the past and don't often go wrong.

f I don't think _____ will make our lives easier because it will distract us and cause accidents.

g I don't think _____ on smartphones will ever work because we all have different accents and ways of speaking.

h I don't want to work in a _____; I like having coffee with my colleagues and the social side of work.

5 Each sentence in 4 expresses an opinion. Do you agree? Why / Why not?

6 Look at this sentence from the survey on page 113.

The mobile phone will be the primary Internet connection.

This is a prediction. You express predictions about the future using *will*. Underline other predictions in the article.

7 Do you agree with the predictions in the survey? Discuss them like this:

A *I think there will be strict controls on copyrighted content.*

B *Do you? I don't. / Me too.*

A *I don't think people will be more tolerant than they are today.*

B *Don't you? I do. / Me neither.*

8 What other predictions can you make about the Internet?

In ten years, all banking will be online.

9 Tick yes (Y) or no (N) against the predictions in the chart so that they are true for you. Then discuss them with a partner.

A *Do you think you'll change your job in the next five years?*

B *Yes, I do. I don't really like what I do now. How about you?*

A *No, I don't think I will. Things are going well and I like my job.*

	Next year	Y	N	In five years	Y	N	In the next ten years	Y	N
My life	I'll change jobs.			I'll leave and start my own company.			I'll make a million and retire.		
My company	Our main competitor will go bankrupt.			Everybody will work at home most of the time.			Most employees will be replaced by computers.		
The world	There will be an economic boom.			The USA will have a female president.			There'll be a world government.		

18 E-commerce

Phrase bank: Discussing advantages and disadvantages

What are the pros and cons?

The advantages/benefits/disadvantages/drawbacks are ...

That's a negative/positive factor.

Security is an issue.

Another point is ...

Having a good job is one thing, but earning a lot of money is another.

Vocabulary ▶

Shopping and the Internet

1 Match the verbs (a–f) to their collocations (1–6). Then complete the sentences with the collocations.

a	compare	1	a bill
b	influence	2	the conversation
c	listen to	3	a network
d	run up	4	prices
e	try on	5	the decision
f	access	6	a sweater

a I like to _____ before I buy anything expensive.

b His children have _____ of over $300 by surfing on the Internet all day long.

c When she asked to _____ they told her they didn't have one in her size.

d To _____ you have to obtain a user name and a password from the administrator.

e Did you _____ about restructuring in the canteen yesterday?

f What factors do you think will most _____ on salaries?

2 Complete the anecdote using the words in the box.

button	came	charge	clicked	complain	crashed	download
email	message	online	pay	reply	security	website

Why I will never buy anything on the Internet again

Ask most people how shopping will be in the future and inevitably they will mention the Internet. Well, the other day I had a bad enough experience shopping (a) _____ to put me off for life. I heard about a book you could download from a (b) _____ before it was published and sold in bookshops. As it was by an author I adore, I decided to investigate.

I found the page and read the information. They charged 30 euros for the (c) _____. Not a massive amount but you had to use a credit card. I completed the form with the endless details requested, including my (d) _____ address.

Finally I entered my credit card number, because they solemnly promised that there was no (e) _____ risk. When the payment was authorized – it took about a minute – a new screen appeared with a (f) _____ which said 'Download now'. I (g) _____ on the button but nothing happened so I clicked again. Then a (h) _____ came up saying 'Download suspended due to network overload. Please try again later.'

Finally the system (i) _____ and I had to turn off the computer. When I reconnected, the same forms as before (j) _____ up but I didn't want to risk paying again, so I wrote an email to the company explaining the problem. I never got a (k) _____.

I assumed that as I never got the book I wouldn't have to (l) _____, but when I got my credit card statement at the end of the month I saw the (m) _____ for 30 euros was there. It was too late to do anything and there was no one to (n) _____ to. Okay, so it was only 30 euros – no big deal – but the question I ask myself is this: why risk buying online when it amounts to what is basically an act of faith? In any case, it will be a long time before I try buying something over the Internet again.

Grammar ▶

will for future predictions

Affirmative			Negative			Interrogative		
I You He She It We They	**will** **'ll**	work.	I You He She It We They	**will not** **won't**	work.	**Will** **Won't**	I you he she it we they	work?

You can use *will* + infinitive to express predictions or beliefs about the future.

- *This year the economy* **will grow** *by 3%.*
- *I'm sure we* **will finish** *the order on time.*

The negative of *will* is *won't*.

- *I'm sorry, but things* **won't get** *any better.*
- *No, there* **won't be** *a recession.*

Put *will* before the subject to make questions.

- **Will** *people use the Internet for most of their shopping in the future?*
- **Will** *the economy recover by next year?*

You often introduce predictions with *I think* …

- *I think the DVD will replace the CD.*
- *I think the meeting will end on time.*

Avoid saying *I think … won't …*
Use *I don't think … will …*

- *I don't think the keyboard* **will** *become obsolete.*
  (NOT ~~I think the keyboard won't become obsolete.~~)
- *I don't think the meeting* **will** *end on time.*
  (NOT ~~I think the meeting won't end on time.~~)

Practice 1

Join the sentence beginnings with the endings using *will* + the verbs in the box.

| affect | arrive | be | continue | get | go | have | retire | take |

a Prices …   *will continue*   … public by next year.
b There …   … with a massive golden handshake soon.
c The managing director …   … better.
d The government …   … a boom in the economy.
e Young George …   … late as usual.
f The company …   … measures against inflation.
g Life here …   … a very successful career, I'm sure.
h The plane …   … to rise.
i The political situation …   … the economy.

Practice 2

Reorganize the words to make correct sentences.

a any new you system won't with have problems the
   You won't have any problems with the new system.

b information think the Internet I you'll on find the
   _____

c Berlin you'll good have time think I a in
   _____

d Juan Montes think see you'll there don't I
   _____

e think do write report time you'll the you to have?
   _____

f time you what arrive will?
   _____

g long how us it will get there take to?
   _____

h we'll shopping I to think go time any don't have
   _____

i make think money I he'll lot a of
   _____

j want people see buy will always to products they before them most
   _____

Practice 3

Make questions with *do you think … will …?* and then write answers that are true for you.

a What time / get home tonight?
   What time do you think you'll get home tonight? About 7.30.

b What / have / dinner?
   _____

c Where / go / next holiday?
   _____

d change / jobs / next five years?
   _____

e lose / weight / this month?
   _____

f How long / take / do this exercise?
   _____

g ever have / own business?
   _____

h ever drive / Ferrari?
   _____

i work as hard / five years from now?
   _____

19

E-work

Do you ever work from home? Do you prefer it to working in the office?

1 One type of e-work is telecommuting. Discuss these questions with a partner.
a What is telecommuting?
b What kind of people in a company telecommute? Are there some jobs which are more suited to telework?
c Is the number of people that telecommute increasing?
d How highly is the opportunity to telework valued by workers?

2 Read the article and compare the author's findings with your answers in 1.

WORK, HOME *or* WORK FROM HOME?

Today, people don't have to clock in at the office every weekday. Now the jobs go where the talents are.

Telecommuting, the practice of working from home, is on the rise, and more companies are trusting their employees to be more productive in their own home offices than they might be at the workplace. Wrike, a company that makes collaboration software, conducted a survey with 1,074 respondents, asking them a variety of questions about working from home.

According to the survey, 83% of the respondents said they work remotely at least part of the day. Of the 1,074 respondents in the survey, 36% were team members, 33% were managers, 15% were business owners and 15% were executives.

The survey showed that people see a rising trend in the future of remote collaboration: 43% of respondents worked remotely less often two to three years ago, and 66% believe their office may go fully virtual in one to five years.

The survey also found the higher the position in the company, the more time the person spends working outside the office.

Business owners worked nearly 30 hours a week from home, executives worked about 20 hours, managers worked between 10 and 20 hours, while team members worked up to about 10 hours.

When asked how much we are ready to 'pay' for the opportunity to work remotely:
● 78% would forego free meals
● 54% would forego employer-paid cellphone plans
● 31% would accept a reduction in paid vacation
● 25% would accept a reduction in salary.

The survey also found 89% of respondents consider the opportunity to work remotely as one of three main perks, the other two being salary and reputation.

When asked if consumer social communication tools help in remote collaboration, 91% said they would happily abandon social communication tools. The survey found that people spend no more than one hour a day on Facebook, Twitter and Skype™.

Good and bad aspects of remote collaboration
Perceived benefits, according to the survey, include:
● saving time (41%)
● increased productivity (29%)
● focus on work, not office policies (10%).

The 'challenges' include:
● lack of direct communication (37%)
● data accessibility is hindered (21%)
● poor visibility into colleagues' activity (1%).

3 Decide if the following statements are true (*T*) or false (*F*) according to the article.

a Companies allow telecommuting because they believe it is more productive. ☐

b The survey only included people who worked for themselves. ☐

c The biggest group of telecommuters in the survey were executives. ☐

d Nearly half of the participants in the survey work from home more often than four years ago. ☐

e People in top positions spend less time working outside the office than those lower down. ☐

f Most people would be prepared to earn less if they could work from home. ☐

g Social networks like Facebook are very important to telecommuters. ☐

4 Which of the figures in the survey do you find surprising? Discuss with a partner.

Working at home

1 🔘 **2.37–2.38** Listen to two interviews with people who telework. Which speaker:

a has children? _____

b lives in the country? _____

c doesn't have fixed hours? _____

d gets up later than before? _____

e wears her slippers to work? _____

f is self-employed? _____

g works for a company? _____

2 🔘 **2.37–2.38** Listen again and complete the chart.

	Speaker 1	Speaker 2
Country		
What did she do before?		
What does she do now?		
What are the advantages of her new work?		
What are the advantages for her employers/clients?		

3 Which of the speakers is making a better use of technology, in your opinion?

4 Read the advantages and disadvantages of working from home in the magazine article. Put each in the correct category in the chart below. The first one has been done for you.

Does working at home really work?

	Advantages	Disadvantages
Family		1
The workplace		
The working day		
Commuting		
Technology		
Efficiency		
Costs		
Motivation		

WORKING AT HOME

The advantages and disadvantages

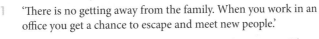

What do people really think about working from home? We interviewed a cross section of people from different industries about their experiences of teleworking. As you will see, there was quite a wide variety of opinions.

1 'There is no getting away from the family. When you work in an office you get a chance to escape and meet new people.'

2 'I think us homeworkers get more done in a shorter time. There are no phone calls or colleagues to slow you down.'

3 'Without the journeys to and from the office you don't get a chance to relax and prepare your mind before you start work, or to wind down before you get home. I miss the separation between home and leisure time.'

4 'You do get to see more of your children. The problem is, though, that you're supposed to be WORKING.'

5 'You don't have to sit in traffic jams or walk to work in the rain. Or listen to people talking loudly on their mobiles on the train.'

6 'I think financially you miss out on perks like subsidized refreshments or travel.'

7 'Life is definitely cheaper for the employee. You save on things like transport and smart clothes. It's also cheaper to have lunch at home.'

8 'It's a bit dangerous for workaholics. You can easily find your working time creeping into your leisure time.'

9 'Sharing ideas and problems with your colleagues can make you more productive in some jobs. And the gossip can be really inspiring!'

10 'Space can be a problem. Rooms can become an unpleasant mix of home and office.'

11 'You don't have to work with those obsolete office computers and the company intranet which always seems to be down.'

12 'The flexibility is great. You can work at five in the morning or on a Sunday afternoon.'

13 'I like the freedom. You can open the window, play music and generally make yourself comfortable.'

14 'It can be difficult to get down to work. You have to be very self-disciplined.'

15 'If you have a technical problem, you're on your own. There's no IT expert to call on.'

16 'No boss cracking the whip!'

5 Look at the chart on page 138 and check your answers.

6 Find words and phrases in the article in 4 which mean the same as the following:

a relax   _____

b queues of cars and lorries unable to move forward   _____

c benefits not included in your salary   _____

d people who can't stop working   _____

e informal exchange of news and information   _____

f out-of-date and no longer useful   _____

g start   _____

h trying to make people work harder   _____

7 Complete the sentences with the words and phrases from 6.

a As I have to travel so much I don't hear any of the office _____.

b When I get home, I like to _____ by listening to some classical music.

c My boss is a complete _____. She just doesn't know how to relax and turn off.

d It's better to have a higher salary than _____ like a company car or free meals.

e The problem with buying a computer is that in a couple of years it's _____.

f I find it difficult to _____ the accounts and usually leave them until the last minute.

g I leave home very early to avoid getting caught in _____ on the way to work.

h _____ is part of any manager's work.

8 Are the sentences in 7 true for you? Why / Why not? Discuss them with a partner.

Stay at home and get rich?

1 There are a lot of adverts for e-work on the Internet. Look at the example on the right. Have you ever seen an advert like this? How do you think you can make money working from home?

2 ⊙ **2.39** Listen to a conversation in which two people discuss the advert in 1 and answer the questions.

a Do the speakers think that the advert is about a real job?

b What do they think are the advantages of working at home?

c What do they think are the disadvantages?

> Make MONEY while you work at home.
>
> NO SKILL required.

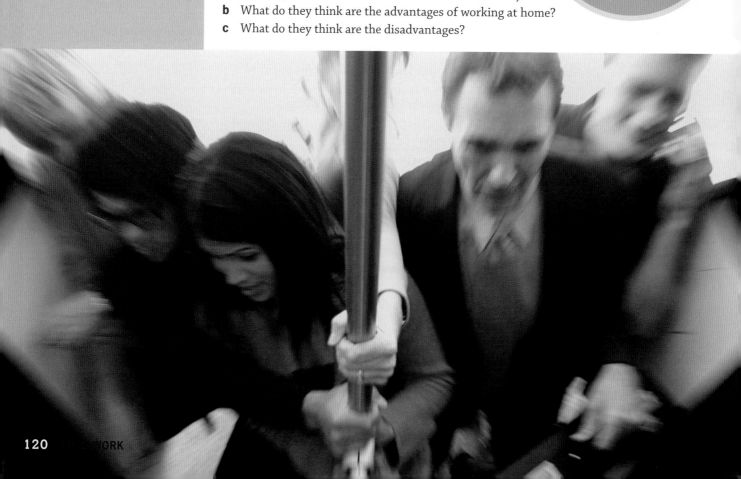

3 🔘 **2.39** Complete the phrases from the dialogue with the missing words. There is a gap for each word – contractions count as one word. Then listen again to check your answers.

a If it _____ so easy, everyone _____ do it.

b That's a shame. I _____ mind working at home if I _____ the opportunity.

c I'm not so sure. I wouldn't miss travelling in to work every day, but if I _____ at home, _____ _____ the contact with people here.

d That's true, but if you _____ just come in a couple of days a week, it _____ _____ okay. On the other hand, unless you _____ somewhere quiet to work, it _____ be difficult to get anything done.

e Do you think _____ be disciplined enough? I don't know. I _____ if it _____ my own business, but otherwise, who knows?

f They do talk about telework a lot these days. Some people say that if people _____ commuting, it _____ be much better for the environment.

4 The phrases in 3 are all examples of how we use *if* + past + *would/could* to talk about hypothetical or imagined situations. Complete the phrases with your own words.

a If I worked at home / If I didn't work at home, my life _____ .

b I'd be happier about my job if _____ .

c I wouldn't be happy about work if _____ .

d If my company introduced / stopped flexible working _____ .

e If I spoke fluent English, _____ .

f I would say 'no' if _____ .

g My company would be more efficient if _____ .

h If people could predict the future, _____ .

5 A company manager is sitting in his office dreaming about how he could change his life. Put his ideas into a chain of conditionals to recreate his dream like this:

If I left my job, I'd spend more time at home. If I spent more time at home, …

be an enormous success	be completely stressed out again	be more relaxed
come up with a really great business idea	have a lot of responsibilities	have time to think
have to work harder than I want to	set up a company	

6 In what circumstances would you:

• start your own business?
• stop working altogether?
• change jobs?
• refuse a promotion?
• ask for a pay rise?
• accept a cut in pay?

Discuss with a partner.

I'd start my own business if I had a good idea.

7 Work with a partner and perform the following roleplay about the advantages of working at home or in the office. Use the phrases in the box and the phrases in 3 and 4 to help you.

Speaker A: You are a manager in your company. You are negotiating with the unions to introduce e-work in your company. Convince your partner of the advantages of working at home.

Speaker B: You are a union representative in speaker A's company. The management wants to introduce working from home, but you are against it. Convince your partner of the advantages of office work.

In company interviews
Units 17–19

If people worked from home, …   Most people find / would find that …
From the worker's / company's point of view, it would mean …
At the moment, people have to … There'd be all sorts of problems if …
I agree with that, but … That's not necessarily true, because if …

19 E-work

Vocabulary

Teleworking

Complete the extract from an article about teleworking using the words in the box.

| commute | desk | flexibility | home | local | office |

The key word for the future is (a) _____. We're not suddenly going to see massive numbers of people working from (b) _____ instead of going into the (c) _____. We'll see a much more hybrid existence where some of the time people are in the office, maybe at a shared (d) _____, and some of the time at home. And there are of course 'telecentres' – serviced offices which provide an intermediate stage where people can find a (e) _____ office instead of having to (f) _____ into a town or city centre.

Grammar

Conditionals (future reference)

You can use *if* + past + *would / could* to talk about hypothetical or imagined situations in the future. This is often called the 'second conditional'. Look at these examples:

Condition	Consequence
If I knew the answer,	*I'd tell you.*
If we got the order,	*we'd have years of work.*

Compare these two sentences:

• *If the factory shuts, over 200 people will lose their jobs.* (The speaker thinks the situation is likely to happen in the future.)

• *If the factory shut, over 200 people would lose their jobs.* (The speaker thinks the situation is unlikely or improbable in the future. It is imagined or hypothetical.)

Practice 1

Match the sentence beginnings (a–g) with the endings (1–7).

a If we worked from home, …

b If I spent less time travelling, …

c The company would save money …

d People would need good computers …

e Our quality of life would improve …

f If I never saw my colleagues, …

g There'd be problems with this plan …

1 … I'd have more time with my family.

2 … if the staff didn't agree with it.

3 … if they had to work from home.

4 … if we didn't have to commute.

5 … I'd miss the personal contact.

6 … we'd spend less time travelling.

7 … if it invested in homeworking.

a	b	c	d	e	f	g

Practice 2

Complete the conversation using the verbs in the brackets in the appropiate tense.

Sarah: Why don't we move out of the city into the country? I'm fed up with living here. It's so stressful.

David: If we (a) _____ (live) in the country, it (b) _____ (take) about ten minutes for you to get bored with it.

S: No it wouldn't. We (c) _____ (get) a nice big house. The kids (d) _____ (go) to a little village school, and we (e) _____ (forget) about all the street violence, traffic and pollution.

D: But they (f) _____ (like) living in the city, and they (g) _____ (miss) their friends. Also, if we (h) _____ (move) into the country, we (i) _____ (spend) all our time in the car travelling in and out to work.

S: Not necessarily. If you (j) _____ (ask) your company, they (k) _____ (let) you work from home some of the time, and mine would, too.

D: I don't think so. I (l) _____ (have) to be in contact with people in my job. Anyway, if I (m) _____ (be) in the house all day, I (n) _____ (go) crazy.

S: Don't be so negative. If you (o) _____ (spend) more time at home, we (p) _____ (see) more of you. You (q) _____ (have) a better quality of life.

D: I'm sorry. I just don't think you're being realistic. It (r) _____ (be) a dream.

S: If you (s) _____ (be) less selfish, you'd at least think about it.

D: Okay, I promise I (t) _____ (give) it some thought if that's what you want.

Practice 3

Write conditional sentences using the prompts.

a He doesn't work hard so he isn't very successful.
If he worked harder, he'd be more successful.

b You don't have enough experience so we can't give you the job.

c He can't drive so he has to take taxis all the time.

d I don't have the information so I can't help you.

e I don't like sport so I don't go to the gym.

f He works long hours because he enjoys his job.

g She only does the job because she hasn't got any choice.

h My car is in the garage so I can't take you to the airport.

i Things take him a long time because he isn't very organized.

j He drives an expensive car because he can afford it.

Practice 4

Give advice by completing the sentences.

a If you got up earlier, *you wouldn't be late to work so often.*

b If you did a computer course,

c You would make a better impression

d If you had a mobile phone,

e You wouldn't be so stressed

f If you used the Internet,

g You'd do better at the interview

h If you didn't complain all the time,

Practice 5

Reorganize the words to form questions.

a job do what would you if choose you could
What job would you do if you could choose?

b live you abroad you where if would to had go

c treat people boss how you would were if you the

d didn't language study would what you English you if learn

e would earn how a you the wasn't living salary if important

Practice 6

Respond to the sentences using the prompts. Decide if the situation is real or imaginary.

a Are you going to tell the boss about it? (If / tell / she / sack me)
No way. If I told her about it, she'd sack me.

b Do you think he is going to get the job? (Unless / get nervous / interview / not have / problems)
Yes, I think so. _____

c Are you going to invite Sarah to the party? (If / invite / Dave / have to invite Sarah too)
I don't have any choice. _____

d Are you going to invite Su to the party? (If / invite / Su / have to invite Dave too)
No, I can't. _____
and Jane would be upset.

e I've got an awful headache but we haven't got any aspirin. (If / take / aspirin / you / feel better.)
Oh, dear. _____

f In this job you haven't got enough time to take up a hobby. (If / have / time / do some gardening)
Yes, it's a shame. _____

g He almost had a accident again on Friday. (Unless / stop / driving like a maniac / hurt himself)
What, again? _____

h Can you give me his mobile number? (If / know / give / it / you)
No, I can't I'm afraid. _____

Working lunch

How often do you have a business lunch?

1 Look at the quote on the left and discuss the questions with a partner.

a Do you try to plan conversation topics when you go to a business lunch?

b What other tips do you have for a successful business lunch? Compare your ideas with the article on page 139.

2 🔘 2.40 Neil Klein and Satomi Tanaka are having a working lunch at a restaurant in Japan. Listen to their conversation and answer the questions.

a Why does Neil like the restaurant?

b Who orders the food?

c What does Neil want to eat?

d What does Neil decide to eat?

3 🔘 2.40 Put the lines of the conversation in 2 in the correct order. Then listen again and check.

Neil Klein

☐ 1 This looks like a very nice place, Satomi.

☐ I'll try the unagi, then.

☐ Okay. Sounds good.

☐ What's that?

☐ Yes, I really like the décor. Er, could you order for both of us, Satomi?

☐ Hmm, I'm sure it is. Actually, do you think I could have a steak?

☐ No, no, let's have some sake.

Satomi Tanaka

☐ And then I think you should try some unagi.

☐ It's eel – grilled and served on a bed of rice. It's delicious.

☐ Yes, I thought you would like it.

☐ Well, I'm afraid they don't serve steak here.

☐ Fine. Would you like some sake, or would you prefer some tea?

☐ Of course. I think we could have some miso soup to start with. They do it very well here.

☐ 14 Right. Sake it is, then.

4

a Make a list of some of the typical dishes which restaurants serve in your area, using the local name.

It's	a type of	fish.
		meat.
		vegetable.
		pie.
	a	rice dish.
		pasta dish.
	made with made from	eggs.
		fruit.
	served with	vegetables.
		a salad.
		potatoes.
		a sauce.
	cooked	with garlic.
		with spices.
		with herbs.
		in olive oil.

Learning objectives: Unit 20

People skills Discussing the business lunch; Describing food; Using the correct business etiquette; Roleplay: Successful business sale

Reading Article about business etiquette in Japan

Listening Conversations at a restaurant

b   Imagine you are entertaining a visitor. Sometimes you can translate the names of dishes, but you may also have to explain how they are cooked. Act out a conversation with a partner and explain what each dish consists of. Use the phrases in 4a to help you.

Down to business

1 🔘 **2.41** Listen to Neil Klein talking to Jeff Segram when he returned to head office, and answer the questions.

a   Was the trip a success?

b   What do you think happened when they got down to business?

2 🔘 **2.42** Now listen to the conversation between Neil and Satomi. What do you think Neil did wrong?

3 Read the information below about doing business in Japan. Does this confirm your ideas in 2?

The Hard Sell

A hard sell is often seen as offensive in Japan. Japanese businesspeople may think that you are trying to convince them because your product is no good. It is better to use a low-key sales pitch and give them objective information. The Japanese are not accustomed to aggressive American techniques that use a persuasive 'winning' argument. If you are not completely honest about your product, your credibility will be damaged and what you say will lose influence. Don't say that yours is 'the best on the market'. It is better to say, 'We sold two million units last year. As you know, our closest competitor sold less than a million.' At the same time, be careful not to criticize competing products. In fact, the Japanese will respect you if you mention the assets of the competition.

Useful language:
Sales
It's true that our competitors ...

We think that sales for the last two years show ....

Our sales have increased ... in your market ...

We have a lot of new orders on our books ...

4 Act out the conversation between Neil and Satomi, but this time Neil should follow the advice in the text.

5 Do you have any similar experiences of doing business with different cultures? What other differences in the way of doing business do you know about?

meet someone halfway

to solve a problem or end an argument in which both sides accept they cannot have everything they want

The deal depends heavily on you agreeing to meet them halfway.

Learning objectives: Workplace Scenario E

Business communication skills Discussing music in the workplace; Roleplay: Negotiating a compromise
Reading Article on music in the workplace
▶ **In company in action**
E1: Dispute in the office;
E2: Meet me halfway

Meet me halfway

1 Read the article and discuss the questions with a partner.

a According to the article, does music have a positive or negative effect on the majority of staff in the workplace?

b What does the article say many managers object to?

c What problems do you think might be caused by workers listening to music using headphones?

d Why might songs with lyrics be more distracting than instrumental music?

e Do you listen to music at work? Does your company have any rules about this?

MUSIC AT WORK
by Jeff Caslow

home
news
reviews

25th August

'If music be the food of love, play on,' wrote Shakespeare. That might be a good rule for life in general, but what about in the workplace? In a recent survey 77% of businesses in the UK said that playing music increased staff morale and also improved the working atmosphere. Today, rules about listening to music at work are changing, in a world where nearly everyone has a smartphone or an mp3 player and employees can choose their own private playlists. However, many managers are still unhappy about the idea of members of their team listening to music, using headphones at their desks and being cut off from their colleagues.

For those who do listen to music at work, another debate centres around the type of music workers should listen to in order to increase their productivity. A summary of recent research from Taiwan shows while some background music can increase worker satisfaction and productivity, music with lyrics can have a negative effect on concentration and attention. The study concluded that music without lyrics is preferable, as listening to songs with words is likely to reduce worker attention and performance.

Comments (21) | share

In company in action

2 Ralph Becker and Claudia López, two colleagues in the Sales and Marketing department, have a disagreement. Watch video E1 and answer the questions.

a What does Ralph object to?

b Why doesn't Claudia wear headphones to listen to music?

c What do they each say about 'respect'?

d In your opinion, is either of them right? Who do you agree with the most and why?

3 Later, Ralph wrote an email to Serena Ortega, the HR Director. Read the email and answer the questions.

a Why does Ralph want to see Serena?

b Do you think he is being reasonable?

c He says 'I don't want to make a fuss'. What do you think that means?

d How do you think Ralph and Claudia can 'meet halfway' on this issue?

Music in the office

Dear Serena,

I'm writing this email in anger! I really think the company needs to have a look at its policy on music in the office. I've just had a disagreement with Claudia about it; she insists on having loud music on and it's driving me crazy. She turns it down when I ask but somehow, after a while, the volume always seems to go up again. I find it really distracting. I don't want to make a fuss, but it's something that's been annoying me for a while. Could we have a meeting to discuss the issue? I'd like to propose a change in our policy, or at least find a way for both sides to meet halfway.

Best wishes,
Ralph

---

4 The next day both Ralph and Claudia regret their disagreement and would like to apologize to each other. However, they also want to find a solution to the problem to avoid more arguments in the future. Work with a partner and roleplay their conversation.

Speaker A: Look at page 140.
Speaker B: Look at page 141.

5 Evaluate your performance using the form on page 145.

In company in action

6 Now watch video E2 to see what happened when Ralph and Claudia tried to negotiate a compromise. Repeat your roleplay, but this time swap roles. Use the notes from your evaluation form and as many of the useful phrases from your roleplays in 4 as you can.

7 Have you experienced any similar issues at work that caused a disagreement or conflict? How did you resolve them? Would you do anything differently now?

8 With a partner, choose one of the situations below and each take an opposing view. Have a similar conversation to the one you roleplayed in 4, where you both need to meet each other halfway. Can you find a solution?

- level of air conditioning or heating
- having a window open
- buying coffee and biscuits for the kitchen
- your own idea

Irregular verb list

Verb	Past Simple	Past Participle	Verb	Past Simple	Past Participle
arise	arose	arisen	flee	fled	fled
be	was, were	been	fly	flew	flown
bear	bore	born	forbid	forbade	forbidden
beat	beat	beaten	forecast	forecast	forecast
become	became	become	forget	forgot	forgotten
begin	began	begun	forgive	forgave	forgiven
bend	bent	bent	freeze	froze	frozen
bet	bet	bet/betted	get	got	got/gotten
bid	bid	bid	give	gave	given
bind	bound	bound	go	went	gone
bite	bit	bitten/bit	grind	ground	ground
bleed	bled	bled	grow	grew	grown
blow	blew	blown	hang	hung	hung
break	broke	broken	have	had	had
breed	bred	bred	hear	heard	heard
bring	brought	brought	hide	hid	hidden
broadcast	broadcast	broadcast	hit	hit	hit
build	built	built	hold	held	held
burn	burnt/burned	burnt/burned	hurt	hurt	hurt
burst	burst	burst	keep	kept	kept
buy	bought	bought	kneel	knelt/kneeled	knelt/kneeled
catch	caught	caught	know	knew	known
choose	chose	chosen	lay	laid	laid
come	came	come	lead	led	led
cost	cost	cost	lean	leant/leaned	leant/leaned
creep	crept	crept	leap	leapt/leaped	leapt/leaped
cut	cut	cut	learn	learnt/learned	learnt/learned
deal	dealt	dealt	leave	left	left
dig	dug	dug	lend	lent	lent
do	did	done	let	let	let
draw	drew	drawn	lie	lay	lay
dream	dreamt/dreamed	dreamt/dreamed	light	lit/lighted	lit/lighted
drink	drank	drunk	lose	lost	lost
drive	drove	driven	make	made	made
eat	ate	eaten	mean	meant	meant
fall	fell	fallen	meet	met	met
feed	fed	fed	mislead	misled	misled
feel	felt	felt	misspell	misspelt/misspelled	misspelt/misspelled
fight	fought	fought	misunderstand	misunderstood	misunderstood
find	found	found	overcome	overcame	overcome

Verb	Past Simple	Past Participle
overhear	overheard	overheard
overspend	overspent	overspent
overtake	overtook	overtaken
pay	paid	paid
prove	proved	proven/proved
put	put	put
quit	quit	quit
read	read	read
ride	rode	ridden
ring	rang	rung
rise	rose	risen
run	ran	run
say	said	said
see	saw	seen
seek	sought	sought
sell	sold	sold
send	sent	sent
set	set	set
sew	sewed	sewn
shake	shook	shaken
shine	shone	shone
shoot	shot	shot
show	showed	shown
shrink	shrank	shrunk
shut	shut	shut
sing	sang	sung
sit	sat	sat
sleep	slept	slept
slide	slid	slid
smell	smelt/smelled	smelt/smelled
speak	spoke	spoken
speed	sped/speeded	sped/speeded
spell	spelt/spelled	spelt/spelled
spend	spent	spent
spill	spilt/spilled	spilt/spilled
spin	spun	spun
spit	spat	spat
split	split	split
spoil	spoilt/spoiled	spoilt/spoiled
spread	spread	spread

Verb	Past Simple	Past Participle
spring	sprang	sprung
stand	stood	stood
steal	stole	stolen
stick	stuck	stuck
sting	stung	stung
strike	struck	struck
swear	swore	sworn
sweep	swept	swept
swim	swam	swum
swing	swung	swung
take	took	taken
teach	taught	taught
tear	tore	torn
tell	told	told
think	thought	thought
throw	threw	thrown
understand	understood	understood
wake	woke	woken
wear	wore	worn
weep	wept	wept
win	won	won
wind	wound	wound
withdraw	withdrew	withdrawn
withhold	withheld	withheld
write	wrote	written

Note: where two alternative forms are given, the second form is used in American English.

Additional material

02 Work–life balance
Work–life balance (p13, ex2)

a 2 **b** 3 **c** 48 **d** 1,625 **e** 76,700

03 Telephone talk
Polite questions (p20, ex2)

A InterAir / help?

B Yes, please / like / information / flight / Zurich

A Yes / know / flight number?

B The flight number? / not sure / know / leaves Zurich / 11.25

A yes / IA 624

B Yes / tell / time / arrives?

A arrival / 14.10

B 14.10 / know / delay?

A No / flight / on time

B Right / thank / much

A welcome / goodbye

04 Networking
Answers (p26, ex5)

a Who do you work for?

b Where is your company based?

c Where are you staying?

d Do you speak (German)?

e Who is (Alex) talking to?

f What do you do? / What's your job?

g Have you got any children? / Do you have any children?

h Where are you from? / Where do you come from?

i Are you married?

j Do you play golf?

k Do you know (Adriana Bellini)?

09 Spirit of enterprise
Answers: Language links (p62, Practice 5)

The Inditex group consists of almost a hundred companies dealing with textile design, production and distribution. Its unique management techniques and its successes (a) **have turned** Inditex into one of the world's largest fashion groups.

The first Zara shop (b) **opened** in 1975 in La Coruña in northern Spain. Over the years, the group (c) **has added** other chains to the original Zara, each covering a different market sector. In 1991 the group (d) **created** Pull & Bear, and in 1995 (e) **acquired** 100% of Massimo Dutti. Bershka (f) **started** its activity in 1998, followed by the acquisition of Stradivarius in 1999. Two years later Inditex (g) **launched** Oysho, a chain specializing in fashionable lingerie and underwear. More recent additions (h) **were** Zara Home, a home decoration store, and Uterqüe, which focuses on fashion accessories.

In the last four years, the number of shops in the group (i) **has reached** a figure of over 5,000, and the group now has operations in 82 countries worldwide. In the same period, sales (j) **have increased** by 46% and net profits by 54%.

Despite its size, the group still controls its activities from a logistical centre in Arteixo, a village in the north-west of Spain, but in 2003 it (k) **finished** work on 'Plataforma Europa', a new distribution centre in Zaragoza.

Scenario B, In my shoes
(p.55, ex5)

Speaker B: David McCann, Production and Operations Manager

Claudia calls to complain about her IT problems. Try to use the four-step approach described in 3 on page 55 to deal with the complaint. Use the phrases you categorized in 4 and any others you think will help.

05 Internet histories
Answers: Language links (p36, Practice 5)

a Steve Jobs didn't co-found Google, he co-founded Apple®.

b The Wall Street Crash didn't start a worldwide economic boom, it started an economic depression.

c The six European states didn't sign the Treaty of Madrid, they signed the Treaty of Rome.

d The eleven member states of the European Union didn't adopt the pound as a common currency, they adopted the euro.

e Engineers at Apple didn't produce the Android smartphone, they produced the iPhone.

f Mark Zuckerberg didn't invent Twitter, he invented Facebook.

07 Hotels
Room service (p48, ex3)

Speaker A: Phone room service to make requests for:
- a bottle of sparkling water
- someone to fix the minibar
- someone to explain how the TV pay channels work
- someone to sew on a button
- an extra set of clean towels
- (your own request).

Scenario C, Stick to your guns
(p79, ex4)

Speaker B: Joe Walker, CEO

You think the survey is a good idea but want to make sure Serena has considered all the options. You want to know:
- about the feedback from the Sales and Marketing team.
- if the survey should be online or paper-based.
- if you should ask external consultants to do the survey.
- if you should publish the results of the survey.

Business skill: Making suggestions

So, have you thought about …?

What about the issue of …?

What about using …?

Did you also consider …?

And how about …?

Scenario A, Passing the buck
(p29, ex5)

Speaker A: Serena Ortega, HR Director
- You are taking Joe's advice and have decided to approach Vanessa again.
- You want to find a solution to the problem with the website without being passed onto someone else.
- You agree with Joe that the best way to confirm a verbal agreement is by following it up in writing.

Try to use some of the phrases below.

Business skill: Discussing and fixing a problem

It's about the new website.

You said I should talk to …

I don't mind who …

We really need to get this sorted out.

Am I right in thinking that …?

When can we get this fixed?

It sounds like we've found a solution.

I'll send you an email later to …

06 Orders
Answers (p38, ex7)

A: S-A-G, can I help you?

B: Yes, this is Elena Moretti from Stern Hydraulics. Could I speak to John Bird, please?

A: Oh, hello, Elena. I'm afraid John isn't here at the moment. Can I take a message?

B: Yes, he sent me an order confirmation – the reference is DH010601 – but the delivery date is wrong.

A: Oh, dear. Can you give me the details?

B: Yes, it says 7th July, but the agreed delivery date was 22nd June. It's really important.

A: I see. Well, I'll tell him as soon as he comes in.

B: Thank you. I'm not at all happy about this. A lot depends on this order.

A: Right, Elena, leave it with me. I'm terribly sorry about this.

B: No, it's not your fault. Just ask John to phone me.

A: All right, then. Bye for now.

B: Goodbye.

10 Stressed to the limit
The ten most stressful jobs (p63, ex4)

Measured by level of 21 specific job demands,
in the USA the ten most stressful jobs are:

1   Enlisted soldier
2   Military general
3   Firefighter
4   Airline pilot
5   Public Relations executive
6   Senior corporate executive
7   Photojournalist
8   Newspaper journalist
9   Taxi driver
10 Police officer

02 Work–life balance
What's in a new job (p15, ex3)

Speaker A

Your partner has the missing information. Complete the chart by asking questions like the ones in exercise 2 on page 15.

Name	Janice	Delia
Job title		Director of Retail Sales
Type of company		Chain of clothing stores
Working hours		45
Responsibilities		Leading a team of 25. Accounts and stock control. Maintaining inventory in stores.
Weekend/Late evening work		One evening and one weekend day a week. Sometimes 'on call' with a pager in case of emergencies.
Most enjoys		Satisfying internal clients. People she works with.
Travel		Not often. Trips to different stores. Three trade fairs a year.
Holidays		Two weeks. Three weeks after five years' service.
Ratio of women to men in position/field		60% male, 40% female.

Scenario A Passing the buck
(p29, ex6)

FEEDBACK: Self-assessment

1   How did the roleplay go? *Well / Okay / Badly*
2   **a** Did you resolve the issue of people passing the buck? *Yes / No / Almost*
    b If yes, or almost, what solution did you reach? _____
    If no, why not? _____
3   What solutions to the communication problems did you find? _____
4   Did you use any of the tips on improving communication from the article? Tick the boxes.
    Find something you have in common and use that to relate to your colleagues ☐
    Avoid office gossip; try to stay professional at all times ☐
    Arrange to follow up phone calls and meetings with an email ☐
    Don't let a negative attitude interfere with how you communicate with your colleagues ☐
5   How many useful phrases did you use? _____
6   If you could have the conversation again, what (if anything) would you do differently?
    _____

---

13 Air travel
The negotiation game (p83, ex3)

Speaker A: Buyer

Negotiate with your partner to get the best deal possible. You get points for each category of the deal – price, quantity, delivery time, and so on. For example, if you agree on a price of 6 euros, you get 2 points, or 3 points if the price is 5.5. Add your points for each category to get your score. To be a successful negotiator you have to get at least ten points.

Points	1	2	3	
Price	6.5	6	5.5	€
Quantity	200	150	100	Units
Delivery	3	2	1	Weeks
Payment	30	60	90	Days
Guarantee	6	12	18	Months

14 Hiring and firing
What about the workers? (p90, ex2)

Speaker A

1 Read the article.
2 Find and <u>underline</u> five examples of the passive in the article.
3 Match the five words and phrases in **bold** in the article to five of the definitions below. Ask your partner which words match the other five definitions.

a compensate for _____
b percentage of working population without jobs _____
c employees with training and abilities to do technical tasks _____
d people who are unemployed for a long time _____
e what employees can legally expect from their employers _____
f motivating factors _____
g money paid to people who don't have jobs _____
h all the people who work in a country or for a company _____
i the number of employees a company requires to do its work _____
j workers who have contracts limited to a period of time _____

Daily News   17

Skills shortage linked to job *insecurity*

According to a survey which was carried out by the Confederation of Industry, almost two thirds of the country's companies are experiencing a shortage of **skilled workers**. It is a problem which particularly affects the electronics industry.

The companies claimed that they provided training for their **workforce**, but that this on its own was not sufficient to cover their **staffing needs**.

In an attempt to **make up for** this lack of skilled workers, nearly half of the 670 firms which were contacted said that they had increased their use of **temporary staff**, and over a quarter intended to do the same in the next year.

According to a spokesman for the Confederation, a result of this skills shortage is an increase in feelings of job insecurity among a third of employees. 'It is increasingly difficult to provide people with jobs for life,' he said.

Although over 60% of firms said staff were paid based on their skills and level of competence, the Confederation noted that while salaries at management level were frequently negotiated individually, conditions for clerical and manual workers were usually agreed at a company-wide level. ■

Scenario C, Stick to your guns
(p79, ex4)

Speaker A: Serena Ortega, HR Director

You have researched the benefits of doing a staff satisfaction survey and believe your decisions are the right ones. Stick to your guns! Discuss these points:

- Tell Joe about the negative feedback from the Sales and Marketing team, but confirm that there are lots of reasons you think you should still do the survey.
- The system you are suggesting uses numbers, not names, so it will be completely anonymous.
- An external consultant is too expensive. The survey should be done internally.
- The survey should be online, so it is quick and easy to assess the results.
- The survey should only have questions that ask for a score, with no open-ended answers.
- You don't think there should be a comments section; it will be too difficult to assess the results.
- The results of the survey should be published in the company e-newsletter.

Try to use some of the phrases below.

Business skill: Expressing opinions and defending ideas

Do you want to discuss the points in your email?

The problem is …	I'm not sure I agree …
Even if we say …	I think it would be more successful if …
Isn't it better to …?	Yes, absolutely. The idea is to …
I'm convinced that …	I've thought about that and …

14 Hiring and firing
What about the workers? (p90, ex2)

Speaker B

1 Read the article.
2 Find and <u>underline</u> five examples of the passive in the article.
3 Match the five words and phrases in **bold** in the article to five of the definitions below. Ask your partner which words match the other five definitions.

a compensate for _____

b percentage of working population without jobs _____

c employees with training and abilities to do technical tasks _____

d people who are unemployed for a long time _____

e what employees can legally expect from their employers _____

f motivating factors _____

g money paid to people who don't have jobs _____

h all the people who work in a country or for a company _____

i the number of employees a company requires to do its work _____

j workers who have contracts limited to a period of time _____

Unions general strike threat

The whole of the country will be brought to a halt if plans for a general strike go ahead. The threatened strike has been called by the unions in reaction to the government's attempts to cut **unemployment benefits**. With the proposed changes unemployed workers will have to take one of the first three 'acceptable' job offers which are put to them, if the place of work is within 30 km of their homes. If they refuse, they will lose their benefits. Also, anyone who is sacked from their job but appealing against the decision will lose their salary entitlement during the period of the appeal.

The two main unions, each with over a million members, say that the reforms are a direct attack on **workers' rights**. They say the changes will be especially negative for those who lose their jobs, and the **long-term unemployed**. They also claim that the new law will make it easier and cheaper for companies to lay off staff, and will lead to increased job insecurity.

With an 11.3% **unemployment rate**, the highest in the European Union, the reforms have been defended by the government, which says they are necessary in order to be competitive and provide an open and flexible labour market. It says the measures will help solve the problem of unemployment by increasing the **incentives** for people to find jobs. Although its relations with the labour movement have been generally good for the last six years, trade union officials say that this time the government has gone too far.

Scenario B, In my shoes
(p55, ex5)

Speaker A: Claudia López, Marketing Executive

You are frustrated with the IT problems you have been having, but also with the IT helpdesk. Complain to David about the following:

- The new system hasn't been working since it was updated; it's constantly crashing. You use this system every day.
- It's very frustrating when work can't be completed properly because of IT problems.
- The IT department don't seem willing to help and haven't provided any solutions to the problems.

Try to use some of the phrases below.

Business skill: Expressing concern

I hope you can help.

I have a problem with ... which means ...,

The main issue is ... which ..., I understand ...

I realize that ... but ...,

Look at it from my point of view ...

Put yourself in my shoes, ...

I appreciate your help.

Thanks for your help.

Scenario C Stick to your guns
(p79, ex5)

FEEDBACK: Self-assessment

1   How did the roleplay go? *Well / Okay / Badly*
2   Which of the issues in Joe's email did you discuss? Tick the boxes.

General feedback	☐	Type of questions	☐
Cost	☐	Focus groups	☐
Anonymity	☐	Results	☐
Type of survey	☐		

3   How easy did you find it to stick to your guns during the conversation? *Easy / Okay / Difficult*
4   Were there any issues that you disagreed on? If so, which? _____
5   How many useful phrases did you use? _____
6   If you could have the conversation again, what (if anything) would you do differently? _____

03 Telephone talk
Polite questions (p20, ex4)

Speaker B

You were just about to send this email to a colleague, when they call you with Internet access problems. Answer their questions.

Sales Meeting with Mr Fuentes

To:

From:

Subject: Sales Meeting with Mr Fuentes.

Here are your travel instructions for your sales meeting with Mr Fuentes. You're on flight BA 44362 at 19.55 on 21 January from London Heathrow Terminal 2. When you arrive at your destination, you'll be met at the airport by a taxi which will take you to the factory to meet Mr Fuentes. The factory is about 40 miles from the airport.

You've got one hour with Mr Fuentes to have your meeting. Then you leave to get to the hotel for the special sales conference. You'll need to drive across country; the hotel is quite far away. Avis have either a Range Rover 3.6 or Jeep Grand Cherokee, whichever you prefer to rent. An armed guide will accompany you on your journey. Don't forget that you'll need to carry your passport and international driving licence at all times.

The hotel for the conference is The Lodge. It's in the middle of the forest, twenty miles from the nearest town, and has 5 stars. All the rooms (including the meeting room) have been booked for the whole week.

Scenario A, Passing the buck
(p29, ex8)

Re: Website

Good afternoon Vanessa,

I am writing to confirm what we discussed in our meeting this morning about the website. The section where people can upload their CVs and complete an application form is missing. We agreed that as you have responsibility for the site, you will speak to Eric to resolve the problem. As you have a meeting with Eric this afternoon you will discuss the situation then and clarify who is responsible for design and programing. You will then let me know when the application form is available. Please let me know if I have misunderstood anything.

Best wishes,
Serena

18 E-commerce
Answers (p111, ex1)

a When you buy something for yourself with your own money, you're interested in quality and price.

b When you buy something for someone else with your own money, you're interested in price.

c When you buy something for yourself with someone else's money, you're interested in quality.

d When you buy something for someone else with someone else's money, who cares?

03 Telephone talk
Telephone frustrations (p21, ex2)

The five main frustrations customers experience in dealing with telephone staff are:

- taking too long to answer
- being put on hold and forgotten
- being transferred and having to repeat their enquiry
- being answered by voicemail and other machines
- not having calls returned.

Scenario A, Passing the buck
(p29, ex5)

Speaker B: Vanessa Morgan, Sales and Marketing Manager

- As Sales and Marketing Manager you have overall responsibility for the website.
- You are frustrated with the IT department because you really believed that Eric was going to look after the HR section of the site.
- You have already spoken to Eric and have agreed to have a meeting this afternoon to resolve the situation. You can explain this to Serena in your meeting.

Try to use some of the phrases below.

Business skill: Discussing and fixing a problem

What did you want to talk about?

I'm sorry there has been an issue with …

Resolving the problem is in everyone's interests.

Don't worry. In fact, I spoke to…

There was a misunderstanding about …

I think we can agree on what to do next.

Don't worry. We …

I'll send you an email to …

18 E-commerce
The future of the Internet (p113, ex3)

Some experts did not either agree or disagree. In some cases they did not answer and in others they gave a different answer.

	Agree	Disagree
The mobile phone (or smartphone) will be the primary Internet connection and the only one for the majority of people across the world, providing information in a portable, well-connected form at a low price.	77%	22%
People will be more tolerant than they are today, because the Internet and other information and communication technologies will help them to learn about other people. There will be less violence and fewer wars.	32%	56%
There will be strict controls on copyrighted content thanks to new laws and the efforts of the technology industry and media companies. People who use copyrighted materials will automatically pay the content owners, and Internet service providers will notify authorities when they identify clients who illegally share music and films.	31%	60%
People will be more open to sharing personal information, opinions and emotions than they are now. The concept of privacy will change and as their lives become more transparent, people will become more responsible for their own actions.	45%	44%
Virtual worlds and augmented reality will be popular thanks to the rapid evolution of technology. Most well-equipped Internet users will spend some of their day – at work and at play – linked to augmentations of the real world or alternative worlds. It will be more difficult to distinguish between virtual reality and 'real life'.	55%	30%
As all phones, tablets and computers will have built-in voice-recognition, it will be completely normal to hear people talking in public to their computing devices. In addition, these devices will allow you to display a full-size virtual keyboard on any flat surface and it will be common to see people 'air-typing' on a projected keyboard only they can see.	64%	21%
The Internet will still have its original architecture and won't be replaced by a totally new system. It will be more reliable and secure, but unfortunately those who want to commit crimes and cause problems will still be able to do so.	78%	6%
The separation between work hours and personal time will disappear. People won't depend on fixed timetables for work and play. They will perform both their professional and personal duties from wherever they happen to be – home, the gym, the mall or from work, which will often be a virtual office.	56%	29%

Scenario D, Change for the better
(p103, ex7)

Speaker B: Felix Schmidt, Factory foreman

- You are the head of the factory workers.
- David, your line manager, will tell you about some new health and safety regulations for the factory workers.
- You resist the changes at first and you know that the other factory workers will not like the new regulations.
- However, you would like to have more responsibility in your work. This is the kind of managerial task that could help your career.
- Explain to David that you think the staff will be unhappy but make sure he knows that you are willing to help him lead these changes.

Try to use some of the phrases below.

Business skill: responding to change

So, what did you want to see me about?	The team will be very unhappy.
I understand that, but …	I'll try and talk to them.
I'm not sure that's such a good idea.	I'll talk to them, but I don't think it will be easy.
But, it's very important to …	I'll try explaining the situation, but …
I don't think you've thought this through …	

19 E-work

Teleworking (p119, ex5)

Does working at home really work?

	Advantages	Disadvantages
Family	4	1
The workplace	13	10
The working day	12	8
Commuting	5	3
Technology	11	15
Efficiency	2	9
Costs	7	6
Motivation	16	14

06 Orders

Answers: Language links (p42, crossword)

Across

1 delivery
6 prompt
8 informal
9 handwriting
10 fax
13 business
15 correspondence
19 check
21 decision
22 message
24 annoyed
28 welcome
29 down
30 confirm

Down

2 immediately
3 expensive
4 signature
5 details
7 courier
11 apologize
12 reply
14 Internet
16 worried
17 phoning
18 mistake
20 that
23 skills
25 order
26 send
27 cost

13 Air travel

The negotiation game (p83, ex3)

Speaker B: Seller

Negotiate with your partner to get the best deal possible. You get points for each category of the deal – price, quantity, delivery time and so on. For example, if you agree on a price of 6 euros, you get 2 points, or 3 points if the price is 6.5. Add your points for each category to get your score. To be a successful negotiator you have to get at least ten points.

Points	1	2	3	
Price	5.5	6	6.5	€
Quantity	100	150	200	Units
Delivery	1	2	3	Weeks
Payment	90	60	30	Days
Guarantee	18	12	6	Months

20 Working lunch

Discussion (p124, ex1)

A business lunch can be an excellent opportunity to create new contacts, make key business decisions and improve your career prospects. But it can be difficult to know the appropriate etiquette required when you are away from the traditional office environment. Here are a few tips on how to make the most of your business lunch and make sure everything goes to plan.

- Timing is everything! Make sure that you leave plenty of time to travel to the lunch and plan to arrive at the restaurant early so that your guest isn't left waiting. You don't want to give them a bad impression of you before the meal has even started.

- Do your research! If you can, make sure that you find out about your guest's dining requirements or preferences before booking a restaurant. For example, don't take a vegetarian to a steak house! Or if your client particularly likes Asian food, find a great sushi or Thai restaurant.

- Stay focused! Make sure to turn off your mobile phone (or turn it to silent) before arriving at the restaurant. You don't want any distracting noises when you're in the middle of an important conversation, and your guest won't appreciate being ignored whilst you read an email or check your messages at the table.

- Remember your manners! Be polite not only to your guest, but also to the waiter and the restaurant staff. No one wants to do business with someone who is rude and disrespectful, whoever they're dealing with.

- Finish up! If you have hosted the meal always remember to pay the bill and thank your guest for joining you. Even if the business discussions didn't go to plan, it is still important to leave your guest with a good impression of you.

07 Hotels

Answers: World records (p48, ex1)

	Hotel	Location	Detail
Largest	The Palazzo Resort and Casino	Las Vegas, USA	8,108 rooms
Tallest	Burj Al Arab	Dubai, UAE	321 metres
Most expensive	Royal Villa at Grand Resort Lagonissi	Athens, Greece	$50,000 room/night
Highest	Hotel Everest View	Nepal	3,800 metres above sea level
Oldest	Hoshi Ryokan	Awazu, Japan	Opened in 717

02 Work–life balance
What's in a new job (p15, ex3)

Speaker B

Your partner has the missing information. Complete the chart by asking questions like the ones in 2 on page 15.

Name	Janice	Delia
Job title	Production Manager	
Type of company	Software company	
Working hours	Normally 40–50 hours but can be up to 75	
Responsibilities	Managing website. Liaising with international offices.	
Weekend/Late evening work	Not in her present position.	
Most enjoys	Doing something that makes a real difference to the company.	
Travel	Occasional trips to other offices.	
Holidays	Three weeks	
Ratio of women to men in position/field	Half the department are women, but only two have technical skills.	

Scenario E, Meet me halfway
(p127, ex4)

Speaker A: Claudia López, Marketing Executive

- You like listening to music while you work; it makes you happy and you work better when you are less stressed.
- You don't use headphones – you find them uncomfortable and you need to listen for the phone.
- You do understand that listening to music might be annoying for Ralph, and that he doesn't share your taste in music.
- You are prepared to compromise, but think that you should be allowed to listen to music for at least part of the day.
- You prefer pop music to classical music.

Try to use some of the phrases below.

Business skill: Negotiating a compromise

I think we should talk about …	I understand your point of view but …
In my opinion, …	Yes, I see what you mean …
Would you agree to a compromise?	Is that an acceptable compromise?
Let's meet halfway.	We could try …
What about if you …?	Would you consider …?
Would you mind …?	

17 Office gossip
Time to talk (p108, ex9)

Speaker A: You are the personnel manager of the company with the notice below about coffee breaks. A management consultant wants you to change the policy, but you don't think a change is a good thing. Explain why, including:

- You think a lot of time is wasted by people chatting and gossiping when they are supposed to be working.
- You are under pressure from the Managing Director to improve the efficiency of the company.
- Recently there have been a lot of rumours about staff cutbacks. Most of them are false, but some are true, and this is creating a lot of problems.

Company Notice

- **Employees may take up to three coffee breaks per day.**
- **Maximum time at coffee machine: four minutes.**
- **All 'gossip' or discussion of non-work related matters is prohibited.**

Scenario E, Meet me halfway (p127, ex4)

Speaker B: Ralph Becker, Sales Executive

- You know you overreacted yesterday and you want to make up with Claudia.
- You feel you should have spoken to Claudia again before sending an email to Serena, but you were really upset.
- You understand that some people like listening to music and you want to reach a compromise with Claudia.
- You don't want to force her to wear earphones.
- You find songs and music with words especially irritating, but don't really mind instrumental or classical music.

Try to use some of the phrases below.

Business skill: Negotiating a compromise

I think we should talk about …

In my opinion …

Would you agree to a compromise?

Let's meet halfway.

What about if you …?

Would you mind …?

I understand your point of view but …

Yes, I see what you mean …

Is that an acceptable compromise?

We could try …

Would you consider …?

06 Orders
On-the-spot decisions (p41, ex5)
Speaker A

Speaker B will tell you a problem. React using one of the solutions below. Say *Don't worry, I'll …* Then choose a new problem from the table and tell Speaker B.

A *I've got a problem, the battery in my mobile's flat.*

B *Don't worry, I'll lend you mine.*

Problems	Solutions
I can't understand these figures.	I'll look for information on the Internet.
My computer keeps crashing.	I'll send it to you again.
I can't get an answer from the taxi service.	I'll go through it and correct them.
I need to speak to you urgently.	I'll reserve the tickets for you this morning.
The printer is not working properly.	I'll look it up for you.
I don't know how to use this program.	I'll print them out for you.
Our email system isn't working.	I'll get you an aspirin.

07 Hotels
World records (p49, ex3)
Speaker B

City	Chain	Price	City	Chain	Price
Amsterdam	Royal Inn	272	London		476
	Executive International	238			408
	First Class Hotels	195			329
	Travel Express	178			188
Frankfurt		494	New York	Executive International	584
		330		Royal Inn	457
		157		First Class Hotels	268
		152		Travel Express	260
Geneva	First Class Hotels	394	Paris		420
	Royal Inn	357			381
	Executive International	260			361
	Travel Express	148			254

03 Telephone talk

Sales contacts (p23, ex2)

Speaker A

Situation 1

You work as the Publications Officer in the marketing department of Miki-chan Fashion Accessories. You are currently producing your new company brochure. This is a 32 page, full colour brochure on high quality paper. You need 30,000 copies. Phone JD Graphic for an estimate. The only problem is that the brochure needs to be ready in ten days. Can they do it?

Situation 2

You work for JD Graphic. A potential client phones you. Listen to what the customer wants and complete the phone contact form with the necessary information.

 **GRAPHIC**   PHONE CONTACT FORM

DATE:

CALL INITIATED BY:

CALL HANDLER:

CLIENT:

ADDRESS:

CONTACT:

POSITION:

TEL:

EMAIL:

NATURE OF BUSINESS:

PURPOSE OF CALL:

COMMENTS:

ACTION REQUIRED:

BY WHOM:

DATE AND TIME:

15 Time

Wasting time (p95, ex4)

Be sloppy

A good hour or two can be gained every few weeks if you keep your desk in a mess. Friday afternoons and Monday mornings are perfect times to set aside for cleaning up your work area. (28 minutes to an hour once a week)

The computer

Load your computer with unnecessary programs that make your machine run more slowly. While you're waiting for the PC to process information, sit back and relax. If the boss questions you, just say, 'Damn computers.' He'll laugh and agree with you. (Roughly 42 minutes a day)

The Internet

Be very careful misusing the company PC to surf the Net for personal enjoyment. Your boss knows the Internet is a big waste of time and is watching for people who are doing web searches for MP3s and games. The best way is to use it for all research. If you need a phone number for a client across town, use the Internet to find it. Most people just reach for a phone book, which is faster than using the Internet. (Roughly 9 to 33 minutes a day)

Office conversations

Enter business conversations around the office that are taking place in the open. You don't have to be a part of the conversation very much. The important thing is to be there physically. Just listen and nod your head when appropriate. (23 minutes to 1.3 hours)

Meetings

Go to every meeting you can get into. You'd be surprised at how many people miss the opportunity to waste time by avoiding meetings. Once you're in a meeting, it's all about planning your weekend, or thinking about the football game you watched the night before. (According to Office Studies International the average meeting takes 42 minutes and meetings happen every 5 hours. Count on 2–3 meetings a week.)

Adapted from 'Wasting time at work' by Galen Black
Source: www.vgg.com

Scenario D, Change for the better
(p103, ex7)

Speaker A: David McCann, Production and Operations Manager

- You need to tell Felix about the changes to the health and safety regulations.
- Make sure Felix knows that you need his help in communicating these changes to the team and that you understand it will be difficult.
- Use Serena's advice from activity 5 and your own notes from activity 6 to explain the changes to Felix.

Try to use some of the phrases below.

Business skill: leading change

As you know, …

This is what's going to happen, and I need your help with it.

Because of …, we have decided to …

I'm sure you'll agree that …

I need you to make sure that …

Do you think you can help me?

This could be very good for you.

I realize that this will be very unpopular …

I think we should point out the pros as well as the cons.

I'm here if you need anything.

Scenario B In my shoes
(p55, ex6)

FEEDBACK: Self-assessment

1 How did the roleplay go? *Well / Okay / Badly*

2 a Did you successfully put yourself in each other's shoes? *Yes / No / Almost*

　b If yes, or almost, what solution to the problem did you find?

　_____

　If no, why not? _____

3 Which advice from the four-step strategy for keeping people happy did you use in your conversation? Tick the boxes.

Listen with an open mind ☐

Repeat the problem back ☐

Be sympathetic and fair ☐

Follow up promptly ☐

4 On a scale of 1–10 how useful did you find the advice?

1_____10

(Not useful at all)　　　　　　　　　　　　　　(Very useful)

5 How many useful phrases did you use? _____

6 If you could have the conversation again, what (if anything) would you do differently?

_____

06 Orders
Correspondence (p40, ex3)

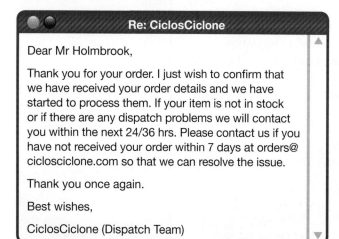

Re: CiclosCiclone

Dear Mr Holmbrook,

Thank you for your order. I just wish to confirm that we have received your order details and we have started to process them. If your item is not in stock or if there are any dispatch problems we will contact you within the next 24/36 hrs. Please contact us if you have not received your order within 7 days at orders@ ciclosciclone.com so that we can resolve the issue.

Thank you once again.

Best wishes,

CiclosCiclone (Dispatch Team)

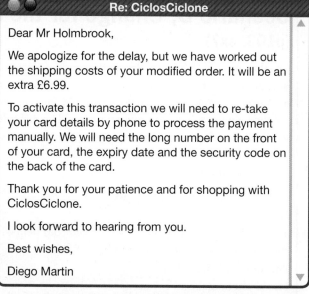

Re: CiclosCiclone

Dear Mr Holmbrook,

We apologize for the delay, but we have worked out the shipping costs of your modified order. It will be an extra £6.99.

To activate this transaction we will need to re-take your card details by phone to process the payment manually. We will need the long number on the front of your card, the expiry date and the security code on the back of the card.

Thank you for your patience and for shopping with CiclosCiclone.

I look forward to hearing from you.

Best wishes,

Diego Martin

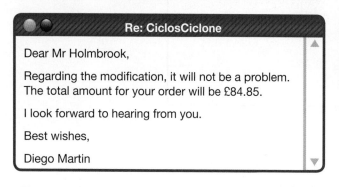

Re: CiclosCiclone

Dear Mr Holmbrook,

Regarding the modification, it will not be a problem. The total amount for your order will be £84.85.

I look forward to hearing from you.

Best wishes,

Diego Martin

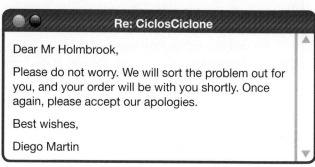

Re: CiclosCiclone

Dear Mr Holmbrook,

Please do not worry. We will sort the problem out for you, and your order will be with you shortly. Once again, please accept our apologies.

Best wishes,

Diego Martin

Scenario D Change for the better
(p103, ex8)

FEEDBACK: Self-assessment

1 How did the roleplay go? *Well / Okay / Badly*

2 a Did you both agree that the changes would be for the better? *Yes / No / Almost*

   b If no, or almost, what did you disagree about? _____

3 Which of the tips on leading change were included in your conversation? Tick the boxes.

   Communicate the vision clearly ☐

   Involve those that are affected in the planning of the change ☐

   Explain the impact of the change for the individual ☐

   Be honest about the pros and cons ☐

   Ask for and listen to feedback ☐

4 How would you describe the general tone of the conversation? Circle the word(s) below.

   Tense   Forceful   Awkward   Neutral   Constructive   Supportive   Friendly

5 How many useful phrases did you use? _____

6 If you could have the conversation again, what (if anything) would you do differently?

   _____

05 Internet histories

Answers: Language links
(Business and the Internet, p35)

a became
b release
c develop
d claim
e estimated
f reach
g announced
h downloaded
i presented
j achieve

06 Orders

An important order (p39, ex9)

Speaker B: You are John Bird. You understand why Elena Moretti is angry. Her company is one of your best customers. Your production department let you down. They promised to meet the delivery date but there was a transport strike and some components didn't arrive. Apologize as much as you can for what happened and invent excuses for everything. Offer to pay for a holiday weekend in London for Elena, but don't make any promises you can't keep.

Scenario E Meet me halfway

(p127, ex5)

FEEDBACK: Self-assessment

1 How did the roleplay go? *Well / Okay / Badly*
2 **a** Did you come to an agreement to meet each other halfway? *Yes / No / Almost*
   b If yes, what did you agree? _____
   If no, or almost, what did you disagree about? _____
3 Did you make any compromises? What were they? _____
4 On a scale of 1–10 how happy were you both with the outcome of the conversation?
   1_____10
   (Very unhappy)   (Very happy)
5 How many useful phrases did you use? _____
6 If you could have the conversation again, what (if anything) would you do differently?
   _____

06 Orders
On-the-spot decisions (p41, ex5)

Problems	Solutions
I've got a headache.	I'll get you an aspirin.
I can't understand these figures.	I'll explain them to you.
My computer keeps crashing.	I'll call the IT technician.
We didn't get your text.	I'll send it to you again.
This report has lots of errors in it.	I'll go through it and correct them.
I can't remember his phone number.	I'll look it up for you.
I need to speak to you urgently.	I'll phone you this afternoon.
I haven't booked my flight to Berlin.	I'll reserve the tickets for you this morning.
The printer is not working properly.	I'll change the ink cartridge.
I don't know how to use this program.	I'll show you how it works.
I need three copies of this proposal.	I'll print them out for you.
I don't know anything about this company.	I'll look for information on the Internet.
Our email system isn't working.	I'll fax the details to you instead.
I can't get an answer from the taxi service.	I'll take you to the airport.

03 Telephone talk
Sales contacts (p23, ex2)

Speaker B
Situation 1
You work for JD Graphic. A potential client phones you. Listen to what the customer wants and complete the phone contact form below with the necessary information.

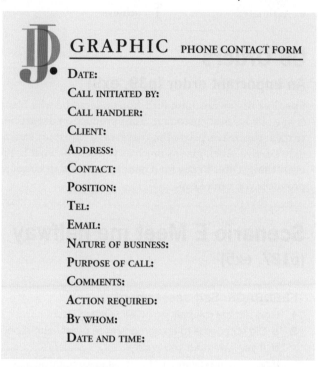

GRAPHIC PHONE CONTACT FORM

DATE:
CALL INITIATED BY:
CALL HANDLER:
CLIENT:
ADDRESS:
CONTACT:
POSITION:
TEL:
EMAIL:
NATURE OF BUSINESS:
PURPOSE OF CALL:
COMMENTS:
ACTION REQUIRED:
BY WHOM:
DATE AND TIME:

Situation 2
You work as the Marketing Manager in the marketing department of a clothes manufacturer, Lewis & Co. You are looking for someone to print some labels for your new range of jeans. The labels have to be printed on quality card in two colours. They also have to be cut to the shape of the company logo. You want 10,000 labels. Phone JD Graphic for an estimate. Invent any other information you need to.

Listening scripts

01 INTRODUCTIONS

 1.01

A: Okay everybody, can we make a start? First of all, allow me to welcome you all to Ashbourne Management College. My name is Mariah Wilson and I am the main tutor for our 'Results Through Collaboration' course. It's always useful to know something about the background of the other participants so we normally begin by asking you to introduce yourself to the rest of the group. Perhaps we could start with you, Jan?

B: Yes, hello. My name is Jan Werner. I work for Metronet Fibre. Our main business is fibre optics. We install urban fibre-optic networks for telecommunication systems all over the world. I'm Director of Communications in the HR department. I'm Norwegian, but I live and work in the Czech Republic. Our headquarters are in Prague. That's where I'm based. At the moment, though, I'm spending a lot of time visiting our other offices in Europe. My job involves organizing and running different management training courses for our senior management.

A: Thank you, Jan. Silvia?

C: Well, I'm Silvia Fortuni. I'm Catalan and I'm from Barcelona. I work for a big retail chain with franchises all over the world. We manufacture and sell clothes and fashion accessories, but my role is related to sales and promotion. I work out of our headquarters in Barcelona and I'm the Regional Director of Marketing there. I'm responsible for our campaigns in the European area. I have to say I love my job and I welcome the opportunity to learn something more about communication skills. I think that's it. If you want to know anything more, you can ask me.

D: My turn? Hi, everybody. My name is Jean-Christophe Marchal, but most people just call me JC. I'm Commercial Director at PPTT Services in Paris. We mainly work with big public companies in the Paris area. My background is in new technologies and I'm responsible for promoting and selling our ideas for online services and products. I'm in charge of quite a large team and good communication is essential. You probably think from my accent that I'm French. Actually, I'm Belgian but I'm based in Paris, where we have our main office.

A: Thank you, JC. Now, Elena, I think it's your turn …

 1.02

Hello, and welcome to *Business Talk*. This month we're looking at the role of ethics in business. According to Richard Reed, co-founder of Innocent Drinks, the company behind award-winning fruit-based smoothies, ethics are fundamental to the company's success. Innocent says that, as well as making money, the objective is always to leave things a little bit better than it finds them, an inspiring way to approach business.

So, how did the success that is Innocent all begin? Innocent was founded back in 1998 by Richard and two friends from Cambridge University. They decided to set up a business together and spent £500 on fruit to make smoothies to sell at a music festival. A sign above their stall said 'Should we give up our jobs to make these smoothies?' They asked people to put their empty bottles in one of two bins marked 'Yes' and 'No'. At the end of the festival the 'Yes' bin was full, so they went into work the next day and resigned.

At first, finding investment was a problem until an American businessman, Maurice Pinto, put up the £250,000 they needed to get started. With a fresh image and careful use of social media for promotion, Innocent soon became one of the fastest growing companies in the UK and enjoyed a significant period of success. However, some of its fans were disappointed when, in April 2009, Coca-Cola® bought a small stake in the company for 30 million pounds. There was further negative publicity when, a year later, the multinational increased its stake to 58% for about 60 million. Innocent now operates from its headquarters in London as a subsidiary of Coca-Cola.

Despite any issues they've had, Innocent continues to innovate and the product range now consists of vegetable pots and other healthy, natural products as well as smoothies, and the company is constantly working on new lines. Innocent sells to over ten thousand retailers in 13 European countries, and its market is constantly growing.

So what is it that makes Innocent an ethical company? Apart from only using packaging that can be recycled, it uses only 100% natural products and each year gives 10% of its profits to charities in the countries where its fruit comes from.

Innocent wasn't the first company to tap into the fruit drink market, but it was one of the first. It's always important to be different from the competition and, with Innocent, the combination of ethics and clever marketing is a recipe for success.

02 WORK–LIFE BALANCE

 1.03

A: Hi, Eddie. How are you?

B: Oh, hello, Jennie. I'm fine. And you?

A: Fine thanks. How's Fiona?

B: Oh, she's okay. She's got a new job.

A: Really? That's good.

B: Well, yes, I suppose so, but I'm worried she's working too hard.

A: Oh, dear. Does it involve long hours?

B: Officially 40 hours, but she often works late. We don't see her at home much.

A: What's she doing?

B: It's the same company – you know, educational software – but she's regional marketing manager for Latin America now.

A: Sounds impressive. What does it involve?

B: Quite a lot! Apart from being in charge of the sales reps she also works on new product development and the whole marketing strategy of the company.

A: Does it mean a lot of travelling?

B: It seems to. At least a couple of trips a month.

A: I see.

B: I don't mind that. It's the weekends that cause problems.

A: Does she have to work weekends?

B: Not every weekend, but we can never make plans.

A: Oh, dear. How much holiday does she get?

B: It's not bad. Three weeks a year. But that's a long way off.

A You're being a bit negative. Does she enjoy it?

B: It's hard work, but I think she enjoys the challenge.

A: But you're not very happy.

B: I'm happy for her. The money's good and it's great for her career, but there is a downside.

A: Well, it's always difficult at the beginning. Anyway, give her my regards. Why don't we go for a drink sometime?

B: Okay, I will and yes, I'd like that.

03 TELEPHONE TALK

 1.04

A

A: Yes?

B: I'd like to speak to Derek LaMotte, please.

A: Who?

B: Derek LaMotte. Is that ILM?

A: What number did you want?

B: 0837 621 882.

A: No, I'm afraid you've got the wrong number.

 1.05

B

You have one message from 903586759 at 18.30 on April 1st: Hi, it's Dave here …

 1.06

C

C: This is the BetaGuide directory service. Donna speaking. Which city?

D: I'm calling from Portsmouth. Can you give me the number of Budget Car Rental, please?

C: Just one moment. I have three numbers.

D: Oh. I need to call them to report a breakdown.

C: Okay. It must be this one.

D: I think the number ...

E: The number you require is 0453678234. The number you require is 0453678234.

 1.07

D

F: UKN Systems. Janet speaking.

G: Morning. My name's Peter Bland from Pressic SA. I arranged to meet Derek LaMotte at a factory out here on the Houghton Industrial Estate, but I can't find it. Could you give me his mobile number so I can ask him where it is?

F: Err, yes. Just one moment.

G: It's probably just around the corner.

F: It's 0766 349 3782.

G: I'm sorry. Could you say that again more slowly?

F: 0766 349 3782.

G: Right. Got it. Thanks.

F: Bye.

G: Yeah. Goodbye.

 1.08

E

Remember, you have the chance to win £1,000. Ring now on 090 238 6980. I'll repeat that for you. If you know the answer, phone us now on 090 238 6980.

 1.09

A

A: InterAir, can I help you?

B: Yes, please. I'd like some information about a flight arriving from Munich.

A: Yes. Do you know what the flight number is?

B: The flight number? I'm not sure. I know it leaves Munich at 17.30.

A: Oh, yes, that's IA 345.

B: Yes, that's it. Could you tell me what time it gets in?

A: Yes, the arrival time is 19.10.

B: 19.10. Do you know if there's any delay?

A: No, the flight is on time.

B: Right, thank you very much.

A: You're welcome. Goodbye.

 1.10

A

A: Can I have extension 305, please?

B: I'm afraid the line is engaged. Will you hold?

 1.11

B

A: Could I just check that? You need 50 units by Friday, and Mr Johansson can contact you on 943 694 726.

B: Yes, that's correct.

A: Right, Mr Smith. I'll give him the message as soon as he's free.

 1.12

C

A: ... and it really isn't good enough.

B: Yes, Mr Wright. I understand what you're saying and I apologize for the error. As soon as Mr Downs is back I'll ask him to get in contact with you. I'm really sorry about this.

A: Right, thank you. I realize it's not your fault.

 1.13

D

A: Could I have the sales department, please?

B: One moment, please. Just putting you through now.

 1.14

E

A: Shonagh Clark speaking.

B: Hello, I'm phoning about your letter of 12th June.

A: Have you got a reference number, please?

 1.15

F

A: This is Jorgen Bode here. Could I speak to Jean Simmons, please?

B: Oh, I'm sorry, Mr Bode, but Ms Simmons isn't in the office right now. Can I ask her to call you back? Or I can contact her on her mobile if it's urgent.

 1.16

A: Hello, could I speak to Barry White, please?

B: Speaking. How can I help you?

A: Hello, Mr White. My name is Schmidt, from AMC Elevator.

B: Yes, I think I've heard of you.

A: I'm in charge of the customer support department. I'm phoning to ask for an estimate. It's for a service manual we're preparing.

B: Oh, yes. I don't think we've done anything for you before.

A: No, that's right. We're in the process of updating all our manuals. If the price is right, it will mean quite a lot of work.

B: I see. Well, could you give me the details, then?

A: Yes, it's for a manual of just over 100 pages.

B: 100 pages. Could you tell me what size?

A: It's in A5. We want to print 20,000. But I'd like estimates for 10,000 and 30,000 as well.

B: Okay. Is it in colour?

A: No, it's in black and white. Mainly text. The cover is in colour, though. I can put it all on a memory stick for you. Is that all right?

B: Yes, that would be perfect. Could I just read my notes back?

A: Yes, go ahead.

B: You want quotes for print runs of 10,000, 20,000 and 30,000 of an A5 100-page manual in black and white. The cover is in colour and you'll be supplying the material on a memory stick.

A: That's right.

B: Would you like me to visit you with some samples?

A: Yes, okay.

B: Would tomorrow morning suit you?

A: No, I'm out of the office tomorrow. How about Friday? About ten o'clock?

B: Friday ... the 16th ... at ten. That's fine. I'll bring the estimates with me and we can discuss the details then.

A: Fine.

B: Oh, could you give me the address?

A: 54 Eisenhower Lane North, Lombard.

B: And your telephone number?

A: 630 953 3340.

B: 630 953 3340. Right. Maybe you could give me your email?

A: Yes, it's schmidt@amcelevator.com

B: Can I just check that? schmidt, at amcelevator, dot, com.

A: Yes, that's right.

B: Okay, then, Mr Schmidt. See you on Friday.

A: Great. Goodbye for now.

B: Bye.

04 NETWORKING

 1.17

Conversation 1

A: Hello, do you mind if I join you?

B: Er, no, not at all.

A: How do you do? My name's Rick Van Looy.

B: Hi. Pleased to meet you. I'm Florent Rondele.

A: Are you from around here, then?

B: No, but my company has a store in town. Actually, I live in France.

A: So, what do you do, Florent?

B: I'm in marketing. I work for a retail company. We deal mainly in leisure goods.

A: Do you mean sports equipment?

B: Well, both sports and casual wear. Clothes, shoes, accessories, stuff like that. We have stores in several countries.

A: Sounds like a big operation. How many stores have you got?

B: Nearly 50 in total. And what line of business are you in, Rick?

A: Well, quite similar really. I'm a sales manager for a large Dutch clothing firm, Verweij Fashion – do you know it?

B: Yes, of course. Are you opening a store here, then?

A: Yes, we're looking at possible sites at the moment.

B: Hmm. That can be a slow process. Rick, do you fancy something to drink?

A: Erm, yeah, thanks.

B: Come on, then. There's a table free over there.

1.18

Conversation 2

A: Excuse me, does this belong to you?

B: Oh, thank you very much.

A: It was on the floor.

B: Yes, I was looking for it just now. I wanted to finish this crossword. I'm feeling a bit groggy, actually.

A: Yes, it's a long flight.

B: Isn't it? Have you got the time?

A: Yes, it's ... erm ... just after midnight.

B: So, do we land soon?

A: Yes, in about half an hour.

B: Oh, good. Do you know Bangkok?

A: Yes, I live there. Is this your first trip there?

B: Yes, it is actually.

A: On business, I suppose?

B: Yes, I'm visiting a supplier.

A: Oh, really? I wonder if I ...

 1.19

A: Do you know Jan Nowacki?

B: Yes, isn't he Director of Business Development at Pepsico in Europe?

A: Not any longer. Now he's the Public Relations Manager at the National Bank of Poland.

B: The National Bank of Poland, that's interesting. Do you have any contact with him in your work?

A: Not really, but I occasionally play golf with him.

B: What's he like?

A: He's a nice guy. You'd like him.

05 INTERNET HISTORIES

1.20

With over one billion downloads, Angry Birds™ is perhaps the largest mobile app success so far. It has been praised for its successful combination of addictive games, humorous style, and low price. There are versions of Angry Birds for personal computers and games consoles, a market for merchandise featuring its characters and even long-term plans for a feature film or television series. Here is its history.

In early 2009 a designer, Jaakko Iisalo, presented the idea for a new game to his colleagues at Finnish computer game developer, Rovio Entertainment. The game featured some angry-looking birds. They liked the basic idea, but decided to give the birds some pigs as an enemy because of an outbreak of 'swine flu' at the time. They estimated the initial costs of developing the game were €100,000. After a long period of development, in December 2009, in partnership with Chillingo, Rovio published Angry Birds on Apple®'s App Store. In March 2010, Angry Birds achieved top-selling app status on the USA's App Store, where it stayed until October that year. Also in March, they launched a version of the game for Facebook. In October 2010, Rovio released the first version of the game for Android, and experienced more than one million downloads in the first 24 hours and two million in its first weekend. Throughout 2010, versions for other platforms appeared. The company claimed revenues of over $100,000 a month just for the advertising on the free version of the game.

In December 2010, on the anniversary of its first release, Rovio announced over 50 million downloads, including 12 million on Apple's iOS devices and 10 million on Android.

In April 2011, the UK Appy Awards named Angry Birds as both the 'Best Game App' and 'App of the Year'. In May 2012, the different versions of the game reached the one billion downloads' mark. At the Electronic Entertainment Expo in Los Angeles in June 2012, Rovio and distribution partner Activision revealed plans to bring Angry Birds and two of its spin-off games (the Angry Birds Trilogy) to the PlayStation 3, Xbox 360 and Nintendo 3DS systems, taking advantage of their unique features, such as glasses-free 3D visuals. It's been quite a success story!

 1.21

How old is the Internet? Different experts suggest different dates. It depends on what they understand the Internet to be.

We know that in 1965, the Advanced Research Projects Agency (ARPA), under the US Department of Defence, began work on a system to connect computers. They called the project ARPANET.

On September 2nd, 1969, in a laboratory at the University of California, Professor Leonard Kleinrock connected the first two machines. For many people, that day the Internet was born. The next month they sent the first message to a computer at Stanford University.

By January 1970, ARPANET connected computers in four American universities, and by the following year there were 23 in the system, connecting different universities and research institutes. In 1973, Ray Tomlinson sent the first email via ARPANET. In the same year the Net went international, connecting computers in England and Norway.

The next step was to connect different networks and to create an 'Internetwork'. In 1974, Bob Kahn and Vincent Cerf invented a software called TCP/IP that connected networks using different operating systems. On January 1st, 1983, this software became the universal language of the Internet – many experts think that this event was the real birth of the Internet because it made it possible to link different networks in one web.

More and more networks joined the system and the number of connected computers increased dramatically, from 10,000 in 1984 to 100,000 in 1987. By the early 1990s, the network was accessible to anyone in the world with a computer. In 1992, the number of hosts reached 1,000,000.

In 1993, two programmers, Marc Andreessen and Eric Bina, launched the first version of Mosaic – the first graphics-based browser of the type we all use today – which made the Internet an easy means to browse websites, get information and spread news.

06 ORDERS

1.22

A: S–A–G, can I help you?

B: Yes, could I speak to John Bird?

A: I'm afraid he's not in the office right now. Can I take a message?

B: Oh dear! It's an urgent order – we need five hydraulic pumps by 22nd June.

A: Just a minute. Could you tell me your name, please?

B: Yes, I'm sorry. It's Elena Moretti, from Stern Hydraulics in Switzerland.

A: Right, I'll take down the details and get John to contact you. Did you say five units?

B: Yes, the reference is SG 94321.

A: SG 94321 – five units.

B: Yes, that's right. But the important thing is the delivery date – 22nd June.

A: I don't think that will be a problem.

B: Good, it's for a new customer.

A: I see. Right, when John comes in, I'll tell him immediately. Could you confirm the order by email?

B: Yes, of course. Thanks very much.

A: You're welcome. Goodbye.

B: Goodbye.

 1.23

A: Could I speak to Elena Moretti, please?

B: Speaking. Is that John?

A: Yes. Hello, Elena. I'm just phoning back about your order.

B: Yes, it's quite urgent; I hope you can help.

A: Don't worry. I've got all the details in your email. No problem – we're happy to help.

B: That's good. I was quite worried about it.

A: It should be fine. Can I help you with anything else?

B: No, thank you. I hope we get more business from this customer.

A: Yes, of course. Okay, I'll be in touch. Bye for now.

B: Goodbye.

1.24

A: S–A–G, can I help you?

B: Yes, this is Elena Moretti from Stern Hydraulics. Could I speak to John Bird, please?

A: Oh, hello, Elena. I'm afraid John isn't here at the moment. Can I take a message?

B: Yes, he sent me an order confirmation – the reference is DH010601 – but the delivery date is wrong.

A: Oh, dear. Can you give me the details?

B: Yes, it says 7th July, but the agreed delivery date was 22nd June. It's really important.

A: I see. Well, I'll tell him as soon as he comes in.

B: Thank you. I'm not at all happy about this. A lot depends on this order.

A: Right, Elena, leave it with me. I'm terribly sorry about this.

B: No, it's not your fault. Just ask John to phone me.

A: All right, then. Bye for now.

B: Goodbye.

🔘 1.25

A: CiclosCiclone, can I help you?

B: Yes, I'm phoning from Ballyclare, in Northern Ireland. Could I speak to Diego Martin, please?

A: I'm afraid he's out of the office right now. Can I help you?

B: Well, I sent him a text message and he hasn't replied. It's really quite urgent.

A: Can you tell me what it's about?

B: It's a bit complicated to explain. I need a copy of a certificate for customs. Maybe he didn't get my message. Can I just check his mobile – 07636 746384?

A: Let me check. Yes, that's the right number. Listen, why don't you send the details to me by email and I'll send you a copy of the certificate as an attached pdf?

B: Yes, that's a good idea. What's your email address?

A: Jim, that's J-I-M, dot, J-F-A, at CiclosCiclone, dot, net. CiclosCiclone is all one word.

B: Can I just check that? Jim, dot, JFA, at CiclosCiclone, dot, net.

A: Yes, that's right.

B: Great. I'll deal with the email straight away. By the way, my name's David, David Holmbrook. And you are, Jim ...?

A: Kutz, Jim Kutz. Don't worry about the certificate. You'll have it by this afternoon.

B: Okay, thanks for your help.

A: You're welcome. Bye.

🔘 1.26

A: Have we got the details of the order from David Holmbrook?

B: No, but don't worry, I'll ring him now.

A: I tried – there's no answer.

B: Well, I'll send him an email, then.

A: You can't – our server is down.

B: Never mind – I'll send him a fax.

A: I don't think he has a fax machine.

B: Well, in that case, I'll write him a letter before I leave the office.

A: Oh, come on, that will take far too long.

B: So, we'll fly out to see him!

A: Oh, that's a bit expensive ...

07 HOTELS

🔘 1.27

A: Hello. My connecting flight, IB621, was delayed so I've missed the flight to Caracas.

B: Yes, sir. I'm sorry about that. You're booked on the next flight.

A: Yes, but it's not until 11 tonight, right?

B: Yes. I'm afraid there's nothing before.

A: That's nearly eight hours to wait. Can you recommend a hotel I could try?

B: You could try the Travel Inn. It's not far from the terminal building.

A: Thanks. I really need somewhere to sleep.

B: Would you like me to phone for you, sir?

A: No, that's okay. I need to stretch my legs anyway. Thanks very much.

🔘 1.28

A: Good afternoon.

B: Good afternoon. Do you have any rooms available?

A: Yes, sir. Is it just for tonight?

B: Yes. Well, actually I have a flight at 11 this evening so I'll check out in a few hours. I really need to get some sleep. Is it possible to pay for a room by the hour? I mean, do you have any reduced rates or anything?

A: Err ... no, sir. I'm afraid not. I have to charge you for the whole night. I'm sorry, but that's the hotel policy.

B: Well, never mind. I'll take it anyway.

A: Okay, could I see your passport please? And I'll need a credit card.

B: Yes, of course. Here you are.

A: Would you like anything sent up to your room?

B: Yes, please. I'd like a tomato and cheese sandwich and a sparkling water. Oh, and I need to send some emails. Is there Internet access available?

A: Yes, of course. You can pick up the hotel Wi-Fi in every room. And I'll have the food sent up right away.

B: Right, thank you.

A: You're welcome. Have a good stay.

🔘 1.29

A: Room service. My name is Johan. Can I help you?

B: Yes, this is room 301. Could I have an early morning call, please?

A: Certainly, sir. What time would you like the call?

B: At half past six.

A: 6.30. No problem. Would you like breakfast sent up to your room?

B: No, thanks. I'll have it in the dining room.

A: The dining room doesn't open for breakfast until 7.30.

B: Oh, in that case I will have it in my room. Just coffee and a croissant.

A: Coffee and a croissant. Anything else?

B: No, that's all.

A: Okay. Good night, sir.

B: Thank you. Good night.

08 TELLING STORIES

🔘 1.30

A: Look at that car!

B: Yes, very nice. It's a Porsche 911.

A: Did I ever tell you about the time I had a ride in a Porsche?

B: No, I don't think so.

A: It was when I was a student. I was hitchhiking in Europe and a man in a

Porsche stopped. He took me all the way across Austria. We went about 220 kilometres an hour all the way.

B: What about the police?

A: Well, they stopped us about four times, but this chap just showed some identity card and they waved us on.

B: Was he someone important, then?

A: I don't know, I didn't ask. I suppose he was some sort of high-ranking official. Anyway, it was the fastest I've ever been in a car.

🔘 1.31

a   Yes, that was a long time ago. It was while I was living in Italy. I had this apartment in the centre of Milan ...

b   I can remember what happened. It was before I started working here. I was working on a temporary basis ...

c   No, it wasn't until much later. It was after I left university. I'd got my degree ...

d   Oh, yes, that reminds me. It was when I was working at ICL. I was in the marketing department ...

e   I had more time in those days. It was before I got married. In fact, I hadn't even met Mary ...

f   The timing was awful. It was just after my children were born. And there I was without ...

g   I'd just arrived in London. I was looking for a job. I bought the paper every day ...

h   Yes, I was still studying at the time. I was doing my Masters in the States. At the Harvard Business School, in fact ...

i   I was 19. I was studying at Cambridge. Things weren't going very well ...

j   No, it was with a different set-up. I was working for a small company north of here. One day the boss walked into ...

k   I was having a gap year after university. I was travelling through Asia. I'd just arrived in Ho Chi Minh City and ...

l   It happened last March. I was staying at the Continental Hotel in Prague. Lovely hotel, I recommend it.

🔘 1.32

1   **A:** Did you ever hitchhike when you were a student?

   B: Yes, but it was a long time ago, and I hated waiting in the rain, so if I could, I took a train ...

2   **A:** Have you ever had a car accident?

   B: No, I'm glad to say, but I nearly had one this morning! I pulled out and didn't see a motorbike. It was too close for comfort.

3   **A:** Have you ever been to Rome?

   B: No, but I'd love to see the Coliseum one day. I once spent a few days in the north of Italy.

4   **A:** Have you ever lost any money on the stock exchange?

   B: No and I've never made any either. I don't own any shares now.

5   **A:** Did you ever fail an exam at school?

B: Not at school, but I did at university. Actually I arrived late and they didn't even let me take it. It was a disaster.

6 **A:** Have you ever been camping?

B: Yes, lots of times. Actually we bought a camper van last year. We go somewhere most weekends.

7 **A:** Have you ever played a video game in 3D?

B: I didn't know you could. I've seen films with it though. I don't like having to wear those special glasses much.

8 **A:** Have you ever done anything illegal?

B: Not unless you count speeding and parking fines. Unless I've just forgotten something else!

09 SPIRIT OF ENTERPRISE

 1.33

A: ... next on today's programme we talk to David O'Brian about his new book on entrepreneurial success *The Sky is the Limit*. So David, are entrepreneurs born or created?

B: Well, I think they're basically born, but obviously for an enterprise to be a success there are certain key business skills which have to be learnt. Business studies courses provide an opportunity for the potential entrepreneur to get the skills without taking any risks while they do it. In other words, they can learn from the mistakes and experience of others.

A: So you don't think the classic MBA course does any harm?

B: No, not at all, but on the other hand an MBA is probably more important when you want to get a job working for someone else and not set up your own business.

A: Tell us about some of the people you feature in the book.

B: Well, Mike Clare, the founder of the bed shop chain, Dreams, and Michael Welch, the entrepreneur behind car tyre distributor, Blackcircles.com, are both good examples of people who started work when they left school. They first picked up knowledge and skills while they worked for someone else, but each knew that his real mission in life was to be an entrepreneur – to set up a business, take risks and make a lot of money.

A: Apart from their first names, do they have anything else in common?

B: Well, Welch started his business when he was a lot younger, but actually they do have certain things in common. For example, both have made customer service a major selling point. This sounds obvious, but bad customer service is often the reason why businesses fail. Both businesses rely on efficient distribution and they've been successful at building up their networks.

A: Surely there is more to it than that?

B: Well yes, of course. They both saw an opportunity in a market where they felt they could do something better than the competition and had the confidence to take a risk. There is always a certain amount of luck involved, but the other thing I think they have in common is a capacity for hard work. They have worked incredibly hard to get where they are today.

 1.34

Inditex is a global fashion retailer with headquarters in Arteixo, Spain. It owns several retailers, including its flagship store, Zara. The multinational company has over 5,000 stores worldwide with 120,000 employees. The origins of Inditex go back to 1963 when Amancio Ortega Gaona started his career as a clothing manufacturer. Business was good for the young Spaniard, with several factories opening in the next decade. Finally, in 1975, the first Zara opened its doors in downtown La Coruña in Galicia, Spain.

From the start, Ortega wanted to make affordable and fashionable clothes, and this has remained at the core of Zara's business model. There are four key factors which are central to the company's business process and which have contributed to the huge success of this clothing chain. The first is turnover. In order to keep up with the latest fashions, Zara clothing has a very short shelf life. While competitors such as H&M and The Gap may be restricted to seasonal fashion trends, Zara's stock changes regularly in order to meet customer needs. With 60% of production taking place in Arteixo, that demand can be met quickly and efficiently.

The next two factors are variety and quantity, which are just as important as each other. The company makes small batches of each product, which removes the expense of large storage warehouses and ensures that stock can be sold at full price – sales rarely happen in Zara stores. Finally, Zara prides itself on communication with its end-users and has invested in an IT system which can track purchases from store to store and maintain contact with in-house managers who get feedback directly from the customer.

The customer remained central to Inditex's business philosophy throughout its expansion in the 1990s and 2000s. During this time it created and acquired additional retailers such as Pull & Bear, Massimo Dutti, Bershka, Stradivarius, Oysho, Zara Home and Uterqüe. Under the watchful eye of Ortega and current CEO Pablo Isla, Inditex's sales for 2012 were an astounding €13.79 billion. The only question now is, what next?

The obvious next step would be to continue with international expansion; regions such as the Middle East, Asia and South and North America are all potential growth markets for Inditex. However, what they gain in profit may be lost by high operating costs and increased competition, and the Inditex system and brand could become diluted. One option is to raise the company's online presence, which offers the freedom to expand without the financial burden.

One thing is for certain: Inditex is a company which is constantly moving forward, and always looking for new opportunities and ways to grow. It seems inevitable that the company will continue to expand and, with Zara leading the 'fast fashion' movement and appearing on more and more high streets across the world, Inditex will be a retail powerhouse long into the future.

10 STRESSED TO THE LIMIT

 1.35
Interview 1

A: According to statistics, around 75% of all visits to the doctor are the result of work-related stress. Do you think you suffer from stress? That's the question we're asking in the streets of Edinburgh. Excuse me, I'm from the radio programme *Work Today*. We're doing a survey on stress. Would you mind answering some questions?

B: Eh, well, actually, I'm in a bit of a hurry, but ... erm ... go on, then.

A: Thank you. What's your job?

B: I'm an accountant.

A: Do you suffer from stress in your work?

B: Eh, yes, I do, I think.

A: What symptoms do you notice?

B: Erm, I get a lot of headaches and I sleep very badly.

A: And what causes your stress?

B: It's my boss. He's a real ... well, let's just say he doesn't exactly make life easy. He always wants things done for yesterday.

A: Thank you very much.

 1.36
Interview 2

A: ... and what do you do?

C: I work in a shop.

A: Do you suffer from stress?

C: No, not at work, I don't. I find being at home more stressful.

A: Why's that?

C: Well, I've got three children and my mother's ill. She lives with us. And my husband ... well, he doesn't help much.

A: And do you have any physical symptoms?

C: Well, I get a bit on edge at times and then I get this horrible rash on my neck.

A: So, stress is a problem in your life.

C: Yes, definitely.

 1.37
Interview 3

A: ... and you, sir. Do you suffer from stress?

D: Well, to tell the truth, I'm off work at the moment because of it.

A: Really, what do you do?

D: I'm a teacher. I work with teenagers and I don't know why, but every year they seem to get worse.

A: Yes, that does sound stressful.

D: Everyone thinks teaching's an easy option because of the holidays, but you get to a point where you just can't handle it any longer. You lose control.

A: Well, I hope things get better for you.

D: Thanks, but I think that basically the solution is probably to change jobs. Fortunately, I'm still young enough to do that.

A: Right. Good luck, then.

 1.38

Interview 4

A: Can I ask you if you suffer from stress?

E: Who? Me? No, not at all. I don't understand what it is, really.

A: And what do you do for a living?

E: I'm a self-employed architect. I work for myself.

A: I see, and what's your secret?

E: I'm sorry?

A: I mean, how do you avoid getting stressed?

E: I think it's all down to a philosophy of life. I just take each day as it comes. I don't worry about things. What I say is that if you've got a problem, solve it. And if you can't because there's no solution, there's no point in worrying because that won't help.

A: So, you think avoiding stress is to do with mental attitude, not what you do?

E: Yes, that's basically it.

A: Well, thanks very much.

E: Not at all.

11 TOP JOBS

 2.01

In July 2012, Marcos Galperin, founder and CEO of MercadoLibre, was named as an 'Ernst and Young World Entrepreneur of the Year'. His company is the world's second-largest online auction site. Since September 2001, it has been a partner company of the US auctioneer, eBay™, which acquired 19.5% of MercadoLibre in exchange for its Brazilian subsidiary, Ibazar.com.br.

Galperin grew up in Buenos Aires, but went to college in the United States. After graduating, he returned home and worked for three and a half years at the largest oil company in Argentina. He then went back to the United States to do an MBA at Stanford. While Galperin was there, he pitched his ideas for an Internet company to John Muse, the founder of a private equity fund. Muse thought the ideas showed potential and agreed to invest.

Galperin has known the co-founder of MercadoLibre, Hernan Kazar, since they were students together at Stanford. In fact, after creating the business plan and securing financing, Galperin recruited several classmates there to help manage the business. Since its creation in 1999, MercadoLibre has grown dramatically to become the largest online commerce platform in Latin America, with sites across nine countries, including Brazil, Argentina and Mexico.

Back in the 1990s there were many start-up companies trying to become the Latin American eBay. Galperin was different to the others in that he focused more on IT and the platform and less on marketing or

PR. As a result, his company flourished while the rest went bankrupt. Following the rise of smartphones and tablet computers, it modified its original technology so it could run its services on mobile devices and allow external developers to build applications. Company sales grew 37% between 2007 and 2011, and MercadoLibre is the eighth highest-ranked retail site for traffic in the world. During 2011, there were almost 53 million products sold, an increase of 35% from 2010. Every month the company manages more than 1.2 million transactions, attracting 750,000 buyers, and business has more than doubled every year for the last five years.

 2.02

A: Good morning. Could I speak to Peter Davis, please?

B: Speaking.

A: Oh, hello, Mr Davis. My name is John Lindsay.

B: What can I do for you, Mr Lindsay?

A: It's more a case of what I can do for you ... Erm, how long have you worked for Blueprint International, Mr Davis?

B: For about six years. Why do you ask?

A: And before that you worked for Navigate for three years?

B: Yes, I joined them as a trainee manager when I left university. But ... what is this about?

A: And you were made head of the International Division a year ago. How's it going?

B: Very well, thank you. Now, could you tell me what you want, Mr Lindsay?

A: I'd like to talk to you about an extremely interesting career opportunity. I work for People Search, the management consultants. We've been approached by a client who's looking for someone with just your professional profile.

B: Oh, I see. So that's what it's about. Listen, Mr Lindsay, I'm really quite busy and ...

A: Yes, I understand that, but you should know I'm talking about a considerable salary increase. You've been married for a couple of years now and recently became a father, I believe.

B: What's that got to do with it?

A: Well, think about your family and the financial possibilities of an advantageous career move at this moment in your life. I think you should at least talk to me.

B: Erm, well, I suppose so. What's the name of the company?

A: I'd rather not say over the phone. Perhaps we could meet to discuss things further?

B: I'm not sure I'm that interested ... Blueprint International have been very good to me.

A: Oh, come on, Peter! What are the real prospects in your present post? You've got as far as you can in Blueprint. Do you want to be in the same place ten

years from now? At least find the time to talk to us.

B: I'd like to think about it. Can I phone you back?

A: No, I'd prefer to phone you back myself in a couple of days. In the meantime, think about what I've said. A more stimulating work situation, not to mention a considerable rise in salary ... Talk it over with your wife.

B: Fair enough.

A: Oh, and one more thing, Peter. I'd appreciate it if you didn't mention this call to anyone in your company, okay?

B: Yes, yes, all right. So, you'll call me, then?

A: That's right. In a couple of days. We'll arrange a meeting somewhere. Bye for now, then.

B: Bye.

12 CONVERSATION GAMBITS

 2.03

Conversation 1

A: Excuse me, are you here for the ITM conference?

B: Yes, that's right.

A: Me too. Do you know where to register?

B: I think it's over there.

A: Oh, yes, right. I'm Paulo, by the way.

B: Hello, Paulo, I'm Kate. Let's go and register.

 2.04

Conversation 2

C: Phew! Is it me, or is it boiling in here?

D: Yes, they always seem to have the heating on full.

C: So, it's not your first time?

D: No, it's my fourth time here.

C: Oh, right, so you're an old hand. I'm Boris.

D: David. Pleased to meet you.

 2.05

Conversation 3

E: Is it my mobile phone, or is there some problem with coverage here?

F: Oh, hang on. No, mine seems to be working okay.

E: Typical – flat batteries and nowhere to charge up.

F: Can I lend you mine?

E: Oh, that's very kind, but I was expecting a call on this number.

F: I see.

E: My name's Nadine, by the way. From Xanadu Electronics.

F: Pleased to meet you. I'm Miko.

 2.06

Conversation 4

G: Excuse me, do you know anything about this speaker?

H: No, I'm sorry, I don't.

G: I can't find my programme notes.

H: Oh, here. Borrow mine.

G: Thanks. By the way, I'm Bill Smart from Silicon Technologies.

H: Right, how do you do? I'm Kazuo Yamada from Lexico.

 2.07

A: Excuse me. Would you mind if I had a quick look at your newspaper?

B: Er, no, go ahead. I've finished with it.

A: There's just something I want to check out.

B: No problem. Take your time.

A: Thanks. By the way, my name's Allan.

B: Nice to meet you.

A: Here's your paper then. Thanks very much.

B: Don't mention it.

A: I'm glad to say we won.

B: Sorry?

A: The football results.

B: Oh, I see.

A: I think I'll have a coffee. Can I get you something? If you don't have anything else to do, that is.

B: I was just about to go, actually, but … yes, why not, … Al, I think you said your name was?

A: Allan, Allan Vilkas.

 2.08

B: I'm Sean, Sean O'Malley.

A: Pleased to meet you, Sean. Can I get you something?

B: A coffee, please.

A: Right. Two coffees, please.

C: Right, sir.

B: So, Allan, where are you from?

A: Well, I was born in Lithuania, but I've lived in Germany most of my life. Are you from here?

B: Yes. What do you think of Belfast?

A: Well, I've only just arrived today and it's my first visit, but it seems very nice. Lots of character.

B: Are you here on business?

A: Yes, that's right. I have a meeting tomorrow. I'm a bit nervous about it.

B: I'm sure it'll go all right. How long are you staying?

A: Just a couple of days. I go back on Thursday morning. I was just looking at your paper to see how Bayern Munich did yesterday. Do you like football?

B: If it's a good match, but I'm not that keen. Actually, I prefer golf myself.

A: Do you mean you play golf?

B: That's right.

A: I play myself, but not very seriously. I find it relaxing though.

B: Yes so do I, I love spending … Oh, well, Allan, it's getting late. I have to be off. Thanks for the drink, and good luck with your meeting.

A: Right, it was nice talking to you.

B: It was nice talking to you too. Cheerio, then.

A: Bye.

13 AIR TRAVEL

 2.09

Conversation 1

A: Good morning. Is this where I check in for flight RA 264?

B: Yes. Can you give me your reference number, please?

A: I'm afraid I've lost the paper I had it on, but here's my passport.

B: I'm sorry, but if you haven't got the reference number, I can't check you in. You'll have to go to the main desk over there. They'll give it to you.

A: But can't you look it up? You've got my name.

B: I'm afraid not, Sir.

A: Do I have to queue up again?

B: No. Just come to the front.

A: Okay.

B: Next, please.

 2.10

Conversation 2

A: Can I have your reference number and passport, please?

B: Here you are.

A: You've just got one suitcase to check in?

B: Yes, this one.

A: I'm afraid it's over 15 kilos. You'll have to pay excess baggage.

B: It's only just over, isn't it?

A: Actually it's 17 kilos.

B: Are you sure? How much will it cost me?

A: It'll be £30, but you have to pay over there at the main desk.

B: What, over there? There's a really long queue. Can't I pay here?

A: No, I'm sorry. But come straight to the front when you come back.

B: Okay. Thanks.

 2.11

Book as early as possible – within three weeks of the flight. With an early booking you can choose the seat you want. However, if you book months in advance, you'll be too early for a seat assignment.

If you use a travel agent, make sure they have a record of your seating preferences – aisle or window. Tell them you want to sit close to the front. If you sit at the front, you'll get on and off the plane faster.

When you receive your ticket and boarding pass or e-ticket confirmation, check the seat assignment. Mistakes happen. If you have time, cross reference with the airline seating chart.

If you are unable to confirm a seat, be sure to get to the airport early – at least 45 to 60 minutes before the flight.

If you do have an assignment for your preferred seat, don't check in too late. Those few minutes reading magazines at the newsstand can translate into hours of discomfort in the air.

Finally, the gate check-in attendant can be your best friend. Ask politely if there is a better seat available. Saying that you are claustrophobic might not hurt, but don't

feign an illness or say you're pregnant if you're not. There's no point in feeling guilty the entire flight.

If, in spite of your best efforts, you end up with the middle seat, here are some tips to cope:

If you are late boarding and have your choice of middle seats, go for the one up front near the exit.

Check out the aisle and window passengers. Do they look like they will be self-contained and give you plenty of room? Observe their body language and trust your instincts.

Capture as much personal space as you can right away. Dominate the two armrests. This will force your seatmates to give you more space. Be polite, but establish your territory. After all, they have 'personal space' on either side.

Don't work on your laptop during the flight. A cramped space becomes even more claustrophobic when you bring out the hardware. And don't try to read a newspaper. Stick to small paperbacks.

Although it is important to keep hydrated in the air, don't drink water by the gallon. If you climb over seatmates repeatedly to get to the bathroom, they'll get annoyed.

Get up once during the flight to stretch your legs, even if you don't have to use the restroom. This time away will allow your companions to move around as well and refresh the whole row.

 2.12

A: If I order 100 units, will you give me a price of 5.5 euros?

B: No, I'm sorry. I can't do that. On 150 units I'll give you a price of six euros.

A: Six euros. And what about payment?

B: Payment is within 60 days.

A: If we pay within 30 days, will you lower the price?

B: I'll go down to 5.5 euros if you order 200 units or more. That's my best offer.

A: Well, what about the guarantee?

14 HIRING AND FIRING

 2.13

Speaker 1

I think that these days you have to really sell yourself. Certainly this is what employers expect in the USA. You should show them how great and self-confident you are. Modesty isn't going to get you anywhere and no one is going to mind if you exaggerate a bit and dress things up to sound more impressive. Make the potential employer feel that, although this is the job you always wanted and of course you are the ideal person for it, if they don't snap you up, someone else will. So, they had better hire you before they lose the chance.

 2.14

Speaker 2

It's not often that qualifications and experience totally match up to an advertised post, so it's preferable to emphasize other qualities, like your willingness to learn and the fact that you work hard. In fact, you should be careful not to give the impression you are overqualified for the job. I think that employers are often more interested in things like loyalty and ability to fit in. A high-flier who knows too much can create a bad working atmosphere and break a team. Personally, I want the employer to think that I am going to be easy to work with and won't create too many waves.

 2.15

Speaker 3

No one likes a 'big head' but, on the other hand, don't be falsely modest either. Basically, your qualifications and experience tell their own story, so you're not going to impress anyone by adding a lot of adjectives like 'excellent' and 'outstanding' to your CV. Usually this will make an experienced recruitment officer suspicious. It doesn't hurt to acknowledge one or two weaknesses either – areas that you would like to improve and you want a chance to develop. Above all, be honest, because if you exaggerate or lie, in the end someone is going to catch you out and you'll end up looking stupid.

 2.16

Speaker 4

People's motivations interest employers. If you want to work for a specific company, tell them why, especially if you are changing jobs. Valid reasons would be that you are frustrated by the limitations of your present post, or that you can't fulfil the potential of your background and education. Don't whine, though, and don't blame your current employers: you've learnt a lot with them, but it's time to move on. Tell potential employers that you have a lot to offer, and all you need is an opportunity to show it. If someone gives you a break, they won't be disappointed.

 2.17

A: Right, shall we make a start? My name is Philip Rickett. I work in the human resources department and I'm responsible for recruitment.

B: Pleased to meet you.

A: Did you find us all right?

B: Yes, the map you sent me was very clear.

A: Good. Now, this is just a preliminary interview to check out some details. If you're successful, you'll go on to a more in-depth interview this afternoon. Is that all right?

B: Yes, I don't have to be back at work until tomorrow morning, so as long as I have time to drive back this evening, that's fine.

A: Do your present employers know where you are?

B: No. I asked for a day's unpaid leave for personal reasons. I didn't say why.

A: What don't you like about your current position?

B: Actually, there are a lot of things I do like about it, but no job is perfect. I think I am ready for more responsibility and when I saw your advert, I thought I should apply.

A: You know this job is a managerial position. How much managerial experience do you have? It's not very clear from your CV.

B: Well, in my present job I'm a management team coordinator.

A: Yes. Does that mean you're the leader of the team?

B: Not exactly. I assist the general manager in running the department.

A: Oh, I see. Are you a kind of personal assistant?

B: No, I think it's a bit more than that …

A: But are you a manager?

B: I suppose not.

A: It says in your CV that in your previous position you were an 'SPC professional'. What exactly does that mean? Is Sales Productivity Centre basically a sales department?

B: Yes, we provided backup for 20 salespeople from different sectors of the company.

A: Are you saying you were directly involved in sales?

B: No, it was more about providing support to help drive sales and increase productivity.

A: I see. So, what sort of work did the job involve?

B: I'd say it was a position that required a lot of time management skills and prioritizing of tasks. It gave me a lot of insight into the sales process.

A: Can you be a bit more specific, please?

B: Well, to be honest, some of the work was secretarial, but I am applying for your post because I'm capable of doing far more. I'd like more responsibility and to be able to use my studies and my languages.

A: Yes, your English is obviously excellent and you speak Spanish. Is your Spanish as good as your English?

B: Yes, it's not bad.

A: Could you tell me about your degree course … in Spanish?

B: I'm sorry? Oh, I beg your pardon … Well, I need a little time to think … Let's see …

15 TIME

 2.18

A: Hello.

B: Hello, is that Domingo?

A: Yes, speaking.

B: Hi, this is Joe. Look, I need you to tell me something about the new database. We're worried because it's behind schedule. What's the situation?

A: Well, yes, I'm sorry about the delay but there have been some problems with the application.

B: I appreciate that, but the system was supposed to be online last October. You didn't meet the deadline and it's now February. My boss is getting a bit nervous. And so am I.

A: Okay, okay. But you modified the requirements and the old system is not compatible with the new design. That means we have a different time frame.

B: What do you mean? How long is it going to take?

A: We need to make sure that migrating the data from the old database is going to go smoothly. We don't want to lose anything important. And then there are the security issues, but I think we should be ready by October.

B: I don't understand. Are you saying that the schedule for all this is now next October?

A: Yeah. It shouldn't take longer than that.

B: You're joking.

A: No, I'm not actually. It really is much more complicated than anyone anticipated.

B: Can you guarantee that you're giving us priority on this? Will it be on time?

A: Yeah, sure, you're at the top of the list.

B: Okay. Listen, is Jorgen there? I'd like to speak to him.

A: Hang on, I'll see if he's available.

 2.19

Conversation 1

A: Where are you going?

B: Well, I've finished everything I had to do so I'm going to leave early.

A: What about the sales predictions for next month?

B: Oh, I'd forgotten about that. I'll start on them tomorrow first thing. I've arranged to meet someone at five.

 2.20

Conversation 2

C: Have you planned Mr Logan's visit? What about lunch tomorrow?

D: I'm going to take him to The Redwing.

C: I seem to remember he's a vegetarian.

D: Is he? In that case, I'll phone to check they have a vegetarian menu.

 2.21

Conversation 3

E: Is everything confirmed for your trip to San Sebastián?

F: Yes, the plane goes to Bilbao. I'm going to take the train from there.

E: No, don't do that – it takes forever. The bus is much faster.

F: Is it? Well, I'll take the bus, then.

 2.22

Good afternoon. The subject of my presentation today is 'The Myth of Time Management'. There are thousands of books and online courses on the market which are designed to help people be better managers of their time. They all suggest techniques for using our time more efficiently. They recommend making 'to do' lists, prioritizing and not answering the phone as ways to make us more time efficient. But do these techniques really work?

They say that time is money, but time is not like other resources which we manage, such as materials and machines. Use of time depends to a large extent on personality and attitude, but also factors outside our control. Sometimes we can change our own behaviour, but time management really depends on changing the behaviour of the people around us and the demands they make on our time. This is always difficult and often impossible. As a result, you can be a very efficient user of your time – disciplined, organized and choosing the right moment to do vital tasks, yet still feel stressed and overworked. In fact, in many cases this is simply because you are being asked to do more than is possible in the time available.

The reality is that our use of time is usually about making choices that we don't in fact have. One of the recommended techniques is to close your door at certain times, or leave your voicemail to deal with calls. That's all very well, but if interruptions and dealing with unpredictable human problems are part of your work, then those techniques don't help very much.

Another time-management technique is to analyze what you are doing and decide if it is important or not. Well, I think most people of average intelligence can normally see the difference between activity which is useful and activity which is a waste of time. Unless they dislike their job or their employer, they will do useful things in their work time.

Time management may work with jobs with very defined tasks, where procedures and processes are very clear. Machine operators, for example, don't have to worry much about managing their time because the pace of work is imposed from outside. On the other hand, if you are faced with a task which involves creativity or problem-solving, how exactly to perform the task may not be clear. It could also be that you are in a job where you lack either the necessary skills or appropriate training to carry out your duties.

We have to remember that there will always be more work than time. This is what keeps us employed. How effectively you use your time is a question of ability, training and proper planning. But above all, it is about having a positive attitude towards your work, combined with reasonable expectations about how much you can do.

16 GETTING THINGS DONE

 2.23

Conversation 1

A: Oh, look outside!

B: What's up?

A: I've got to go to the Post Office to pick something up and it's raining. Could you lend me your umbrella?

B: Of course. As long as you don't lose it.

A: Oh, right. Don't worry, I won't.

 2.24

Conversation 2

C: Gert, I have a meeting with an agent this afternoon, and they're decorating my office.

D: Lucky you.

C: The thing is that I need somewhere quiet where we won't be interrupted. Could I use your office?

D: All right, as long as it's free by four. I've got a meeting myself.

C: Don't worry, it won't take that long.

 2.25

A: Richard, I wonder if I could ask you a favour?

B: Depends what it is.

A: I've got to go over to the warehouse to do something, and I haven't got my car. Would you lend me yours?

B: No way!

A: What?

B: I never lend my car! In any case, where's your car?

A: It's in the garage. Eh, I had a little accident.

B: And you expect me to trust you with mine?

A: It's just a minor scratch. Oh, don't worry. I'll think of something else.

 2.26

A: Sandra, we need someone to answer the phone from 2.00 till 4.00 while Julia is off sick. Could you do it?

B: From 2.00 to 4.00? It's not my hours.

A: I know, but you can take the time later on.

B: It's not the time. I'll have to get someone to pick the kids up from school. Isn't there anyone else?

A: No, there isn't. Look, I know it's inconvenient, but I can't think of any other solution.

B: Well, can't we just put the answering machine on for a couple of hours?

A: Not really. It creates such a bad impression. Listen, I'd do it myself, but I've got to be somewhere else.

B: I'm sure you would, but it's not my problem, is it?

A: No, it isn't, and obviously I can't force you to do it, but …

B: But?

A: … but on the other hand, if you do it, I'll see it as a personal favour.

B: I see. I don't really have much choice, do I? I hope it's just this time …

A: Yes, in principle, yes. But you never know. Your contract is up for renewal next month. Enough said?

B: Yeah, enough said.

 2.27

Conversation 1

A: Good afternoon, sir.

B: Hello. I'm on flight IB 603. I was wondering if there's any chance of an upgrade to business class?

A: Well, I don't know. It depends how crowded the flight is.

B: Yes, I quite understand, but I'd really appreciate it if you could have a look. I don't mind paying the extra. It's just that I've had a really hard day and it'd be

really nice to have a bit more space and comfort.

A: Just a minute, sir.

B: I'm sorry to put you to any trouble.

A: No, that's okay. Oh, yes, there's lots of space in business class. I think we can do it.

B: Oh, fantastic. How much is that?

A: That's all right, sir. Don't worry.

B: Oh, thank you ever so much.

A: You're welcome. Have a good flight.

 2.28

Conversation 2

A: Good evening, sir.

B: Look, I'm not at all happy with the room you've given me. It's on the wrong side of the hotel. It faces onto the road and it's far too noisy.

A: I'm sorry, sir. No one has ever said anything before.

B: I can't believe that. Are you going to change it?

A: I don't think I can, sir. We're a bit full tonight.

B: Look, I'm really tired, and the last thing I want to do is argue about my room. If you don't change it, I'll tell my company not to use this hotel again.

A: I'm sorry. There's no other room available.

B: Oh, come on.

A: There's nothing I can do.

B: What about some sort of discount, then?

A: I'm afraid I'm not authorized to offer a discount on your room.

B: So, I have to pay the full price for a noisy room. Great!

A: Sir, if you want, I can call you a taxi …

17 OFFICE GOSSIP

 2.29

A: Hi Quin. How's it going?

B: Trixy! Where have you been?

A: I had a few days' holiday owing to me.

B: Go anywhere interesting?

A: I wish! No, I went up north to stay with my parents.

B: So, you haven't heard the news.

A: What news?

B: About the 'restructuring'.

A: What restructuring?

B: They want to reorganize marketing and sales.

A: No! Really? Is it official?

B: No, but somebody overheard Gary talking to one of the management consultants.

A: What did he say?

B: Apparently he said that we were overstaffed in some areas.

A: Never!

B: Yes, this consultant told him they would have to let some people go.

A: But that's awful.

B: Yes, Gary asked him how many people it involved.

A: And what did he say?

B: He said it depended on individual performance and attitude.

A: Does that include Maureen?

B: What do you mean?

A: Well, you know what they say about her and Gary.

B: Go on …

A: I'm not saying who, but someone told me he often sees them in the Café Au Lait.

B: That little café on Oxford Road?

A: That's right.

B: Well I never! The other day he asked her if she would stay behind to work on a report.

A: There you are, then. There's no smoke without fire.

B: Listen, don't tell anyone I told you.

A: Now, come on, Quin, you know me better than that.

B: Back to work, then.

A: Right. Catch you later.

B: Bye.

 2.30

Conversation 1

A: Jeff, have you finished last month's production figures?

B: No, Jane, I'm sorry. Can I give them to you this afternoon?

A: It's no good being sorry. There's always some excuse. If they're not on my desk by 4 o'clock, I'll have to speak to Mr Bradley.

B: Yes, Jane. I'll start straight away.

 2.31

Conversation 2

C: David, have you got a minute? There's something I want to discuss with you … in my office.

D: What's it about?

C: Oh, well, we're missing a laptop computer from the store.

D: What has that got to do with me?

C: Well, you are the only other person with a key to the store and …

 2.32

Conversation 3

E: Marie, the figures you need are ready.

F: Thanks, Pedro. Is everything okay?

E: Yes, no problems. Would you like to look at them with me?

F: Yes, but I'm a bit busy this afternoon.

E: Me too. Er, do you know that new café they've just opened? It's nice and quiet. We can go through them there after work.

F: Oh, I suppose so, but I won't be able to stay for long.

E: Great. See you there at about six, then?

F: Yes, all right. See you there.

 2.33

Conversation 4

G: Hi, Monica.

H: Oh, hello Jim. How are things going?

G: Great. In fact, you can be the first to congratulate me.

H: Yes, you look very pleased with yourself. What's up?

G: I'm the new head of the eastern sales team.

H: Oh, really? What salary are you on now, then?

G: Sixty grand a year.

H: I can't believe it. Sixty thousand!

G: And they're giving me a new company car.

H: Oh, really? Congratulations, then. The drinks are on you. See you later.

G: Yes. Bye.

 2.34

A: In this week's *Business Today*, we talk to Karina Schmidt. Karina is the author of a report by the Industrial Society which looks at workplace relations, and how they've changed over the years. Karina, first of all, welcome to the programme.

B: Thank you, it's a pleasure to be here.

A: In your report, you say that many companies nowadays have abandoned some useful institutions which allowed for social interaction.

B: Yes, these days there's less opportunity to gossip and socialize. For example, often the tea trolley has been scrapped, and having a chat in the tea break was an important part of the working day. Going for a drink after work around the corner is another example.

A: And why do you think these things have disappeared?

B: I think it's all part of the revolution in human resources. Some of these traditions have become unfashionable. Talking about things not connected to work is now seen as bad and as wasting time. There are even theories about removing chairs from meeting rooms, so that the meetings are more efficient and finish quickly.

A: And are we more efficient now, then?

B: Well, that's a good question, but in any case, something has been lost from the workplace which is very important. And perhaps in the long term, with these drives for efficiency, companies are making false economies.

A: In what way?

B: The difference between a good job and a bad job are the human, emotional elements. In other words, happy employees are productive employees. People enjoy the social aspects of work, the personal interaction with colleagues, the friendships …

A: And the gossip!

B: And the gossip. Yes, in some ways gossip is the glue that holds the organization together. Providing communal space such as coffee areas or lunch rooms allows employees to share information and build relationships that benefit both the company and the employees.

A: Are you saying that gossip should be encouraged?

B: Not exactly, it's obviously a question of balance. All gossip and chatting doesn't make for an efficient company, but neither does no gossip or chat. All I'm saying is that I think companies would do well to remember this when trying to improve efficiency and bring down costs.

A: Karina, I'm afraid that's all we've got time for. Thank you very much for talking to us. It's been very interesting.

B: Thank you for inviting me.

A: That's all for now from *Business Today*. So, until next week, goodbye.

18 E-COMMERCE

2.35

I: For most listeners, Amazon, eBay™ and PayPal will of course be household names, and bring to mind books, music and shopping on the world wide web. According to latest surveys, three out of five Europeans have at some time bought goods on the Internet and online sales have doubled annually over the last five years. But will this growth continue? And what will the state of online trading and shopping be ten years from now? Our guests today – Paul Bradley and Johan Webb – are both well-known commentators and bloggers on business and online technology. Paul, how do you see the future of e-commerce? What are the pros and cons?

P: It's difficult to say because things move so fast, but I think the future is quite bright. I'm pretty sure that e-commerce will become the normal way to buy and trade, not in all products, but in a fairly wide range of goods. The advantages for the customer are obvious: access to products that may not be available locally, in online shops open 24 hours a day, seven days a week and 365 days a year, with delivery to your doorstep.

J: Yes, for the customer the benefits are clear – convenience and lower prices. And the seller can do business with anyone in the world connected to the Internet. In fact, the only limitations are transport and delivery costs.

P: That's absolutely right, but there are other drawbacks as well. When you buy online you have to wait for the goods to arrive – a lot of us just don't have the patience. There is also the possibility the goods won't arrive as expected and when there are problems they can be difficult to sort out. Returning goods is not easy. With a product like a computer or high-definition TV for example, people like to have a shop where they can take it back to if something goes wrong. After-sales service is still a negative factor.

J: On the plus side, the seller can deal directly with the manufacturer and offer a cheaper price as a result. For the customer, of course, the price difference has to be enough to make it worth taking the risk.

I: Is payment a problem?

P: For me, security is still the big issue in people's minds. They're scared of identity theft and what happens to the information they give online. For the moment it's something which is slowing down growth.

J: There are solutions out there. Payment systems like PayPal offer guarantees and security. If something goes wrong you can get your money back quite easily.

I: What about the type of products that can be sold?

J: Well, except for perhaps making your order at the local supermarket via a webpage, I don't think buying food is ever going to take off. Books and DVDs are one thing, but fruit and vegetables are another.

P: Yes, and buying online makes the groceries more expensive, so what's the point? Actually, this highlights another limitation. You can see pictures, read text and hear sounds on the Internet, but you can't smell a flower or feel the quality of cloth online. There will always be some products that people will want to touch and feel before they buy.

J: Not only that, but when you go to a shop and pick something up, you choose what to look at and how to look at it. On the Internet, you only see what the seller wants you to see. That's why people are more comfortable buying products like DVDs, books and electronic gadgets. Often you've already seen them in a shop before and you're just looking for a better price. Personally, for example, I won't buy clothes online unless I know it's something I want because I've been able to try it on to see if it fits.

I: Can we go back to the use of credit cards? Apart from security, are there any other issues?

P: Well, yes. Credit cards are an added cost for the seller, but you can't pay cash over the Internet.

J: There's another point here. Because payment is by credit card, very small or very large transactions tend not to be conducted online.

P: And that brings us back to what e-commerce is all about: buying and selling products which are suitable for package delivery, where compared to traditional retail, the costs of selling, payment and transport make it worth doing business online for both buyer and seller.

I: Well, Paul, Johan, thank you both very much. If you would like to comment on anything you've heard, don't forget you can email us at …

🔘 2.36

a The right qualifications for a job are one thing, but having experience is another.

b A high turnover is one thing, but making good profits is another.

c Having a good idea is one thing, but putting it into practice is another.

d High productivity is one thing, but improving staff motivation is another.

e Creating a good product is one thing, but selling it is another.

19 E-WORK

🔘 2.37

Interview 1

A: The Internet and other new technologies have changed the way we work and the titles of our jobs. For example, instead of the secretary, meet Jill Spencer, a 'virtual assistant'. Jill, what exactly is a virtual assistant?

B: Virtual assistants, or VAs, work from home. We offer services to businesses which don't have sufficient work to justify employing someone full-time.

A: Why did you decide to be a virtual assistant?

B: I retired from my job as a conference organizer, but I wanted to earn some extra money. I became a VA because it meant I didn't have to leave my country home down here in Cornwall.

A: Yes, it's a lovely place – I can understand why you didn't want to move away. So, how did you start?

B: I had a lot of contacts from my previous work. I began by providing things like bookkeeping, but now I offer a range of services for clients all over the UK.

A: It's going well, then?

B: Yes, I wasn't looking to earn a fantastic amount of money. The biggest advantage is that you can do as little or as much as you want. If it's a lovely sunny day, I can sit out in the garden and do the work in the evening.

A: What do you need to get started?

B: The basic tools are a computer with an Internet connection, a scanner and a mobile phone. Anyone with basic office skills could do the job. Apart from that it depends on the kind of services you're going to offer and what the clients want.

A: And what's in it for the companies?

B: Companies get a huge amount out of it because they only use a virtual assistant when they need one. Also, they can perhaps get someone with a higher professional level than they could get if they had to pay someone full-time. There's also no problem of office hours. A businessman can be out of the office all day, but his assistant is still available in the evening if he needs to discuss things. I think it could make a big difference to everyone's lifestyle.

🔘 2.38

Interview 2

A: Anna, what exactly do you do?

B: I'm a concierge at the Westin Hotel in Santa Clara, California.

A: What was life like before you became a teleworker?

B: I had to get up at three in the morning so I could shower and dress, take my kids to my mother's, and set off to work by 4.30.

A: 4.30!

B: Yes, there was a lot of traffic. On a good day I got there by 6.30. That gave me half an hour to relax before starting my shift at seven o'clock.

A: It sounds awful.

B: Yes, I was getting up in the dark and getting home in the dark. I never saw my husband or children. I liked my job, but my life was a nightmare.

A: And what is life like now?

B: Oh, I feel like the luckiest person alive. I now get up at 5.30. My mother still looks after the children but I don't have the 80-mile drive to work along Highway 101. We've set up my workplace in one of the bedrooms. I sit down in front of a camera, pin on a microphone and I'm ready for business.

A: How does it work at the hotel?

B: Guests still go up to the concierge desk, but instead of me in person, they see me on a giant TV screen. They can only see my head and shoulders, so I can wear my slippers while I work.

A: What do your employers think about it?

B: Oh, they're happy because they can't afford to lose me. In the hotel industry we don't have the high salaries of Cisco, Palm or Sun Micro, so there's a high turnover of staff. With unemployment around here so low it's hard to replace workers. It cost them $50,000 but they thought it was worth a try.

A: And the guests?

B: They're happy. Apart from anything else they don't have to leave a tip!

🔘 2.39

A: Have you seen this?

B: What?

A: 'Make money while you work at home. No skill required.'

B: Oh, it's not really about working at home. You sign up to a scheme where they say they will pay you to reply to emails or visit pages on the Internet. Then you're supposed to persuade your friends and family to do it.

A: Oh, so it's like pyramid selling.

B: Yes, the more people you get to do it, the more money you make. The idea is to show potential advertisers that they have an audience. I doubt it really works. If it was so easy, everyone would do it.

A: That's a shame. I wouldn't mind working at home if I had the opportunity.

B: I'm not so sure. I wouldn't miss travelling in to work every day but if I was at home, I'd miss the contact with the people here.

A: That's true, but if you could just come in a couple of days a week it would be okay. On the other hand, unless you had somewhere quiet to work, it would be difficult to get anything done.

B: Do you think you'd be disciplined enough?

A: I don't know. I would if it was my own business, but otherwise, who knows? It probably sounds more attractive than it would be in reality.

B: They do talk about telework a lot these days. Some people say that if people stopped commuting, it would be much better for the environment.

A: That's probably right but in the end, I think it depends on the type of job you have.

A: Er ... about two million dollars' worth worldwide.

B: Could I see the documentation?

A: Well, I'm afraid that's confidential, but listen, if we can make a deal today, I can offer you an even better discount.

20 WORKING LUNCH

🔘 2.40

A: This looks like a very nice place, Satomi.

B: Yes, I thought you would like it.

A: Yes, I really like the décor. Er, could you order for both of us, Satomi?

B: Of course. I think we could have some miso soup to start with. They do it very well here.

A: Okay. Sounds good.

B: And then I think you should try some unagi.

A: What's that?

B: It's eel – grilled and served on a bed of rice. It's delicious.

A: Hmm, I'm sure it is. Actually, do you think I could have a steak?

B: Well, I'm afraid they don't serve steak here.

A: I'll try the unagi, then.

B: Fine. Would you like some sake, or would you prefer some tea?

A: No, no, let's have some sake.

B: Right. Sake it is, then.

🔘 2.41

C: So, any news from Tokyo, Neil?

A: No, I'm afraid not, Jeff. It looks like they're not interested.

C: How did it go with Ms Tanaka?

A: Oh, she was really nice. She took me to a great restaurant. Actually, everything went okay until we got down to business.

C: What happened?

A: I don't know. I thought the sale was a sure thing, but she seemed to lose interest. I don't know what I did wrong.

🔘 2.42

A: Mmm, that was delicious.

B: I'm glad you enjoyed it. So, Neil, tell me about this digital control software. Why do you think we should be interested?

A: Because it's easily the best program for the job on the market.

B: The system we use at the moment works okay. Why should we change?

A: It's a question of costs. It could save you up to 30%. If you look at the competition, there's just no comparison.

B: Can you give me some information about your sales?